David Frost

Other books by Willi Frischauer

The Aga Khans
European Commuter
Goering
Grand Hotels of Europe
Himmler
The Man Who Came Back
The Nazis at War
Onassis
Twilight in Vienna
The Navy's Here (with Robert Jackson)

David Frost

by

Willi Frischauer

MICHAEL JOSEPH LONDON

First published in Great Britain by Michael Joseph Ltd
52 Bedford Square, London W.C.1
1972

7181 1005 6

Reproduced and printed in Great Britain by
Redwood Press Limited, Trowbridge & London
Bound by James Burn

Acknowledgments

My THANKS TO ALL who have submitted patiently to my Frost-like questioning about David Frost—including David Frost himself. His contemporaries at Cambridge University, his personal friends, his business associates, and television executives on both sides of the Atlantic have helped me to obtain material and to trace documents, letters, and scripts, none more untiringly, tactfully, and sweetly than Joan Pugh. I have coped as best I could with David's ten mammoth volumes of press clippings and with one that came into being as I worked—largely to avoid repeating much that has already been said except where I have specifically quoted reviews and other references to him.

As much as possible I have also eschewed duplicating what he has written in his own books, but Ned Sherrin and Anthony Jay, his coauthors at one time or another, have elucidated some points in conversation with me and added much that was new. Wallace Reyburn has diligently delved into David's pre-American activities, but I had to go over some ground he has covered if only to clarify points in the light of later events and to record David's new thoughts on some subjects. His mother, Mrs. Mona Frost, has kindly talked to me about the family background and her son's early years, of which she is the most valuable witness.

Rather than take up a position on the outside looking in, I have sought David's cooperation and received it in generous measure. He has answered innumerable questions about his private and professional life and, in the spirit of his own craft, has evaded

few, although true to his character, he has put the best construction on what he and others have said or done in the passage
of time. I have watched him in full flight for many days in London,
New York, and Hollywood—and at a height of thirty thousand
feet above the ground, where he spends so much time jetting
from one end of the world to the other.

David's detractors, of whom there are fewer than his spectacular success would seem likely to breed, have disappointed me
by their inability or unwillingness to make specific points other
than insignificant quibbles (most of which I have noted). His
many friends embarrassed me by talking about him in such
extravagant terms that they hardly bear repeating. The consensus
was best expressed by Ian Davidson, who said with a hint of
exasperation: "It's his Christianity!"

I am grateful to Bernard Levin for permitting me to quote
from his splendid book about the sixties, *The Pendulum Years*
(London: Jonathan Cape, 1970). Some of the other volumes I
have consulted are listed in the Bibliography. As usual, my wife
has helped enormously with the research on both sides of the
Atlantic.

W. F.

London and New York, 1971

Contents

Photographs appear on pp. 105–120.

CHAPTER 1

David's Eyrie

IN THE CRAMPED, almost claustrophobic office on the third floor of New York City's Little Theatre, off Times Square, David Frost sits behind his small, cluttered desk, ear glued to the telephone, hand covering the receiver from time to time while he dictates to Cate Ryan, his attractive little secretary, or responds to callers who put their heads round the door. His eyes look sleepy; an occasional yawn distorts his features, which are handsome and more delicate than they appear on the television screen. The voice is even, slightly nasal, and sometimes raised—in harness with the eyebrows—with the studied emphasis of a typical Frost expression: "Super! That's great!" He smiles easily, showing his rather prominent gleaming white teeth. Now and then he reaches for a small cigar but, if he lights it at all, puts it down after a few desultory puffs.

Behind him the wall is dominated by a colorful but diffuse portrait of Frost, looking thinner and more thoughtful than the original, painted in a few short minutes of one show by Australian Rolf Harris. On his left is a photograph of Frost talking, with an articulate hand underlining his point. In the corner the Emmy award has a coveted place.

The shelves are half-empty or rather half-filled with a higgledy-piggledy collection of books, each with a bearing on some of the more than fifteen hundred subjects he has dealt with in his first two years as host of the *David Frost Show*. A Westinghouse (Group W Productions) show, it goes out on Channel 5 in New York at the peak time of 8:30 to 10 P.M. five times a week and is

1

syndicated to almost a hundred stations, including almost all the fifty key stations, independent and network, which are the industry's measure of success. Dotted around the office are a few pieces of pop art and framed awards and testimonials, and on the wall facing David there is a Plexiglas arrangement with colored cards indicating scheduled guests for future shows. Only Cate Ryan, with an office next door, shares David's eyrie, which he—and only he—reaches via a tiny elevator whose third-floor button is marked "Do Not Press."

In the seclusion of his office, which he reaches soon after breakfast most Mondays through Thursdays, he studies briefs prepared by his team which tell him everything there is to know about the evening's principal guest and about the pop stars, guitarists, comics, and whoever else is booked to appear on his show. He consults the literature pertaining to his guests, rapidly skimming the pages of fat volumes and thin pamphlets. If it's a senator, David will have read a biography and his most important speeches before meeting him in the studio. In the case of showbiz personalities, he will have viewed the film or seen the show of which they are the stars.

Within easy reach by his side are two leather bags, bulging with scripts, books, magazines, and correspondence, which go wherever he goes. They are his memory bank, his inspiration, his repertoire, his last resource. Most of the documents he wants to consult can usually be extracted almost without looking, but what slips to the bottom of the bags may be out of reach for months, though it is never really lost. Television work—and not only work on talk shows—thrives on talk, and David frequently picks up the intercom to clarify points with Neil Shand, his chief idea man on whose perceptive notes David relies to frame his questions, or with Peter Baker, producer of the *David Frost Show*, both English and both Frost associates of many years' standing.

At 6 P.M. the long queue outside the Little Theatre is admitted, many of them young women anxious to see their idol in the flesh. ("I get some incredible letters from ladies," David confesses.) At 6:30, the time the taping is due to start, the telephone rings, and David is told that the studio audience and the crew are ready and awaiting his presence. David nods and picks up the receiver to make a call of his own. He continues to talk to his visitor—there is always a visitor—while making signs to Cate Ryan, which only she understands.

Ten minutes later, without any show of haste, David rises, stretches his wiry, athletic body, and disappears into his dressing room, only to turn up in the doorway a minute later in his shirt and underpants and stockinged feet, continuing to shout instructions to Cate. The next time he appears it is 6:50, and he is wearing his favorite black-suede shoes and a well-cut suit, courtesy of Hardy Amies, who makes all his stage clothes. The shirt is vivid, either with bold stripes or all red, the tie modishly wide. His very pale skin is covered with liquid bronzer. London is calling in the person of Joan Pugh, his English secretary; there is another call, from his New York agent; and when the phone rings for a third time, it is Hollywood, and since David's face is wreathed in sweetness, anyone can guess who is at the other end of the line.

"David's lateness—" says the president of Group W Productions, which runs the *David Frost Show,* "we've learned to live with it, love it—and pay for it!" About 7 P.M., half an hour after the scheduled start of the taping, David takes the elevator to the studio, sweeping his visitor along in his wake. He carries a clipboard with his notes, his only ammunition.

In front of the big mirror downstairs he checks his appearance. There is just the slightest hint of tension before he draws a deep breath that seems to fill him with buoyant strength. As he crosses an invisible line on the way to the stage, the adrenaline begins to flow. The tiredness visibly lifts from his shoulders. The eyes sparkle; the skin glows; the chest expands. The step is light and springy even for a man of thirty-two with a passion for ball games.

He waits until Billy Taylor—leader of the show's band, a fine musician and spirited talker—finishes his warming-up act, which puts the studio audience in the right mood. The band intones the signature tune, and with the last note, David Frost himself appears on stage, sometimes literally leaping forward, head slightly inclined, viewing the audience with a gently coy, intimate, even affectionate glance before throwing out his chin to announce in his confident, urgent, distinctive voice: "Tonight we have the pleasure and the privilege to welcome to the studio . . . !"

American television shows are an incestuous business, with the principal characters hopping in and out of each other's "specials."

They may feel like murdering their rivals, but for the benefit of the viewers they do not stab—they pat—each other's back. David Frost had no sooner entered the ranks of the talk masters when he garnered a fair harvest of outstanding television personalities as guests for his show. Hugh Downs, Arthur Godfrey, Walter Cronkite, Merv Griffin, Johnny Carson, and Chet Huntley are only a half dozen among the many professional talkers who have joined David on camera and basked in the reflected glory of his novel approach. Ed Sullivan was more articulate on the *David Frost Show* than on his own, and Johnny Carson, a rival, gave David one of his most memorable ninety minutes.

It was not long before the tables were reversed and David became a hot favorite, often called on to brighten the shows of other top performers—but with a difference. David, the interviewer, was now familiar to millions of American viewers. Though by the summer of 1970 only a few dimly remembered him as the chief satirist and comic of the American version of *That Was the Week That Was,* which first introduced him to a U.S. audience, this was the David Frost producers were anxious to present on their shows. He taped an appearance for Petula Clark's song and dance special, then early in August starred with Flip Wilson in his hit premiere. At the end of August he was once more bound for the West Coast and the N.B.C. Studios in beautiful downtown Burbank to inject a little satire into the *Dean Martin Show.*

To make up for his absence from New York, he arranged to tape two sessions of his own show, one after another, on a Wednesday afternoon, a total of 180 minutes on camera. He conducted a major interview with Birch Bayh, the young senator from Indiana who had recently challenged President Richard Nixon over the Supreme Court nominations of Clement F. Haynsworth, Jr., and G. Harrold Carswell. Another of David's guests was Mel Torme, who talked about his book on Judy Garland. It was a piquant situation, because Mel is married to Janette Scott, who was David's first great love.

After the two tapings and a quick dinner at Sardi's Restaurant, next door to The Little Theatre, David went to his apartment on the seventh floor of the Lombardy Hotel and worked on the proofs of his latest book, *The Americans,* a collection of his best

American interviews, which has since been published by Stein and Day. It was past 4 A.M. when he finally went to sleep. Four hours later, his early morning call having gone unheard, he was still asleep. The breakfast tray, with a small cup of black coffee, grapefruit juice, and strawberries—he's always been mad about strawberries—was untouched on the table.

David's Lincoln limousine was outside the hotel at 8 A.M., just early enough for a comfortable ride to Kennedy Airport to catch the 9 A.M. United Airlines flight, which (allowing for the three hours' time difference) would get him to Los Angeles at eleven. As usual, chauffeur Tom Cronin ("Ireland's gift to America") called from downstairs, and David acknowledged the call with a sleepy-voiced "Good morning." He had obviously only just opened his eyes.

Twenty minutes later, Tom went up to the apartment to tell David that it was getting late and that traffic was liable to be heavy. David was out of bed and brushing his teeth. There was no time to shave because he still had to gather up some clothes to put in his suitcases and select half-a-dozen ties. He nibbled at a strawberry and took a sip of coffee, then called Cate Ryan at home and asked her to advise the airport that he would definitely be taking the flight on which he was booked.

It was 8:35 when David was on his way at last. The Lincoln went like a rocket, smoothly gliding in and out of lanes, cunningly avoiding concentrations of other cars. Incredibly it made Kennedy and the United Airlines departure lounge one minute before nine. Greeting David like an old friend, the receptionist told him: "I have made out a ticket for you, Mr. Frost."

"You are a great human being." David grinned. "Thank you very much." In a low voice he added: "Thank you, thank you, but I already have a ticket."

An airline official buttonholed him to say how much he enjoyed the *David Frost Show*, then picked up the telephone and tried to reach the runway. After a hasty conversation his face fell: "The aircraft has just left the departure area, Mr. Frost—so sorry, but we can't get it back."

Not a flicker of disappointment showed in David's face. "I did want to catch this plane," he said quietly. The next scheduled flight to the coast was forty-five minutes later by T.W.A.

The receptionist, obviously well versed in the Frost routine, was already on the phone to T.W.A. to make a reservation. Porters took David's bags, including the ones with scripts, newspapers, books, and magazines, to the car. "You are all terrific," David cooed, and everybody assured him that it was he who was terrific.

Safely installed in the V.I.P. lounge of the T.W.A. terminal, David was instantly on the telephone to Cate, asking her to advise Los Angeles of the change. He made another call, talking in whispers and manifestly enjoying himself. While David poured himself a cup of coffee—which he never got around to drinking—and dialed one more number, an air hostess appeared to say that the plane was about to depart.

The aircraft's engines were already running when he slid into his seat. By the time the plane was rolling down the runway David had already taken off on the wings of sleep. He did not notice the passenger in the seat behind who tried to nudge him with a copy of the current *New Yorker* magazine, which carried a David Frost cartoon ("You know how David Frost always asks what your most memorable experience was?" a man is saying to his wife in bed beside him. "Well, I've been lying here for three solid hours, and I can't think of a single damn thing."). The air hostess gave him a searching but fondly approving look and covered him with a blanket. He was slumbering like a baby.

Four hours later and only twenty minutes from Los Angeles, David woke up, went to wash and shave, and emerged spick and span, rested and lively. As the plane came down to land, he had a cup of coffee at last. There were fond farewells from the air hostess, friendly looks of recognition from fellow passengers, and a kind word to the lady with the *New Yorker*, who managed to attract his attention after all. An electric baggage cart was waiting to carry him and his luggage to the big black Mercedes 600 (with color TV, refrigerator, bar, and telephone) that he uses whenever he is on the Coast. Ex-Marine Tony Valentino, who drives the huge limousine whenever David is in Los Angeles, triples as his valet, secretary, and factotum.

At the Beverly Hills Hotel, where the Mercedes disgorged David, the reception was spontaneous and warm. "David Frost!" A television producer emerged from the crowd, embraced him, and suggested he might want to do a spot on his show.

"Love to," David said, "but at the moment I have a whole batch of things to get through. . . . Call me in New York. . . . I am so glad you asked me." A lady pushed an autograph book under his nose. "How very kind of you to ask me," David said—it was not clear whether he was talking to her or still to the TV producer.

His luggage was whisked away to his regular bungalow (Number One, of course), and he followed, shaking hands all around. "There was one thing on your show I didn't like, David," a perfect stranger told him, "but then, you are not responsible for everything, are you?"

David answered sweetly: "As long as there is a reaction, I am quite content." He was not yet fully inside the bungalow when he began to shed his shirt. He donned an electric-blue number, blue with blue stripes, changed into a milk-coffee–colored suit, and was off to a luncheon party only thirty minutes behind schedule.

By 2:30 he was in his star dressing room (same corridor as Dean Martin and Peter Ustinov) on the N.B.C. lot, already in deep discussion with two scriptwriters, to one of whom Bob Hope owes many of his most successful gags. David was putting his six-minute monologue together. "Not this one," he was saying, "I never joke about sickness." He objected to another item with a political flavor: "I can't say that—it is not my view!" ("David is a professional," scriptwriters say. "He knows what he wants, never knocks the material, but states his reasons whenever he turns down an idea.")

With the help of several funny stories and a few bits and pieces from David's own two leather bags, a sequence emerged that satisfied them all. They laughed when he told his joke about the man who was jailed for making big money—"He made it just a fraction of an inch too big"—and when he produced a new one about the fact that 48 percent of American women are now taking the Pill—(looking at his watch) "And it is only nine-thirty P.M.!"

On his way to the set for a run-through a lady harpist stopped him: "You know, Mr. Frost, my daughter has some marital difficulties just now . . ."—David looked apprehensive until she continued—"and only yesterday she said that if it weren't for the *David Frost Show*, she wouldn't know what to do."

"I am sorry about her difficulties," David said kindly, "but give her my love, will you?"

Rattling off his monologue without even glancing at the idiot boards, David elicited laughs from the pros in the show, the hardest audience to please. Dean Martin appeared, shook hands with David, embraced and kissed every chorus girl in sight, and disappeared again. The bigger the star, the less he rehearses. David, who also figured in some sketches, was not required again on the set until the next day, but he took time for a quick lesson from the musical director, who tried to teach him to play the violin badly—with little success.

In a mix-up about dressing rooms Wilfrid Hyde-White appeared, apparently with instructions to share David's dressing room. After a fond all-British reunion he and David decided they were better apart. Both wanted to use the telephone—no major television star wants to be out of touch with his business manager, stockbroker, real-estate administrator, agent, secretary, and paramour for a minute longer than his presence on the stage demands.

When his turn came at the taping the next day, David, introduced by the strains of his own theme song, went through his monologue with the ease of a practiced performer, next did a sketch about a launderette with Dean Martin and Barbara (*Get Smart*) Feldon, then joined a line-up of the stars in a hint of a dance routine. He was not specific, but when he left the set, his day's work done, he was several thousand dollars richer. Awaiting him was the ravishing Diahann Carroll ("Julia," of the TV series) and an evening at Chasen's with Peter Ustinov and a few showbiz entrepreneurs. "I have a big thing on," he said. He always has.

"David thinks huge. He is a great initiator with a tremendous feeling for an opportunity." The man speaking is a very vigorous, intense Etonian in his early forties, Richard Armitage, head of a theatrical agency and a big figure in the entertainment industry who has considerable interests both in Britain and in the United States. Armitage is the man who discovered David Frost and guided his first steps to fame as his agent and adviser. Now David's closest business associate, he is the managing director of five Frost companies in Britain and the head of another five in the United States.

Though David conducts his affairs from his beautiful house in

London's Knightsbridge district, only a stone's throw from Harrods, his English companies operate from elegant offices in Mayfair where he chairs board meetings and attends production conferences. These are his lesser-known activities, and yet they fill a great part of his professional life.

Besides being a performer and talk-show host David is also an impresario and entrepreneur. In England he has made stars of unknowns overnight. In the United States his "specials" have introduced a galaxy of the world's leading performers to American television, Noel Coward and Frankie Howerd among them. In one single presentation ("The Best of the English Theater") he brought Alec Guinness, Nicol Williamson, Jill Bennett, Vanessa Redgrave, Sybil Thorndike, and many others to American TV screens. In another special television production he did a song-and-dance act with Queen Elizabeth's brother-in-law, the Earl of Snowdon. David Frost is a film producer (*The Rise and Rise of Michael Rimmer, Futtock's End*) and owns music and stage-production companies. He is the author of several books that have been on best-seller lists on both sides of the Atlantic and for a time was the biggest individual stockholder in London Weekend Television, one of Britain's leading commercial-television companies.

The Frost empire comprises five companies in England, most of them named after his father's and his own middle name, Paradine: Paradine Limited, David Paradine Productions, David Paradine Films, David Paradine Plays, and Glebe Music Company. The chairman of them all is David Frost; the deputy chairman or managing director is Richard Armitage. In the United States Frost operates David Paradine Productions, Inc., David Paradine Records, Inc., Beccles Music Company (Beccles is David's home-town in England), Bungay Music Company (Bungay is another small town five miles away), and the David Frost Show, Inc., all similarly run by David Frost and Richard Armitage. There is another American firm, Exclamation, in which David has an interest, and one, Hellespont, incorporated in Curaçao, which controls his overseas services and those of some of his collaborators.

The income from his variegated activities is considerable. Apart from his earnings as a talk-show host in the States, which are around half a million dollars a year and constantly rising as new outlets take up the show (plus his constantly rising fees as a performer on English television), each of his firms contributes liberally to his growing fortune. He is known to have invested astutely. David Frost has been a millionaire for some years—dollars or sterling, take your pick.

In his native England his fame as a television personality is unrivaled. According to an opinion poll, only the Queen and the Prime Minister are as well known as he. As the first Englishman to host a major talk-show on American television, it has taken him less than two years to become a household word in the United States as well, the subject of a hundred cover stories and a thousand items in news reports, gossip columns, and the feature pages of newspapers and magazines across the country, so that Westinghouse could claim without blushing: "He is as American as apple pie."

Recognition and awards have been showered on him, making him the most honored television star in the history of the medium. It started with the Golden Rose of Montreux, a coveted international award, which went to the *Frost Report*, one of his early English shows. In one memorable week in 1970 he won the Emmy for the *David Frost Show*, received an honorary doctorate in the States, and was awarded the Order of the British Empire, which he received from the Queen at Buckingham Palace later in the year while his mother looked on proudly.

Before the year was out, he told his mother: "I was able to take you to Buckingham Palace. Now I would like you to come to the White House!" Introduced by President Nixon, David Frost entertained a distinguished gathering at the White House with a Frost Christmas show specially produced for the occasion.

The date: Thursday, September 17, 1970. The time: 8:30 P.M. The place: The Little Theatre, New York.

The day's show safely on tape, David Frost takes leave of his guests and goes up to his office to remove his makeup and change, talking to Peter Baker and Neil Shand all the while. Cate Ryan keeps breaking in to remind him of the trip ahead. "Your plane leaves Kennedy at *ten*, David!" she says several times. David smiles acknowledgment. He rummages in his bags to check the material he is taking with him to London on the first stage of another of those incredible working tours that have become routine to him but to nobody else. ("Getting him on a plane is one of our major worries," Cate Ryan says.) Cate puts a call through to Joan Pugh in London: "David is due at Heathrow Airport at nine forty A.M.," she tells her.

Cate and Joan are still talking across the Atlantic when David leaves for Sardi's for a quick bite and half a bottle of claret. A reporter from a midwestern newspaper is waiting for an interview. Unless he summons them for breakfast at the Algonquin Hotel, David often meets journalists and business associates at Sardi's, which is home away from home to him.

As soon as the reporter departs, his chair is taken by Marc Merson, the former C.B.S. executive who is head of David Paradine Productions, Inc., and looks after David's American business affairs. Together they study a sheaf of documents while David eats his meal hurriedly and without showing much interest in the food. He nods, interjects an idea, voices a gentle protest— whatever he does is done gently, but the manner is deceptive, and he does not budge easily from his views.

Cate Ryan turns up with a few more notes for the trip which she has just completed. David has some final requests and instructions for her. At long last he is on his way to the airport to catch the 10 P.M. plane for London, but just barely.

Even before the aircraft takes off he is already immersed in his reading matter. One item is a slim volume of poems by Mary Wilson, wife of Britain's recently deposed Labour Prime Minister; Harold and Mary Wilson will be David's guests on the first show of his new London series. By his side lies the bulky autobiography of Nazi war criminal Albert Speer, who was Hitler's confidant and armaments minister. Among other material within easy reach are some of Vice-President Spiro Agnew's recent speeches. (Agnew is to appear on David's New York show in a few days.)

A couple of hours later, David snuggles more deeply into his seat and falls asleep. When he wakes up, the aircraft is about to land at Heathrow. He is well rested and alert. The time, five hours ahead of New York, is nearly 10 A.M. (Friday, September 18). With no other luggage except his two bags he is quickly through customs and is greeted by Joan Pugh and Bob Lambert, his faithful chauffeur and confidant. While David discusses the day's schedule with Joan, Bob walks ahead to the Bentley.

Within minutes they are gliding down the M-4 motorway,

making for the offices of London Weekend Television in Wembley, where David joins Geoffrey Hughes, his London producer, and Nicholas Barrett, editor of the *Frost Programme*. The topic of discussion is David's Saturday night show. "We'll have Mary Wilson on first," he says. "I hope she will agree to read some of her poems." He is genuinely curious about the sentiments behind each of the poems and has selected a few he wants her to read and explain on camera. In the second half of the show he will be talking on quite different topics to Harold Wilson.

The conversation with Geoffrey and Nicholas turns on the most effective line of questioning. It continues during a quick lunch, after which David is driven to Vincent Square, Westminster, to the former Prime Minister's temporary home, where he spends an hour or so going over the details of the show. From Vincent Square, he goes to the Paradine H.Q. on Davies Street, Mayfair, for a meeting with his executives, who are working on future Frost "specials." His company produces four a year for Westinghouse.

It is evening when he reaches his house on Egerton Crescent, and he has just enough time to change before going out. Where? "Private dinner." His diary records "private dinners" for most days of the week. The term covers a multitude of sins, and neither he nor his staff will breathe a word about them. Privacy, so hard to come by for a man like David Frost, is a jealously guarded commodity.

He is up early next morning (Saturday, September 19) and reads the English newspapers before coming down to the big drawing room–*cum*-study in his pajamas and robe to work, dictate to Joan Pugh, and telephone. It is midday before he dresses and takes a lonely lunch in the ground-floor dining room. By 2 P.M. he is once more on his way to the London Weekend studios to work on the show. Seven hours later he is at the door to greet Harold and Mary Wilson but does not join the small welcoming party in the hospitality room.

At 10 P.M. sharp he and Mary Wilson settle down before the cameras. Ten minutes later, David opens the proceedings by greeting the ex–Prime Minister's wife warmly, and some say fulsomely, and with exuberant enthusiasm, which the English critics will put down to American influences. Mary Wilson obliges by reading a few poems, and David's response—overenthusiastic or not—reflects popular reaction, which is what he aims at. Mary Wilson's poems impress the studio audience, the viewers, the whole country. Within weeks her little book has outsold every other book of contemporary poetry in England.

Harold Wilson has been a guest on David's show before, and there has always been a certain rapport between them. It is not different on this occasion. After the show a cold buffet and drinks await David and his guests. He is full of praise for their performance. Shortly after the Wilsons' departure David makes his own farewells. It is 1 A.M. (Sunday, September 20) when he gets home and to bed at last.

Roused six hours later by Luisa, his Spanish housekeeper, David reaches for a strawberry ("He loves strawberries, but he won't like these," Luisa says, sighing. "They are frozen.") and leaves the rest. He dresses in leisurely fashion and is ready in good time to catch the 8:55 A.M. flight to Frankfurt, his mind on Albert Speer, whom he will meet a few hours later in the old German university town of Heidelberg. For once, he makes Heathrow Airport comfortably, meeting Geoffrey Hughes, who is producing the Speer show, but the departure of the flight is delayed one hour, two hours—Frost observes that the delay does not encourage punctuality. David spends the spare time delving deeper into the Speer autobiography and continues his study on the plane, which arrives in Frankfurt at noon, squeezing his schedule tighter than before.

He has three and a half hours to get to Heidelberg Castle, fifty miles away, where Speer is waiting, tape a one-hour show, and get back to Frankfurt for the 3:45 plane to New York. This is David's second interview with a major war criminal—his first was with Hitler Youth leader Baldur von Schirach, who was Speer's fellow prisoner at Spandau during most of their twenty-year confinement. Speer, whose autobiography reeks with self-abasement and abstract admissions of guilt but is well written and illuminating about Hitler and the Nazi clique, looks every inch a well-fed, prosperous, serious-minded German bourgeois and obviously copes well with his remorse. David decides to employ a technique similar to his approach to Schirach, which is not to put Speer in the dock all over again but to extract as much information as possible.

"What were Hitler's good points?" is one of his first questions.

"There weren't really many good points," Speer admits.

They talk about Hitler and his death-bed bride, Eva Braun, and about rumors that Hitler was a homosexual—but Speer is the last person likely to admit that. "Was Hitler mad?," "What about Hitler and religion?," and "Was Hitler the most evil man who ever lived?" are some of David's other questions. The interview touches on the disputed death of Martin Bormann ("Bormann was a drink addict," says Speer about Hitler's evil genius), on Hermann Göring's suicide at Nuremberg, and on Rudolf Hess, who is still confined at Spandau. "Fascinating!" is how David acknowledges some of Speer's replies, and that is what his audience thought when the interview was screened. One of the last questions is whether Speer hopes for forgiveness.

"That's up to God" is the answer.

"It's been a great experience to talk to you," David says in conclusion, "and I think we understand at least a little more as a result of it."

There is no time for niceties—not that David is in the mood for small talk, anyway. Without much ado he returns to his car and is off to Frankfurt airport. At 3:45 his T.W.A. flight leaves for New York—via London. Predictably, David uses the London stopover between 5 and 6 P.M. to talk to two business associates who had been alerted to meet him in the V.I.P. "Ambassadors Lounge" for a conference that goes on until minutes—or rather seconds—before the aircraft takes off for New York. At 9:05 P.M., almost exactly seventy-two hours—three crowded days—after leaving New York, David alights again at Kennedy Airport. He reaches his hotel by ten and there is still time for dinner with friends before he goes to bed to catch a few hours' rest.

Another day dawns (Monday, September 21), and David arrives at the Little Theatre early to prepare the afternoon's taping session. It is a difficult one. His guests are Vice-President Spiro Agnew and four college student leaders, highly critical of the Nixon Administration, who will meet face to face in the studio, David Frost presiding. It is a very American occasion, far removed from David's encounters with the Wilsons and with Albert Speer in the last two days, a confrontation between establishment and protest, the big issue of American politics.

David will need his sangfroid to keep the temperature of the discussion at a tolerable level.

The four students—Stephen Bright, University of Kentucky, Greg Craig, Yale Law School, Eva Jefferson, Northwestern University, and Richard Silverman, University of Washington—do not mince words. Violence and campus disorders, the Vietnam war, and Agnew's idiosyncratic rhetoric are subjects bound to inflame tempers. Sparks begin to fly as soon as the lights go on and the cameras turn. Agnew's adversaries call him "one of the greatest precursors of violence in the country," but the Vice-President retorts that there was campus violence long before he assumed office. Going over to the counterattack, he blames "the disgusting permissive attitudes of the people in charge of campuses."

Alternatively acting as stimulus or safety valve, David keeps the argument from getting bogged down and makes sure that the Vice-President gets a fair hearing but is equally quick to press him for an answer when he tries to evade a question. The verbal battle sways to and fro. The Vice-President denies that he condoned the killings at Kent State University but adds that in his view students started the violence. Many other issues are raised, turning the ninety-minute debate into a fine television accomplishment that the world press reports under big headlines a few days later—it is rare for a talk show to make international news on such a scale.

Having completed three major interviews in three different countries in three days, David might be expected to give himself a little respite. He doesn't, however. It is 6 P.M. when the Agnew-student confrontation ends, 6:30 when the Vice-President leaves. David has two hours to spare: one hour to rest (which means attending to other business) and one hour to prepare himself for a second taping session that same evening.

At 8:30 his guests are waiting as usual for the summons to face their interrogator on stage. The change of background, subject, and mood is perplexing. The principal characters of this edition of the *David Frost Show* are journalist Bob Considine and author Truman Capote. Next on the evening's schedule are the two Japanese most closely associated with the attack on Pearl Harbor: Commander Minuro Genda, who devised it, and Commander

Mitsuo Fuchido, who led it. Two American naval men make up David's round for the evening.

Two ninety- and two sixty-minute shows in three days! Perhaps the next day (Tuesday, September 22) is a day of rest? Not for David. At noon on Tuesday he is at New York City's Plaza Hotel, moderating Wagner International's Symposium on Public Relations and the Media before an audience of leading television, magazine, and newspaper journalists. By 6:30 he is back at the studio to do his daily stint, his chief guests being Art Carney and Pat O'Brien. Then he returns to the Plaza for dinner—no "private dinner" this. He is there to act as master of ceremonies at a function honoring Senator Margaret Chase Smith, of Maine.

In the words of the show that first made David Frost famous: That was the week that was.

> Man of the Sixties! How many coveted that title, sought it, wooed it, pursued it! One young man would perhaps be offered the title by many judges—not yet, but when the dust and the anxieties have sufficiently settled for us to see the decade's shape more clearly. Perhaps David Frost grasped earlier than most the quality of the Sixties. Always one jump further on than where he was expected, ever exploiting a new medium, a new technique, a new hairstyle, Frost divined by a remarkable instinct what the age demanded, and gave it. . . .
>
> Young enough to remain for many years in the public eye, flexible enough to move on again and yet again, aggressive enough to battle on behalf of the future yet wise enough to keep on his side those who feared it, with all the most modern techniques for getting audiences and keeping them. David (as we may presume to call him, lest we be constrained to call him Dave) at the close of the Sixties could reflect, and probably did, that he had done well out of the decade, and that it had done none too badly out of him.

This remarkable testimonial by Bernard Levin, one of Britain's outstanding writers (in The Pendulum Years, which brilliantly surveys Britain in the last decade), was penned even before David Frost stormed "Fortress America," conquered it, and became the compleat transatlantic man. His years in America have not remained without impact on the Frost mentality, the Frost approach, and the Frost technique, which English critics eagerly prospect for American elements. To some of them, David Frost's manners and attitudes seem to have taken on an American gloss, even though Americans never cease to remark on the Englishness of the only Englishman ever to become a major talk-show host in the United States.

These are superficialities, however. There is no question about David Frost's roots, which are English to the core. However swiftly it has developed, his success has its origin in his background, his boyhood, his student years, and his start as the first English youngster to go straight from the university into television.

Much of what David Frost says or does takes us back to his beginnings.

CHAPTER 2

The Boy David

"W. W. FROST, Halesworth's Premier Ironmongery," said the sign over the shop in the little Suffolk town some hundred miles northeast of London. Grandfather Frost was doing reasonably well for himself. He was the proud father of three sons: George, born in 1888, Robert, who followed two years later, and Wilfrid (David's father), who arrived after another ten years, on May 10, 1900.

George was the bright boy of the family. Nowadays, with all three brothers dead, details of his career are hard to come by, but in some mysterious way he is remembered as an outstanding fellow in drab and undistinguished surroundings. He trained as a mining engineer and was by all accounts very able, with great drive and imagination. Suffolk could not hold him. George Frost was still a young man when he went overseas and met up with another mining engineer, named Herbert Hoover, who worked in Australia and China before becoming President of the United States.

"It's from his Uncle George that David gets his brains," said David's mother. She never met her legendary brother-in-law but remembers her husband telling her that George's letters brought a whiff of romance to the Frost home. A red marble ashtray, a souvenir of George's travels which he gave to his youngest brother, still has a place of honor in her home. George also bought Wilfrid his first bicycle, a kindness never forgotten.

Family lore has it that Hoover had such a high regard for

19

George Frost that he wanted to keep him in the United States. George was in the reserves, however, and he returned to Britain at the outbreak of World War I, joined up, and was killed in action in France. Not much later his younger brother Robert met the same fate.

The third and youngest of the family, Wilfrid John Paradine Frost was fourteen years old when he joined his father's business. His mother was hard of hearing, and to enable her to lip-read the boy enunciated slowly and clearly, a habit he retained in adult life. Sunday, after the week's hard work, he always went to church—to a Congregational church. He was a placid youngster who kept his feelings well under control, a description that perfectly fits David.

Wilfrid had just turned twenty-two when he met "Mona" Aldrich, one of eleven children of a farm family from the village of Darsham. Her real name was Maud, but her mother, who was not well enough to attend the christening, did not like it and called her Mona instead. All the family were staunch Methodists; Methodism means intense personal involvement for every believer and engages the layman almost as much as the minister.

Mona had lost her mother when she was eleven years old. Five years later her father died, and the Aldrich farm was sold; her share was just over sixteen hundred pounds. A vital girl with lots of energy and stamina—qualities which have also come down to David—she married Wilfrid Paradine Frost in 1922, when she was nineteen, and soon persuaded him to join the Methodist Church. They had two girls: Jean, who was born in 1923, and Margaret, who came two years later.

The couple's closest friend was Ezra Ramm, the local Methodist preacher, who became a frequent visitor to their house on London Road. Religion, a subject close to Mona's heart, was the main topic of conversation, and Wilfrid was deeply stirred. It was Ezra Ramm who inspired the "deep spiritual experiences" that Wilfrid underwent at that time. When he was twenty-seven years old, he heard the call of God. He made up his mind then and there to commit himself completely to the faith and devote himself to preaching His word.

Wilfrid Frost decided to become a minister and, though lacking in formal education, studied hard, passed his examinations, sold his house, and took up work as a probationary minister in

Horsham, in the county of Sussex. It was something of a precedent twice over because Methodist ministers usually went to college and then joined the ministry unmarried. An itinerant life with no hope of material reward awaited Wilfrid and his wife. The financial prospects were bleak: The minister's stipend was less than five pounds (twenty dollars) a week, and for the rest of his income he was dependent on the generosity of the congregation.

"We had our faith," Mona Frost recalled. She had to make do and mend things, but her peace of mind made up for the hard life.

"The Lord will provide," her husband said.

Their daughters were growing up, and they were anxious to give them a good start in life. The proceeds from the sale of the house dwindled. Much of it was expended on the education of the two girls.

From Horsham the Reverend Mr. Frost went to Burnley, in the north of England, and south again four years later to Tenterden, a small town in the county of Kent. In 1938, thirteen years after Mona had had her last baby, she had news for her husband which was at once exciting and disconcerting. She was expecting another child. "The thought of starting a family all over again!" she exclaimed. "I was rather upset."

Wilfrid was overjoyed and prayed for a boy. When her time came, he drove his wife in their ramshackle old car to Kenchhill Nursing Home, then returned to his manse. At 10:30 A.M. the following morning, Good Friday, April 7, 1939—the day Benito Mussolini invaded Albania—a baby boy was born to Mona Frost: "The most wonderful thing that ever happened," she said.

Her husband received the news just before the 11 A.M. service. Said the doctor who told him, "He was so pleased, he had wings."

"What a boy he was!" said Mona Frost. They called him David.

"Tenterden," says the guidebook, "nestles in the Weald of Kent . . . an attractive enough town with good shops. . . . A veritable hotbed of religion."

"Tenterden," said David Frost about the town of his birth, "is a very nice place. I left it when I was nine months old, and when I returned many years later, people always said to me, 'My, how you have grown!'"

David was an attractive baby with fair curls. He was plump—"too plump, in fact," Mrs. Frost thought. Her husband adored him. The Reverend Kenneth Aldrich, Mona's brother, officiated at the christening. Wilfrid heated the sacramental water and stood by with a handkerchief to dry the baby's head lest he catch cold. As soon as the boy could talk, he was taught his prayers and taken to Sunday services and Sunday school. From the time he was three, he said grace before his meals and sometimes still does.

Kempston, where the Reverend W. J. Paradine Frost and his family settled next, is a suburb of Bedford. The Methodist minister, a big, pink-cheeked, cheerful man, became a popular figure in the town. Touring his parish on a bicycle, he often carried little David in a seat in front of him, specially built to accommodate the boy.

David was only four when he was sent to Crescent and Froebel House, Bedford—the Froebel method, named after the German educator who invented the kindergarten, dispenses with strict discipline and gives children a great deal of latitude. (A boy called Thorne, David remembers, kept jumping up in the middle of class, shouting, "Dick Barton, special agent"—the Batman of his time—and sitting down again. He was not rebuked.) Such an education, which puts emphasis on self-reliance, helps to build character. To the kindergarten department of the school we owe the first "Frost report" (spring, 1944):

> David has settled down happily at school and has made good progress during the term. His gentle nature and generosity have helped him to establish a friendly relationship with other children. He is a little inclined to be too dependent and is being encouraged to make more efforts to solve his own little problems. He shows promise of good ability in the beginnings of number and language work and is responsive to all activities. He is a willing and helpful member of his group.
>
> [Signed] [Mistress] M. Breasley
> [Headmistress] M. Spence

With two big sisters and a fond mother, David's early years were a little woman-bound. He was greatly indulged, but Mrs.

Frost kept a good grip on affairs—and has not relaxed it to this day: "David was a good boy," she said, "but not too good." His sisters did extremely well, and their parents, who had sacrificed so much for their education, had the satisfaction of seeing Jean win a scholarship to Liverpool University. Margaret trained as a children's nurse.

By this time the Reverend Mr. Frost was on the move again. Gillingham, in the county of Kent, became the biggest station on his circuit. While his father read the lesson to a growing congregation, David spent most of his time reading comics. "Don't you want to read some good books?" his father used to ask. The boy and his comics were not easily separated, however. It was some time before he grew out of them and "graduated" to football annuals.

"When worried mothers tell me their boys will read nothing but comics," said Mrs. Frost, "I tell them about David."

On weekends his father often took him to the local railway station to watch the trains and locomotives, which fascinated David. He became a devoted engine-watcher and meticulously noted the numbers and names of the big monsters as they roared by. A talent for imitating people which David developed sometimes caused embarrassment. Nothing and nobody was sacred. "Coming home from church," his mother recalled, "he even picked up things Daddy said in the pulpit and made fun of them." His father did not mind, really, and father-son relations could not have been happier.

David warmly reciprocated the affection showered upon him: "Father was a marvelous man," he said recently. "So liberal, so tolerant, without ever giving up his basic, almost fundamental faith."

The youngster could take a scolding without bitterness and never bore grudges. (He is still inclined to offer the other cheek and embrace—or employ—his enemies rather than fight them.) He was enrolled at Gillingham Barsole Road County Primary Junior Boys' School, which he remembers as "an ordinary school, a sensible school where they belted you."

There were forty-seven in the class, and he might not have been well received had he not been strongly recommended: "He is an intelligent boy, and his father is a minister," the headmaster told a reluctant teacher.

Rosy-cheeked and still well rounded, David was strong with an excess of energy and did not take kindly to the switch from Froebel freedom to normal school discipline. Overworked teachers had difficulty controlling him: "He was always bobbing up and down," one of them recorded.

Still, he was well liked and made friends easily. His schoolmates called him Jack—in England every Frost is called Jack after Jack Frost, the storybook character who personifies cold weather. Teachers also had fun with his name: "Paradine Frost?" one of them quipped, "or Paradise Lost? Ha ha ha!"

David was soccer mad; he lived and breathed it. He was a great supporter of the local team: "My weekends were entirely dependent on whether the Gills's forward line scored and won," he said. He toasted them in orange juice, showered them with potato chips instead of confetti, and shouted, "Up the Gills!"

For him, though, soccer was not just a spectator sport. He played the game with great skill: "I always kicked a ball around—I only learned to read so as to follow the league football results." He was carried away with fantasies of fame, and his favorite character was a larger-than-life soccer player in a popular comic book.

Once David settled down, his progress in school was steady. The school report on David Frost for the summer term, 1950, boasted a long line of A's and B's, broken only by a solitary C for geography: "He has distinguished himself both as an enthusiastic sportsman and an aspiring scholar. The Grammar School is the right place for him, and no doubt in time he will be one of its chief ornaments."

Was Gillingham the right place for him? There was no alternative. Although the minister's stipend rose a little—to five pounds, fifteen shillings (then less than twenty-five dollars) a week—funds were desperately short at the manse. Mrs. Frost had to watch every penny; it was years since she had had a new coat. Yet there was talk of sending David to a private school, a rather expensive business.

"When Father and Mother opened the question," he recalled, "I somehow realized that sending me to a boarding school would mean a vast burden. Besides, life at home at the manse was far too interesting." After some heart-searching the plan was abandoned. Was David disappointed? "It was not a big crisis in my life," he said. "I was still very young. A week or so later I hardly remembered."

As a boy he was very thrifty. When he was given money on his birthday or at Christmas, it went straight into the savings bank. He liked collecting money—not only for himself but also for the church—and was so good at raising pennies that he earned several medals.

Pranks and practical jokes kept him and his schoolmates amused. They sharpened their schoolboy wits at the expense of other people. One of David's favorite ploys, far from original, was to stop a man in the street and ask, "Haven't we met in Johannesburg?" When the stranger replied that he had never been to Johannesburg, the boy would blurt out, "Neither have I—it must have been two other people," and run off.

David was fifteen when the Reverend Mr. Frost was transferred to Raunds, a little Northamptonshire town, his income climbing up slowly toward a peak of ten pounds, ten shillings (or about forty dollars) a week. Faith and football dominated David's life. He entered Wellingborough Grammar School, which had a long and distinguished rugby tradition and also had a cricket team—but no soccer. For David this posed a grave dilemma.

Like most English boys, he took naturally to cricket, and doing well at whatever he attempted, performed well enough at rugby. He was careful, however, not to play so well as to qualify for the school rugby team, which competed against the other schools on Saturdays, for on Saturdays David joined the Raunds soccer team, which had a place in a minor league.

This Saturday game was the highlight of his week. News of the accomplished young player spread until the scout of a well-known soccer club came to watch him and tried to sign him as a professional; had he accepted, he might even then have earned more than his father. For David, his soccer success remains a matter of pride which television's greatest honors have not put in the shade. "I was a natural ball-player" is one of his rare boasts. He still cannot resist kicking a ball around and sometimes crosses the Atlantic for no other reason than to play in a showbiz charity football match in England.

On a visit to Devon he dived into the sea with boyish exuberance, but swimming was not his sport. Venturing out of his depth, he was overwhelmed by the waves and nearly drowned. He was rescued in the nick of time and never forgot his terror: "My whole past life flashed before me at that moment, as it was supposed to do," he remembered, "but unfortunately, I was only thirteen at the time, so there wasn't much to flash and it wasn't much fun. Now, today . . ." Hard as he tried, water was the only element in which he could never keep afloat.

He was still up to his pranks. In his last year at Wellingborough he started writing spoof letters to local newspapers; some of them were actually printed. In one letter he demanded that all public parks should be closed, in another that a nude statue in the town should be draped.

London seemed a faraway place, and a trip to the capital, even by bus, was a luxury the minister's family could not often afford. At Easter, 1954, however, David and his parents were among the busloads of people from all over England who converged on London—and Harringay Arena—to attend the opening of the Reverend Billy Graham's Greater London Crusade. David was spellbound. Thousands responded to the handsome preacher from the American Bible Belt. "I didn't actually go forward," David said, but his encounter with Billy Graham's fervent evangelism helped to trigger off an intense religious period in his young life.

The family went to London to hear Billy Graham once more, and then one of his evangelist associates, Grady Wilson, came to speak at the Reverend Mr. Frost's church. "I had been exposed to religion all my life," David later remarked, "yet it was around that time that the whole religious thing got through to me." "The whole religious thing" has remained with him ever since. David's Christianity has come through in many of his interviews with church leaders, among them Billy Graham, who has been a guest on his shows in London and New York.

Young Methodists often come forward and say that they would like to start preaching. As a minister's son David soon joined the queue. Having grown up in a manse, preaching came to him naturally, and he felt quite at home in the pulpit. By the time he was seventeen, he was an accomplished lay preacher. "He made up the whole order of the service and chose the hymns and the passages from the Bible to match for reading," his mother said. "At one time Daddy thought David might like to follow in his footsteps, but the boy seemed anxious to go out into the world. His mind was made up."

He took his preaching seriously, nonetheless. Accompanied by a senior layman, he visited surrounding villages to preach and was listened to with respect. His congregations grew to rival those of his father. To the Reverend Wilfrid Frost it was a matter of pride.

What was so appealing about David's sermons was the humor with which he flavored them. The style he developed remains a characteristic of his television appearances. Once, taking leave of his congregation, he told them not to worry: "After all, I am only going to be two hours away," he said, and after a pregnant pause added, with a pointed reference to the distant local station, "One hour on the train, and one hour to get home from the station."

Some of his jokes were a little racier. One of his favorite stories was about the preacher whose theme was the parable of the Wise and the Foolish Virgins and who challenged his congregation: "Well, my friends, what are we going to do? Are we going to stay alert with the wise virgins, or are we going to sleep with the foolish virgins?"

A couple of years ago, after he had won fame, David discovered among a stack of invitations to speak at functions all over the country one signed by Geoffrey W. Cooksey, who invited him to address his school in the north of England. "I shall be delighted" was David's prompt reply. He fondly remembered Geoffrey Cooksey as the tall, studious young man with a shock of dark hair who was one of his teachers—his favorite teacher—at Wellingborough. David feels he owes him a great deal: "He ignited my interest in language, in communication," he said. "He was a very good teacher." Mr. Cooksey held his classes in the school library, and David remembers him talking, for instance, about the various English newspapers, comparing them and discussing the different approaches of papers like the conservative *Daily Telegraph* and the comparatively radical *Daily Mirror*. David soon toyed with the idea of becoming a journalist.

If Mr. Cooksey awakened his interest in language, a neighbor with a television set—a luxury David's father's manse could not boast—can take credit for having infected David with the television bug. At every opportunity he put his head around the door of the home of Mrs. Gladys Lawrence—"Auntie Gladys"—a handsome woman who was a member of Mr. Frost's congregation. Auntie Gladys may have thought that David had a crush on her, but if he was infatuated, it was with the television set. He could not tear himself away and sat for hours studying television personalities until he was able to imitate them. Another attraction of the Lawrence home was a tape recorder he was allowed to use. He taped his impersonations, listened to the recording, polished his phraseology, and rerecorded his voice until he was satisfied with the way it sounded to him.

He was a natural entertainer. An outlet for his talent was found when he joined the church youth club, which went in for dramatics and other social activities. To organize them and to act as hosts to the congregation were the duties of the Reverend Mr. Frost and his wife. It was not long before they found they could leave arrangements to their precocious son.

During school vacations David took charge of the Methodist concerts, prepared scripts, invented novel party games and competitions, and acted as master of ceremonies. "Some of the social evenings, to be frank," Mona Frost said, "used to be dull as ditchwater. When David took over, they became a huge success. He really made them interesting." The church hall was the scene of his earliest stage triumphs. Behind the church hall he used to meet Margaret, his first girl friend, who made a big impression on him and is not forgotten—David mentioned her in one of his recent shows in New York.

In the summer of 1955 the Reverend Mr. Frost took his family to a Methodist holiday center in Swanage, in the county of Dorset. For the hundred or so holiday-makers David did some of his impersonations of television stars, imitating Eamonn Andrews, of *This Is Your Life,* and Gilbert Harding, of *What's My Line?* The following year at a Methodist holiday camp in Eastbourne he further developed his repertoire.

David is fond of saying that he did not study very hard. One of his teachers remembers that he would not concentrate on any single subject, a failing on which some of his associates still remark. According to another teacher, though, he had "a mind like a vacuum cleaner" and was very quick on the uptake.

He had to be fairly good to qualify, as he did, for a state scholarship to a university. This was more difficult to come by than a scholarship endowed by the university. Cambridge, for which he was heading, could not immediately offer a place, however. David decided to fill in the time as a teacher and found a job with a (secondary modern) school at Irthlingborough, near Raunds. "The town had a shoe factory and a pea factory," he said. "The school got these boys and girls for a brief spell before they were bound for a lifetime working in one or the other."

Fond of children, he enjoyed teaching but was rather critical of the syllabus. Instead of discoursing learnedly about ancient history, he gave his pupils an inkling of current affairs, which were more relevant to their lives. Ill-paid and demanding, the teaching profession in England was always short of young recruits. The headmaster would have liked David Frost to make teaching his career, but as his mother said, his mind was made up: "I shall go into performing and producing," he stated.

David did not have eyes for television only. A fair share of his attention was devoted to the local girls, who were attracted to the gregarious young man with the fresh face and the wiry build; what one American writer described as David's concave chest passes as "athletic" in England. From Margaret, his first love, he switched his affections to a girl called Jennifer, first of the many "young ladies"—as Mrs. Frost describes them—her son brought home. As girls began to play a growing part in his life Jennifer did not remain the only one for long.

Her chief rival was a photograph in an old newspaper or an image on the movie screen, whichever version you prefer. According to one, David's mother brought home the meat from the butcher one day, and David's eye fell on the newspaper wrapping, which showed a photograph of Janette Scott, the pretty and talented young English actress. He promptly fell in love with her. "Untrue!" said Mrs. Frost.

David himself has supplied the authentic story. It was in Raunds that he went to the local Carlton Cinema to see a film, *Now and Forever*, the highlight of which was the youthful star Janette Scott receiving her first screen kiss. "I was inflamed with passion," David says, with his usual touch of self-mockery. "I fancied her like mad!" Photographs of Janette Scott in fan magazines started to compete for his attention with those of his favorite soccer players in the sports columns.

The girls of the family were no longer at home. Having graduated from Liverpool University, David's sister Jean had gone to China in 1949 and married Dr. Andrew Pearson, a missionary doctor who later worked in Nigeria. Margaret, a qualified children's nurse at Great Ormond Street Hospital in London, had married real-estate agent Kenneth Bull in 1953 and gone to live with him at Whitby, in Yorkshire, but distance did not weaken the family bond. David has remained close to his sisters and is an affectionate and generous real-life uncle to his nieces and nephews.

In September, 1958, the Reverend Wilfrid Frost went to Beccles as superintendent minister of the Beccles, Loddon, and Bungay Methodist Circuit. A month later David set out for the mainly masculine realm of Cambridge. Even in the changing social climate of England in the fifties, it was a daunting prospect for an impecunious grammar-school boy with a small-town background. David's greatest asset was the fact that he was completely and blissfully unaware that this might be a handicap.

CHAPTER 3

Freshman Frost

THE WORLD OF Cambridge which David entered in 1958 was precious and sophisticated, but he was not easily overawed. His college was Gonville and Caius, called Caius for short and pronounced "keys." "I arrived in Cambridge at five in the afternoon, and by six I was in the swing of things," he said. It was not quite as simple as that, but he already had (to quote his friend, film producer Bryan Forbes) "that Maxwell House quality of instant friendship," the ability to make new acquaintances feel that they were his best friends in town, in the country, in the world.

Entering Tree Court from Trinity Street, David passed through the Gate of Humility—one of the three gates designed by Dr. John Caius, from whom the college takes its name. The others are the Gate of Virtue, dating back to 1567 and sporting two figures with a palm branch and a horn of plenty (rather appropriate for David, who nowadays has both humility and plenty), and the Gate of Honour, through which students go to receive their degrees—no easy passage for young David, as it turned out.

Sundays he went to chapel but soon missed one service, then another and another, until his visits to chapel became rarer and rarer. Yet whenever he was on vacation in Beccles, he still went to neighboring villages to preach from the pulpit, his enthusiasm and appeal undiminished.

At college the outer door of his room was often closed. This was called sporting the oak and meant that he was working or entertaining a lady and did not wish to be disturbed. He did not

31

lead a retiring life, though—on the contrary—and was recognized wherever he went.

Like many undergraduates, he regularly listened to the radio program *Any Questions?* on which people of distinction—academics, writers, actors—discussed topics before large audiences in English provincial centers. He could visualize the team sitting on a platform and holding forth. . . . Oh, to be one of them! He was a voracious newspaper-reader and well informed on current affairs; he still cannot pass a newsstand without automatically picking up a few papers. At Cambridge he was mainly interested in the university's student publications, among them *Granta,* the leading magazine, and *Varsity,* the newspaper. He was impatient to become a contributor to one or the other—preferably to both. In the solitude of his room he wrote his first satirical piece to offer to the editors; its subject was the *Reader's Digest.*

The Footlights, the university's revue club, was a great attraction, and when he went to see a performance, he was impressed by the clever fellows who wrote and acted out the sketches on the stage. Some of them did imitations much like those he had done at the Methodist youth club. There was John Bird, who became his close friend; Peter Cook, his senior by a year, a fine writer and straight-faced comic; and Eleanor Bron, a stately, handsome girl cut out for the stage. David felt very much at home among them. The stage was his world. The sooner he could join the Footlights, the better. He could not wait to be asked, and he did not have to wait long.

Studying, alas, ran a poor third. And a bad "Third," a disastrously low mark for a state scholar, was the verdict of his teachers when they assessed his progress at the end of his first year. It was touch and go whether he would be expelled. The Reverend Mr. Frost was terribly upset that David might have to leave the university, but David, as he so often did, hung on by his teeth.

He came back for his second year without any intention of reducing his extramural activities. Life at the university was too full of distractions and opportunities for that. The poor boy from the simple manse—no alcohol, no rich food, no Sunday newspapers—was thirsting for all those things. As a first step toward the good life for which he was yearning, he helped to found the

Cabal gourmet club, which was the beginning of his interest in good wine—he rarely drank hard liquor.

Societies, committees, organizations, functions—he loved becoming involved. Many undergraduates avoided the administrative side of college life like the plague, but David reveled in it. Armed with a bag of coins, he occupied the telephone as if he were linked to it by an umbilical cord. (He still has a mania for telephoning.) Friends, editors, television executives, were at the receiving end of his incessant calls.

To some of the younger students the university's literary and theatrical cliques seemed a bit snobbish and remote. Not to David. He did not have to knock at their doors too long. The pieces he wrote for *Varsity* and *Granta* were amusing and readily accepted, including a well-written interview with a voguish publisher which he brought back from a trip to London. He was also interested in the production end of *Granta*, raring to get his hands on it.

When he became editor, it was said that it was because William Dunlop, his predecessor, did not want his reputation dimmed by too eminent a successor—and consequently sponsored David Frost. Similar digs have been made by his sophisticated friends at every stage of his career. David's appointment was announced with a typical spoof "WARNING" by the departing editors:

> Please remember this is not granta but a cheap substitute put together at the same price. . . . The first person opened in this office who can guess the least number of misprints, and simultaneously reveal the whereabouts of granta's new 12-storey office block (mislaid) is invited to tea (or sherry) with next year's editor, funloving laughable DAVID FROST who can be seen already searching . . . for contributions with a butterfly net. . . .

His telltale grammar-school accent became polished—but not affected—producing the classless voice that now appeals to many listeners. It easily earned him a place among the Footlights cast. Like most of the performers, David enjoyed the productions as much as the audiences did, if not more so. He appeared in a number of revues whose topical humor does not travel well across the years. One of the sketches in which he figured was called "Pop Goes Mrs. Jessop," but he was at his best when doing monologues. For the young lay preacher it was easy to make contact across the footlights.

One of his favorite roles was that of a "television announcer" giving details of future "Epilogues," the brief religious broadcasts with which the B.B.C. closed its daily transmissions. One of these spoof epilogues was on the Creation, Crucifixion, and Resurrection and was entitled "God, Son of God, Return of the Son of God." "No," he said, looking back, "they were not particularly irreverent." The theme was later to recur on one of his television shows, creating an uproar.

In a skit on a NATO meeting David made fun of the pomposity and triviality which go hand in hand at international assemblies. Delegates addressed each other by the names of their countries: "Take off your earphones, Holland!" David demanded. He played the German delegate, opposite Peter Cook as the French representative.

Granta and Footlights were ideal shopwindows for literary and show-business talent. David was quickly noticed in both departments. Anglia Television gave him a five-minute spot. The first press reference to David Frost, TV performer, appeared in the Beccles newspaper:

> Mr. David Frost of the Manse, Frederick's Road, Beccles, who recently returned from Cambridge University for the summer vacation, made an appearance on Anglia T.V. on Sunday afternoon. He contributed a recorded five minute satirical feature on the programme "Open Air". As the recording had been made the previous day, Mr. Frost was able to sit at home with his parents, the Rev. W. J. Paradine Frost, the Methodist superintendent minister, and Mrs. Frost and watched the programme.

The Reverend Mr. Frost expected to hear a religious broadcast—"I think someone told father it was Anglican Television," David said with a smile—but he was pleased with his son's debut.

Other opportunities came to David, who invested the financial rewards, small as they were, in gracious living and status symbols. For his stage appearances he bought his first evening clothes, a ready-made tuxedo for the equivalent of seventy-five dollars, but he also wore it on social occasions. The bills he started running up at Miller's Wine Parlour helped to develop his palate. In the best Cambridge tradition, they were settled only some time after he had left the university. Breakfast in bed became one of his indulgences, and he often hired a taxi driver to bring him the Sunday newspapers. When he moved from the college residence into his own apartment, his nocturnal activities kept his landlady awake: "Either he sat up all night writing, or he came in late," she said.

It was not all work. Apart from writing and acting, he cultivated the girls. "I became rather expert at climbing in and out of Newnham and Girton," he said. (Both are girls' colleges. Girton girls have a reputation for courage and unselfishness, but they have something of a reputation for unconventionality and free living too.)

David at this time acquired a special girl friend in Cambridge, named Marion. He remembers her fondly, but during vacations he returned to Beccles and to Jennifer. "They were on-and-off affairs," he said.

Undergraduates took a lively interest in television. Like many of them, David was familiar with the structure of the medium in Britain, where TV was dominated by the B.B.C. (British Broadcasting Corporation), a typically English institution operating under a royal charter, financed by viewers' fees and delicately balanced between official status and a jealously guarded independence from government interference. Hotly competing with the B.B.C. were the commercial television companies, financed by advertising revenue and subject to license by the independent television authority set up under an Act of Parliament. When David first surveyed the scene, eight companies held licenses and were doing so well that the head of one of them described his franchise as "a license to print money."

Rediffusion, the biggest of the eight, made a practice of recruiting new talent from among undergraduates, sending out scouts to find the brightest boy and the brightest girl of the year and to invite them to submit themselves to scrutiny by a selection board.

In 1960 their choice fell on David Frost and Sue Turner, a girl from Reading University. Without a trace of nerves and with every sign of self-assurance, David presented himself to the selection board at Rediffusion headquarters, Television House, in London's Kingsway. He passed the test (so did Sue Turner), which guaranteed him a trainee job after graduation.

In the last week of his last term David took part in a new Footlights revue and was doing his stuff on stage when Richard Armitage, a leading London theatrical agent, visited Cambridge on one of his frequent talent-scouting forays. Armitage is the head of the Noel Gay theatrical agency, named after his famous father, who wrote the score for several London revues produced by Charles Cochran, as well as prewar song hits like "The Lambeth Walk." "I went to Cambridge at the invitation of two other members of the Footlights cast—never mind their names," Armitage said. "After a quarter of an hour I knew that I did not want either." Then it was David Frost's turn, and he reeled off a series of jokes. "They were not very good," Armitage recalled, "but this young man carried his own atmosphere."

"Actually, the material was pretty good," David has said in retrospect, but then there are few things in which he does not find something good. "Many a myth has grown up about my early work."

There was no doubt in Richard Armitage's mind about David himself. He often acted on instinct about performers. Instead of walking out, he stayed and watched. "I very much wanted David," he said. "I sent a note backstage asking him to come and see me."

For David there still remained the minor formality of graduation. He passed his exams, he likes to say with self-mocking bravado, with the help of "purple heart" pills and a few sleepless nights. In the summer of 1961 he graduated from Cambridge with a modest Second Class Honours degree. (Nine years later the family association with Cambridge was resumed when, in the autumn of 1970, Michael Pearson, David's nephew, entered Caius College.)

David's advent in the adult world—he was twenty-one—coincided with a period of profound social change, which he eventually helped to accelerate. After a decade of Tory rule Prime Minister Macmillan's tired administration, lacking in imagination and initiative, was stumbling toward political decline. This was the dawning of the age of irreverence. A gap yawned between ordinary people and the vested interests of politics, authority, church, finance, business, which London writer Henry Fairlie lumped together as "the Establishment."

The mood was expertly captured by four recent university graduates. They were Jonathan Miller, who commuted between the stage and the pathology laboratory; Peter Cook, who had graduated from Cambridge a year ahead of David; the Oxford-reared, donnish Alan Bennett, son of a Leeds butcher; and (also from Oxford) Dudley Moore, a jazz musician whose father was an electrician. The four wrote and starred in a revue, *Beyond the Fringe*, which carried on the tradition of Cambridge's Footlights. It was a tremendous hit when it was first performed at the Edinburgh Festival of 1960 and was even more widely acclaimed when it transferred to the Fortune Theatre in London the following year.

The revue's social commentary and irreverent attitude to sacred cows reflected the frustrations of many people. The author-performers proved that jokes about Harold Macmillan could be as funny as jokes about mothers-in-law. They took on racist South Africa, plodding trade unions, the Church of England, the national anthem, and the Queen. A characteristic sketch portrayed a theatergoer who had seen the same show 850 times craning his neck from a cheap seat in the hope of seeing royalty in the audience. When asked why he did not take a better seat, he answered, "They're not worth it."

The Prime Minister, back from Washington, D.C., was quoted in the show as saying, "I was interested to see that President Kennedy also believes government is a family affair!"

The Queen laughed heartily when she came to a performance. She applauded when one of the actors sighed and said in a philosophical vein, "Life is like a tin of sardines. We are always looking for the key."

The vogue for *Beyond the Fringe* was still strong when Peter Cook brought out the first primitive mimeographed issues of *Private Eye*, an underground paper with some articles then considered outrageous. It circulated in Chelsea pubs and coffee houses but soon came to the surface, stirring up high waves of indignation (and not a few libel actions). In the same vein Cook opened

The Establishment, a nightclub in the striptease belt of Soho, where the political satires performed proceeded to strip the veneer from the high and the mighty. Cook was carrying on where the prewar continental political cabarets had left off. Stand-up comics at The Establishment poked fun at their stuffy audiences, who were largely from the very classes—gluttons for punishment—that were the comics' principal targets. Satire was the shrine at which everybody worshiped. The leading protagonists of this new wave, most of them David's friends, were being extravagantly acclaimed—or savagely attacked.

Poor but hopeful, it was at this stage that David went to London to start his trainee job with Rediffusion. At first he took a room in a mews near Regent's Park, but he soon moved into a bachelor's pad on Churton Street, near Victoria Station, a modest and chaotic place that he shared with his Cambridge friend John Bird, whose adroit stage impersonations were already an integral part of the London scene. With a foothold in television, David prepared to conquer other objectives: to begin with, the press. He had nothing to offer except talent—or perhaps that is not quite correct. He already carried a collection of his manuscripts, short stories, humorous articles, and monologues in his bulging briefcase. As time went on and his production increased, the briefcases grew bigger and stouter; nowadays he is rarely without two or three big bags full of stage and TV material.

One of his first destinations in London was the Noel Gay office on Denmark Street, the heart of the city's Tin Pan Alley. Richard Armitage handed him over to Diana Crawfurd, one of his aides. A strikingly good-looking Scottish girl, Diana had also recently graduated—from secretary to agent—and was looking after two Noel Gay clients. "You take care of Mr. Frost," Armitage instructed her. She was nervous, and David was nervous. "But he was charming," Diana said.

She promised to do what she could. "All he could expect," Diana thought, "was a few shillings for a thousand words." Yet the outposts of the press yielded more quickly than expected. Diana Crawfurd managed to sell some of his contributions to *Queen* and *Strand* magazines, both now defunct. The fees were small, but "Goodnight, Mr. Gladston," a short story by David Frost, has been reprinted as evidence of his early efforts.

Television did not embrace him with open arms. He was

attached to *This Week*, a topical program, and received a salary of fifteen pounds a week. His first jobs were almost menial. It was not unusual for the youngest member of the staff to be sent for coffee or cigarettes, but David made good use of his apprenticeship. He learned to write captions, frame questions for interviews, and research difficult topics; he became familiar with the technique of putting a show together.

Major items for *This Week* were taped some distance away, in Wembley (it so happened that a few years later David was one of the men who assumed control of the Wembley studios), but some studio work for the show was done at Television House, where David worked. He watched the proceedings with a hawk-eye, studied lighting and camera angles, analyzed the cameramen's every move, and acquainted himself with all aspects of the complicated process. No newcomer to the medium showed greater interest in the technicalities of television, and few performers came to know more about them.

His only contact with the big television audience was an occasional assignment to interview people in the street; his voice was heard but his face was not seen. The sad fact was that Cyril Bennett, producer of *This Week*, did not have a very high opinion of the ambitious novice. David's face and teeth seemed to Bennett less than photogenic and made him, in Bennett's view, totally unsuitable as a performer. In television terms the misjudgment was so monumental that the perpetrator has since basked in the doubtful glory of being the man who turned down David Frost. David does not bear grudges. Some years later Bennett popped up in a key post in the television company of which David was by then a major shareholder. Their association continued even after Bennett went into other television ventures.

Though frustrated and angry, David never showed his disappointment. His self-control was already firm—to this day even close associates mistake his ability to master his feelings for emotional immunity. Neither did he give up hope. He was soldiering on at Rediffusion by day but had not lost touch with the satire crowd. He was delighted to receive a call from Peter Cook's Establishment club when one of the star performers was indisposed. David's versatility was most useful, and he stepped into the breach. From then on he was frequently seen on The Establishment's stage.

His refusal to accept defeat at Rediffusion proved justified. Red-haired, bearded Elkan Allan, a former journalist who was in charge of the entertainment department at Rediffusion, was the only executive who sensed David's potential. Without much difficulty, he persuaded Cyril Bennett to let the young television recruit join his own department. David was put to work on a series entitled *Let's Twist.* . . . Soon he and Allan toured London's dance halls and clubs to find young couples for a Twist contest to be held in the Rediffusion studios, with David as master of ceremonies. The program was a big success, and for the second show they moved to Paris, birthplace of the Twist, going on to the South of France for the third and final edition, "Let's Twist on the Riviera."

David, according to Elkan Allan, quickly showed his amazing aptitude for the medium: "His grasp of situations was instantaneous. He absorbed the most complicated instructions at the first time of telling and did not need an auto-cue." The trouble was that he did not look the part. His total lack of interest in clothes, such as many Cambridge men affect, was out of tune with the show. In the Riviera sun his baggy trousers, ill-fitting jacket, and worn suede shoes made him look shabby.

"I shall get you a new outfit on expenses," Elkan Allan insisted. David was reluctant to waste money—even Rediffusion's money— on such trivialities. In any event, he refused to spend more than a few hundred francs on one or two new things. To make David's expense account look more respectable, Allan bought himself an expensive suit and charged it to his account.

On the day of shooting, the sun gave way to clouds and a heavy downpour. Wearing sunglasses and shorts to convey the traditional Côte d'Azur atmosphere, David was drenched as he introduced the show. Completely unperturbed, he spoke his commentary as if all were sunshine and light, ending with a boorish remark by Comrade Nikita Khrushchev which he had dug up for the occasion: "The Twist arouses passions, inflames the lust, and is an enemy of the state." He returned from his sojourn in the South of France looking as if the Mediterranean sun had never touched his pale cheeks (David always comes back from a vacation looking worse than when he started out).

Once the program was shown, David reaped the first harvest of television fame. Raunds promptly staked a claim to its former resident and football star and invited him to judge a Twist competition at the local "Fiesta." It was the first of scores of such invitations, which prompted David's friends to say that the people of Beccles refer to the seasons no longer as spring, summer, fall, and winter but by the occasions of David's visits to open a Christmas bazaar or an Easter parade. When Beccles calls, David never refuses.

For the ex-Footlights star there were also bound to be opportunities in cabarets and nightclubs. Richard Armitage introduced David to a nightclub owner, Max Setty, of the Blue Angel, whose brother, as David put it, "was involved in a sensational murder case in the worst possible way—he was the victim." Setty engaged him for a week's trial at a fee amounting to a hundred dollars. David prepared himself meticulously for his professional debut and wrote a monologue that bristled with topical jokes. He designed a press conference a la Harold Macmillan, then the satirists' indispensable Aunt Sally, the butt of their jokes, to provoke maximum audience participation.

On the opening night he plunged into his act with the nonchalant self-confidence that is the hallmark of the born performer. He could think on his feet. His knack for apt repartee and his ability to deal with the most unexpected situations still remain his outstanding qualities. "What subject do you want me to talk about?" he asked the audience.

Hoping to lure him into some kind of lese majesty, they shouted, "The Queen! The Queen!"

"The Queen is not a subject!" David came back quick as a flash.

"Mr. Frost has to be pretty quick-witted to keep up with events," wrote a critic.

An advertisement Richard Armitage inserted in *The Stage,* the house journal of England's theatrical profession, paid rich dividends and tells the rest of the story:

Noel Gay Artists
congratulate brilliant young comedian
David Frost
on his cabaret debut
booked at the Blue Angel for a week,
retained for two months.

CHAPTER 4

Satire for the Millions

THE CRACKLING FIRE of satire showed no sign of burning itself out. Peter Cook's club, The Establishment, ran into difficulties, but they were largely brought about by the late Lenny Bruce, the American comedian whose blue act was then a few steps ahead of the permissive society and was too liberally sprinkled with four-letter words. *Beyond the Fringe* was bound for the United States, where it was a big hit in Washingon, D.C., and had a most rewarding season in New York. Nonetheless, satire, familiar to English theatergoers and nightclub patrons, had yet to find a national TV platform. Had anyone predicted that it would soon be provided by "Auntie B.B.C.," few people would have believed it.

Rival claims and idle boasts obscure the origin of the plan to let millions of B.B.C. listeners in on the joke. What is certain is that Ned Sherrin, of the smiling eyes and the acid wit, returning from New York to his job as producer in London of the topical B.B.C. news magazine *Tonight*, brought with him a memorandum outlining a new type of show; he and his friends did not like the "satire" label. Who sent him to New York in the first place is difficult to determine. Kenneth Adam, director of B.B.C. Television, claimed that the whole idea began at the top, with him and the "D.G.," the B.B.C.'s director general, Hugh Carleton Greene, who used to be a British newspaper correspondent in Berlin before the war.

Be that as it may, the *Tonight* stable was put to work on the project as soon as Sherrin returned. His show was now brought

43

under the umbrella of current affairs rather than entertainment, and his memo went through Alasdair Milne, editor of *Tonight*, to Donald Baverstock, the gifted, volatile Welshman who backed the program even before it went to the higher echelons of the B.B.C. Adam and Greene finally nodded assent, though according to another version, they did not come into it again until much later. Ned Sherrin was given a small budget to compile a pilot show, assemble ideas, and recruit a few writers and performers. The anchorman who first came to mind was Peter Cook, but when the success of *Beyond the Fringe* carried him across the Atlantic, Ned Sherrin offered the job to John Bird.

Planning to give Bird a second string, Sherrin was looking for suitable candidates when he came across a review of David Frost's act and also saw the Noel Gay advertisement in *The Stage*. The new young comic was obviously worth a closer look. He decided to go to the Blue Angel that night.

A well-known television producer in the audience was enough to galvanize the nightclub and send a current of excitement through the dressing rooms. Everybody was impatient for the beginning of the show, which was at 1:30 A.M. "What time is David Frost coming on?" Sherrin inquired.

The answer was a curt: "Not at all!" The act seemed to have been cut out. It sounded as if it had lost its appeal and the young hopeful had been sacked.

"I decided to stay on just the same," Ned Sherrin said, "because my old friend Hutch, the singer and pianist, was also on the bill." Sherrin seems to remember that an agent by the name of Beatrice Braham persuaded the manager to put David on after all.

"Ned has rewritten history," David said with a smile when asked about the incident. "There never was any question of me not going on that night. Max Setty wouldn't dream of wasting his money like that."

He did go on, of course, and went through his routine with great panache. Ned Sherrin liked him immensely. Once more there was the familiar verdict: "David can think on his feet." He was being discovered for the second time. "Not so," said Sherrin, "David discovered himself."

"Come and see me at Lime Grove"—the B.B.C. studios—Ned told David, who remembers traveling to Shepherd's Bush wearing a turquoise floral plastic raincoat purchased from a corner store for three shillings.

An icy rain was pouring down: "I was drenched to the skin," David said. "Most of our meetings seemed to be accompanied by rain, hail, and sleet."

They went to lunch at Bertorelli's, a favorite hangout of B.B.C. people working at nearby Lime Grove, and were joined by *Tonight*'s assistant producer, Antony Jay, a stimulating writer who was helping to develop the pilot script for the new show. "Ned told me to come and take a look at this lad," Antony Jay recalled.

Restraining his undergraduate ebullience, David did not make an immediate impression. Besides, Sherrin and Jay, ten years older than he, with their air of intellectual authority, were pretty formidable people to meet. "He was a listener rather than an impression-maker," Jay said. "I remember just an intelligent young man from Cambridge." Jay thought that Ned's instinct might well be right, however.

The note about David Frost sent to Donald Baverstock by Sherrin read, "Ex-Footlights (Cambridge), looks promising. Have seen him conducting Press Conference as cabaret turn at a night-club where he was limited by the stupidity of the customers." David at least qualified for a job as a supporting comic.

Producer, writers, performers, were already hard at work on the first pilot show. "It was rather inchoate," according to Tony Jay. "We were clutching at everything. What we aimed at was 'bi-sociation' of light entertainment and politics."

John Bird opted out, lured to the United States by an offer that seemed a safer bet than the embryonic show with which they were toying at Lime Grove. The search for an anchorman was resumed. The choice fell on Brian Redhead, a young journalist. David was asked to preside over the lighter side of the proceedings. Recording was only a week away when he was offered a contract. It was a big opportunity, bigger than he had expected. The show was tailor-made for him, and the genre was one in which he had been artistically reared. *Private Eye* traced its ancestry from troupes at Cambridge (Footlights) and at Oxford (The Salopian) through *Beyond the Fringe* and *Tonight* to Sherrin and Frost.

For the first time but by no means the last David was torn by divided loyalties. Rediffusion, however grudgingly, had given him his first chance. Now, to counter the satire threat from the B.B.C., they decided to launch a similar show of their own, although, operating under the tight charter for commercial television, they could not hope to get away with as much as the B.B.C. Neither had they made an approach to David. He sought advice from the Noel Gay people. "We had long and searching conversations," Diana Crawfurd recalled. "The question was whether David ought to stay with Rediffusion or go over to the B.B.C."

At Rediffusion, when the news of David's defection finally got through, John McMillan, controller of programs, was livid. Through Elkan Allan he offered David a four-year contract at a five-figure salary. The B.B.C. project was still in the balance, and their contract was worth no more than thirteen weeks at fifty pounds per week. Yet David was totally sold on the B.B.C.: "I could never resist a challenge," he said later.

McMillan asked David to come to his office. He did not mince words. "It is thoroughly unethical," he said, "to accept training facilities from one company and switch to another."

It was not a pleasant interview. David reminded McMillan that Rediffusion had not exactly gone out of its way to give him his chance. "I would like to leave when my year's contract expires two weeks from tomorrow," he told McMillan.

"In that case, you're fired as from next Friday," McMillan told him.

"In that case, I resign tomorrow," was David's final word.

"Get out," McMillan said, fuming, "and never come back again!"

David signed with the B.B.C. The contract provided that once the show went on the air, his weekly pay would be almost tripled. David was thrilled. He took a lively interest in the drafting of his first big contract; contracts, not surprisingly, have fascinated him ever since. "He dissected every paragraph," Diana Crawfurd said, "and immediately understood the significance of such things as screen credits, for instance, of which only experienced pros are aware."

When it came to negotiating, though, he let Diana do all the talking and never opened his mouth. "He never put a foot wrong and backed me in every respect," she said, reliving the experience with evident pleasure. "He charmed all the right people at the right time. It was wonderful to negotiate for him."

David was just twenty-three but quite mature for his age. He was also conscious of his talent. As Diana put it, "He was like a Catholic who is aware of his religion." Or, perhaps, more like a Methodist.

The group David joined was, like him, largely unknown. One principal character was *Private Eye* cartoonist William Rushton, a rustic fellow with a touch of eccentricity. The skinny Lance Percival with the nutcracker face was developing his gawky undergraduate humor, and among the other pioneers were Roy Kinnear, who looked like Rushton's twin, Kenneth Cope, and David Kernan. "Millie"—Millicent Martin—a tiny, talented girl, was booked as diseuse, and Bernard Levin, an acerbic political commentator who was also a theater and television critic, prepared to step from the wings onto the stage as a fearless devil's advocate, confronting groups of interested parties—or parties with vested interests.

David's first few days on the set proved that Ned Sherrin had made the right choice. "He had energy and multiplicity," Sherrin said. "He seemed to have a unique ability to switch from wild comedy to straight narration. David was the first of a new sort of television performer coming straight from school or university into the studio and absorbing cameras and cue cards and inlay and overlay and run-up and feed-back as the basic bricks of his trade." His associates tried to analyze him. (Explaining David Frost is still a favorite pastime on both sides of the Atlantic.) Unlike Christopher Booker, another bright youngster who wrote sketches for the pilot but later became highly critical of the television age, David was not really political.

"What David has brought to the medium," said Tony Jay, "is a marvelous ability to accept a situation." It was an ability that David developed to a fine art. Intellectual versatility was married to mastery of the medium.

He helped to edit scripts, suggested solutions to technical problems, and dealt with impromptu crises. The pilot turned out to be a mammoth affair, occupying two hours and thirty minutes and including sketches, monologues, songs, and chitchat of a kind the

B.B.C. would not previously have dreamed of screening or even taping. The highlight was Bernard Levin haranguing a collection of real-life Tory ladies about—well, yes—Prime Minister Harold Macmillan. Levin's criticism exasperated the good ladies: "Mr. Macmillan has always satisfied me!" one of them retorted. It was the time of Harold Macmillan's "night of the long knives," when the Prime Minister sacked more than half his cabinet out of the blue. The "old entertainer" showing his teeth was vintage material for this kind of show.

Altogether it was an uninhibited romp across the political and social landscape by a hilarious gang with the fresh dew of cheerful dilettantism still clinging to their coattails. The getup was highly professional for all that, though. The pillars of the Establishment were the targets for some powerful invective and some bawdy jokes.

When shown the tape, B.B.C. executives chuckled, but clearly this sort of thing was not suitable for public viewing. The tape and the whole project were put in cold storage, but chuckles rippled through studios, bars, and executive suites until the Tory lady's gratuitous testimonial for Mr. Macmillan came to the ears of Director General Hugh Carleton Greene, who demanded to see the pilot—and loved it. It was too long, of course, and some of the items were unsuitable, but it was certainly worth proceeding with the idea. Work on a second pilot was begun. It was not a matter of smoothing out rough edges—a few even rougher items were included. Brian Redhead was dropped, and David naturally slid into the hot seat as the sole linkman. To get more material he and Ned Sherrin went back to the source of much contemporary humor, the universities. They visited the Footlights, and when they heard that the Oxford (University) Theatre Group was staging a revue at Edinburgh, they traveled north to have a look at it.

The Theatre Group's writer-producer, Ian Davidson, a second-year Oxford undergraduate, was particularly proud of an ingenious item that showed a conductor on stage conducting an orchestrated piece of war: mortars firing, guns bellowing, shells bursting (all noises off stage), escalating in perfect rhythm, followed by the humming of approaching aircraft, pianissimo like sweet violins, and rising again to a crescendo with a deafening bomb blast. In the silence that followed a bird was heard twittering until the conductor gave the signal for a gun—*bang!*—to blast it away. Although unmusical to the point of tone-deafness, David adopted the piece enthusiastically and made a technical improvement that enabled him to coordinate his conducting and the complicated off-stage sounds with an electric button. It became a television classic.

The second pilot did the trick. Ned Sherrin and his merry men were given the go-ahead. Scheduled for late Saturday night, repository of tired old films and unfunny old music-hall acts, the new show promised to stir things up with bold comment on current topics. It was given the title *That Was the Week That Was*.

With many sketches already in the bag, work on the topical commentaries for the opening show started on Monday, November 19, 1962, with a meeting of the principal performers and writers, who were often identical. David had a finger in all the cream pies diligently prepared to hit the Establishment smack in the face. With Christopher Booker he wrote the opening political sketch, and he collaborated with Caryl Brahms, whose thoughtful verses and ballades gave a lift to the show. Many of the lines written by ex-*Daily Mirror* writer Keith Waterhouse and by Willis Hall were fashioned to be spoken by David. He resumed cooperation with Peter Cook, the pioneer of the satirical mode, whom he had already partnered at Cambridge. He worked closely with Michael Frayn, a young playwright of soon-to-be-fulfilled promise.

As the show gathered momentum the list of contributors grew longer. One sentence in the script qualified you for a credit, which became the butt of many jokes but was a tempting incentive for creative talent. Before long it was not unusual for the list of credits to read something like this (in alphabetical order): Albury, Antrobus, Birdsall, Booker, Bradbury, Brahms, Braine, Crewe, Dobereiner, Frost, Gillespie, Glanville, Hall, Kaufman, Kretzmer, Lewis, Lewsen, Levin, Mallory, Mason, Morley, Nathan, Nobbs, Potter, Roth, Rushton, Shaffer, Sherrin, Tynan, Vinaver, Waterhouse.

The resident staff scoured the newspapers—none more hungrily than David—the week's television programs, and political events at home and abroad, with a sharp eye for the inevitable idiocy, insensitivity, and amorality. Switching abruptly from satire to pathos, from invective to ballad, the writers used slapstick, smut, or sacrilege, anything that came to mind. Being young, they were often rude. Although they denied it in public, some of the offensive stuff was deliberately calculated to stir up dust. The search for material and the pace of invention accelerated on Tuesdays, Wednesdays, and Thursdays, and while some performers were already rehearsing their sketches and memorizing their lines, writers were still producing material and bringing items up to date before the whole script was put on the auto-cue.

Intense and wearying efforts to perfect his part did not stop David from seeking perfection in another respect. Many of his free mornings and not a little of the money he was earning were spent at the dentist. Like many an actor before him, he underwent irritating and extremely painful treatment to straighten his teeth, never hinting at the discomfort he suffered in the process. The result did credit to the dentist—the teeth are among the best that flash on television—and to David's determination to allow nothing to stand in the way of success.

At 11 P.M. sharp on Saturday, November 24, 1962, the show hit the air with a noisy cacophony of near-atonal music, which dissolved into the theme song, belted out with unsuspected power by the dainty Millie Martin: "That was the week that was; it's over, let it go. . . ." (The song and the philosophy anticipated the Beatles' "Let It Be" by half a dozen years.) Brusquely interspersed into Millie's melodious recitation of the last seven days' more outrageous events were pungent, amusing comments from the residents sitting side by side at an enormous desk, David Frost presiding.

The phenomenon of the show was this very young man, this "nonpersonality" (as he was soon described), taking over by sheer force of nonpersonality. Though not in song, he carried on where Millie Martin left off. The new face launched on three million viewers presented itself as a toothy sneer beneath a quiff of hair, and a staccato manner of speaking in a precise, classless voice, with just the right intonation (a bit nasal) for a show with the declared objective of breaking down class barriers.

Most of the material was "shocking," or as Ned Sherrin put it, "thought-provoking." The show ended with David holding up the early editions of the Sunday newspapers and, impromptu, drawing attention to the more glaring bits of nonsense and folly and man's inhumanity to man. It went off without a hitch, but the B.B.C.'s telephones starting ringing long before it was over. Congratulations and complaints were more numerous than for any other new show, complaints outnumbering the plaudits. Keeping the "for" and "against" score became a journalistic pastime.

After the show, the principals went to the Casserole, a restaurant in the King's Road, which was becoming the main artery of swinging London. Some people came to think of them as conspirators who had just caused a revolution; others saw them as a gang of schoolboys who had staged a big prank and were proud of their courage but afraid of retribution. "Neither," David said. "At that time we were not aware of having gotten away with something despite the authorities. All we hoped for was that the show be well received. We were just a few young men having done a first night."

It was in the early hours of Sunday when he climbed the winding stairs to his flat and went to sleep. First thing next morning he reached for the newspapers. "Pat Williams' review in the *Sunday Telegraph* gave us tremendous encouragement," he recalled. Before the day was much older, Ned Sherrin was on the telephone; then David telephoned Christopher Booker, Booker called Rushton, and so on. The wires crisscrossing London between the homes of the young writers and performers were humming with cheers and post-mortems. That afternoon David went to Bromley, a London suburb, to listen to Helen Shapiro singing in a concert. The young star was at the peak of her success. She sang her most popular song, "Walking Back to Happiness," which perfectly fitted David's mood.

By Monday they were all at Lime Grove again to start work on the next show. The discussion was intense, the flow of ideas even richer than before. There was a tug-of-war between the out-and-out satirists and the more serious writers and some arguments about who should do what, but Ned Sherrin had a knack of catering to individual talents. "It's marvelous to work with Ned," David said.

Descending from the executive floor, Donald Baverstock joined the creative people, among whom he felt more at home. His

Welsh voice filled the room with television wisdom, and David did not miss a word. "Baverstock taught me what television was all about," he said. "The duties, the opportunities, the challenge, and the responsibilities; he was the seminal influence."

Baverstock returned the compliment. Young as David was, he drew him into the discussions about the development of the show, about the future of television. "At the time I was not sure whether it had any effect on David." He saw the seeds grow, however. "David," he concluded, "was the most remarkable man to emerge since television began." He called David simply The Television Man. What television is about, Baverstock said, is conversation. Of this, David became the past master.

The thoughts were philosophical, sublime, esoteric. The material which emerged was down to earth, hard-hitting, rough. David was the one who barked most fiercely and showed his teeth—literally—with the greatest ferocity. Even if he had not been the anchorman who pulled it all together and to whom the camera always returned, the show would still have become totally identified with him. To viewers it was immaterial whether offending lines had actually been spoken by him. Frost was responsible. Thirteen members of Parliament—"The Silent Thirteen"—were pilloried because they did not attend the House of Commons very often: "M.P.'s Bitten by Frost" was the comment when they asked that he should be indicted for breach of privilege. Their sense of proportion was restored by one of them, Reginald Paget, who said he was willing to forgive because it was such a delightful and amusing show.

An early item was "Your Consumer Guide" on religion. Basic tests: What do you put into it? What do you get out of it? How much does it cost? Sample: The Roman Catholic Church—Jesus Christ has undertaken personal responsibility for the consumer's misdemeanors. Salvation is almost foolproof. The rule here is "*don't*"—but if you must, confess as soon as possible afterwards. "Best buy"—the Church of England.

Bernard Levin greeted a gathering of farmers in the studio with, "Good evening, peasants," which caused a storm. Not many weeks later a member of the audience rushed on stage and slapped Levin's face. There was another brief uproar when David did a takeoff on a popular newscaster and announced: "The

Royal Barge is sinking in the Pool of London. . . . The Queen, wearing a radiant smile, is swimming for her life . . . and now the Royal Marine Band has struck up 'God *Save* the Queen.' "

Prince William of Gloucester was the next royal personage to get a ribbing, and promptly the House of Commons was asked "to ban references to the royal family and religion on television." No action was taken, and not many weeks passed before David and his colleagues were the guests of eight M.P.'s in the House of Commons. "They are very clever people," said one of their hosts. If he expected to get a pledge of good behavior, though, he was disappointed.

In spite of the protests, or perhaps because of them, religion and monarchy were targets too tempting to be lightly discarded. David presented "The Bible Condensed" in *Reader's Digest* style: "I have heard of natural childbirth, but this is ridiculous!" The story of Mary and Joseph: "Your child may be more gifted than you think." The Resurrection: "You can't keep a good man down!"

With some foreboding, he telephoned his parents in Beccles as soon as he came off the set: "You didn't like that, did you?" He did not really have to ask. Members of the congregation had already been on the telephone to the Reverend Paradine Frost, and others were busy writing angry letters to the manse.

"I am thinking of David as an actor who just speaks the lines put in his mouth," the Reverend Mr. Frost said when asked his views by a reporter. "We did not like it," David's mother recalled, but she felt he was old enough to know what he was doing.

Whatever happened on the show, David carried the can, as they say in England. The newspapers called him "Mr. Outrageous" and "The man you love to hate," "The hatchetman of *TWTWTW*" and "The acid-drop kid." Happily, it all added up to "Britain's number one satirist." "Satirist" became a catchword. To his amusement David received a letter that said, "My son is aged four. When he grows up, I want him to be a satirist. How do I go about it?"

The impact of the show was unprecedented. Within weeks the three million viewers who watched its inauguration were joined by another three million, and in the end the number rose to twelve million. David and his *That Was the Week That Was*—by this time it was very much "his"—were changing the nation's habits. The British, who traditionally devoted Saturday evenings to drink, sex, or sleep (or all three, in that order) now wanted to see *That Was the Week* . . . as well. On what used to be their busiest night some pubs were deserted until they installed TV sets; people would not accept invitations to Saturday-night parties unless their hosts allowed them to watch the show.

Viewers bombarded newspapers with complaints; others rose to David's defense. Letters asking the B.B.C. to drop "this horrible program" were followed by others rejoicing in the vigor of British democracy, which could shrug off the weekly drubbing by the TV satirists. Noel Gay triumphantly advertised their fledgling's success: "Frost is forecast for the whole country in the hour before midnight on Saturdays." The floodgates opened for a tidal wave of puns and clichés "inspired," if that is the word, by the show.

"That was the week that was" became a catchphrase that was mercilessly flogged in every conceivable variation on the theme: "THIS IS DAVID FROST THIS IS" was the *Daily Mail*'s headline for the first interview with the young master of ceremonies. A hundred headlines echoed the *TW3* gimmick.

When Roy Kinnear, in the course of a sketch, said casually, "Seriously, though, you are doing a grand job!" David took up the phrase with incalculable results. "Seriously, though, you are doing a grand job" became another catchphrase impossible to escape. "Seriously, though, you *are* doing a grand job!" people kept telling David. "How very kind of you to say so," he said with unfailing courtesy, even if he was hearing it for the tenth time in as many minutes.

Answering a pointed question about what the show was trying to put across, he had to pick his way delicately through a minefield of menacing clichés. "Well, it's difficult to describe, isn't it?" he said. "It's no good me saying pompously, 'We are making a comment on life,' because it sounds like something out of our program: 'This is a program about life—switch off!'" He thought hard and added, "We are trying to get to the root of things."

Whether or not the show changed the nation's life, there is no question about its impact on David Frost. His fifty-pound-a-week salary was trebled, but he coped better with his new prosperity than the observers at his heels ("David Frost is so rich now he keeps a taxi waiting while he has his hair cut"). With every post and every telephone call came new opportunities. He welcomed them because one career was not enough for him even then. Always quick to capitalize on a name in vogue, the *Daily Mail* invited him to write a regular column. He was asked to write a book. As a matter of fact, he had been working on one book, on the Dutch Resistance, for years—it has yet to be published.

He was much in demand to open fêtes and used to oblige with the odd pun: "Welcome to a fête that is better than death." The nightclubs called, and David accepted an engagement at Quaglino's, in London's West End. "It was an old-fashioned place," he said, "but great fun. There was hardly any space in front of you, but people sat all around you."

David loved the job but was told by a critic to stick to television. Undeterred, the Blue Angel lured him back at three times his erstwhile fee. He amused the customers, many of them Guards officers and their girls. In a way, they amused him, too. "You could see these officers sitting there," he reminisced, "looking at their girls and thinking—this was in the days when seduction was more of an art than it is today—'Have I given her enough to drink yet? And have I maybe had too much myself?' You could see that this was stage one in amatory advances all over the room." Other engagements came from workingmen's clubs in northern England, late-night drinkeries that offered their customers entertainment by star performers and that had mixed audiences and exotic names like La Dolce Vita, in Newcastle. They paid star fees.

A whole *TW3* industry developed around David as the central character. The B.B.C. prepared to sponsor books on the show, records, sheet music. No wonder there was no adverse comment from the management about the crudities and no interference—not yet.

The Frost grin confronted Britain from newspapers, magazines, and posters. The youth of England, who only yesterday favored a hairstyle known as the D.A. (for "duck's ass"), asked their barbers to cut their locks in the D.F. style instead.

One comment on the show, although much along the line of

what had already been said three dozen times, gave a new twist to the Frost saga. It described *TW3* as hard-hitting, witty, pungent, brilliantly conceived, occasionally over-long, with an odd bit of tastelessness in which viciousness is mistaken for wit. "David Frost was fine as emcee," the critic wrote. "He gave an edge to the comment." The review appeared in *Variety*. The long arm of American show business was reaching out for David Frost.

CHAPTER 5

David and Jan

THE LIME GROVE studio where the satirists were sharpening their tongues and brushing up their lines for the next show became such an attraction that long-established television personalities often dropped in to take a peek at the new celebrities. David was rehearsing a monologue when he looked up and found himself face to face with a dream. From the small studio next door the panelists of *Juke Box Jury,* a genteel record show, appeared to pay their respects. One of them was Janette Scott.

Introductions were hardly needed. David and Janette shook hands, looked at each other, and knew. David never wasted time. "Will you have dinner with me tonight?" he asked.

"Yes, I will," Janette answered.

The brief encounter over, both turned on their heels, each making for a telephone. Both had previous engagements. Both canceled them to be with each other.

Had not David, years earlier, spent hours gazing at Janette's photographs? Hadn't he seen every film she ever made? If such a cliché situation were not out of character for a star of *TW3,* it could only be described as love at first sight.

They went out again several times, were seen together, were asked the obvious question, and protested vigorously: "We are just good friends." But then, you cannot get much closer than that. For Jan's sake, David was concerned about the publicity. She was still married to a Canadian actor-singer, Jackie Rae, although they had been living apart for nearly a year. David telephoned half-a-dozen editors and asked them to retract reports of a romance.

The following weekend he took Jan to Beccles, where she made another conquest. The Reverend Mr. Frost was charmed by his son's pretty, unaffected friend. David's mother took to her immediately. "We were hoping David would marry Jan," she said, and has said so several times since. "Naturally, I hope to see David married," Mrs. Frost said recently. "I should like him to have a son to carry on the family name."

David and Jan were frequent visitors at the manse. However busy, he would never refuse an appeal from the Methodist youth club, and when the club organized a Carnival Music Hall in aid of Famine Relief, he promised to appear and bring Jan along. They arrived late: "The traffic was appalling," David said apologetically. He and Jan took the stage together, she reading from a book and he acting out the passages, except for one that said, "He bit his lip until the blood came"—instead, his nostrils began to quiver and dilate.

Apart from their excursions to Beccles, it was a typical showbiz affair, a constant struggle to arrange their separate commitments—rehearsals, shows, public appearances, negotiations with agents and producers—so as to give them time together. Jan was working on a film, *Siege of the Saxons*, in which she played the Queen of England, and David, as if the weekly show were not demanding enough, also collaborated with Ned Sherrin on a book about *TW3* and made a *TW3* record. When he and Millicent Martin autographed copies at Harrods, the Knightsbridge store where the Queen often shops unnoticed, there was such a crush that the police had to keep order.

Press reports no longer troubled them. Janette was by his side when he attended an awards dinner of the Guild of Screen Writers, who gave *TW3* a "Merit" in the "Entertainment" category. In keeping with his new status, David took a bigger apartment on the King's Road, not far from Jan's place, but was too busy to go out and buy household things. When entertaining friends, he poured sherry into tumblers: "No wine glasses. Sorry!"

At parties, in restaurants, even at Lime Grove, he felt happier than at home. He was not good at being alone. Lights were blazing in his apartment at all hours, and to this day his friends note how reluctant he is to let them leave even long after midnight. It is probably his inexhaustibility rather than loneliness, though.

Everybody was aware that David loved people, all kinds of people. He listened to taxi drivers and anyone else who commented on the show. They all had something to contribute, he would say in the spirit of a Turkish proverb he discovered, which perfectly reflected his attitude: "Even a stopped clock is right twice a day." It was also obvious that David wanted people to love him.

At the end of one of their busy weeks, David and Jan met for dinner and decided on the spur of the moment to get away from it all. "We packed a few things, drove to the airport, and took the first plane out of London," David said. Next morning he telephoned his mother, who had been expecting them at Beccles.

"Where are you?" she asked.

"We're in Africa," David told her. "Tangier." They had a glorious weekend before returning to London and the relentless pursuit of their careers.

Their association was cloudless. "David and I really enjoyed the fact that we were young and free of responsibilities—no husbands or wives or children," Janette confided to friends. She was not the only one who was struck by the contrast between David's public persona of a sneering, aggressive castigator of social and political ills and his gentle, unruffled, considerate manner in private. He never quarreled and, Janette discovered, was amazingly unjealous when she went to parties without him. An explanation his friends offered was that he was not beyond a little jealousy-courting escapade. One of his partners was Christine Hargreaves, a young television actress, who promptly had to ward off insinuations with the standard "just good friends" rebuttal.

"I am a firm believer in nonmonogamy," David was fond of saying. He was getting a lot of erotic mail from feminine admirers.

Whether he had eight or two hours sleep—it was rarely more than four or five—there was never a hint of tiredness or weariness when he was in front of the camera. He often looked baggy-eyed and drawn and always waxy and pale a minute before the show. When he crossed an invisible line and stepped into the limelight, however, he became buoyant and vigorous, exuding energy. Television was the mental diet on which he thrived. "It's like a Chinese meal," he would say. "Half an hour later, and I'm hungry again."

His self-control enabled him to stand up to the constant glare off and on stage. Did he ever trip up? Once, perhaps. The brilliant English comedian Frankie Howerd, who then seemed to be out of favor with the public, was booked to appear on *TW3* with his solo act of studied bumbling and carefully improvised patter, compounded of wit and innuendo. It was a triumphal performance to which the studio audience responded with shrieks of laughter. When it was at its loudest, the camera unexpectedly switched to David, who was seen frowning, almost glowering.

No incident involving *TW3* was so small as not to merit the attention of the press. The short glimpse of an apparently antagonistic David Frost led reporters to conclude that he was jealous of Frankie Howerd's highly professional skill and success. "It was one of those occasions," said Ned Sherrin, "when the camera does lie. David was studying his prompt sheet in preparation for the next item and was for once unaware that the camera was on him." Actually, David, as soon as he became an impresario as well as a television performer, engaged Frankie as the star of one of his American TV "specials," a big success for Howerd and Frost.

Presently, from America, came another blast aimed at David. Peter Cook accused him of stealing his best jokes, not an unusual situation in the incestuous comedy business where the same tales in various guises keep turning up in many acts. Had it not been for *TW3*'s prominence in the public eye, the incident would have attracted little notice. As it was, the wire services got a lot of mileage out of it. David and Peter, the old Footlights pals, were depicted as confronting each other with daggers drawn.

The satirists were having fun at each other's expense. *TW3* was cheerfully satirizing other B.B.C. programs, and *Private Eye*, which claimed a sort of illegitimate parentage of the fledgling *TW3*, went to town on David Frost, whose partner on stage was *Private Eye* stalwart William Rushton. In classic "underground" style the attack was decidedly forceful: "THE BUBONIC PLAGIARIST— or there's Methodism in his Badness" was their banner headline over a long recitation of David Frost's sins. "After his latest [*TW3*] show," said the story, "400 people rang up the BooBooC—3 in favour, 4 against and 393 to say they wrote the script"—which seemed a self-defeating comment on their criticism.

The first *TW3* season was drawing to a close, provoking a new outburst of acclaim and condemnation. "A tribute to our political stability" was the verdict of a quality newspaper (*Observer*). "Good-bye to a gang of low schoolboys!" said the mass-circulation *People*.

There was still no time for domesticity. "David did not really know how to fend for himself," Janette said. He would not keep his apartment tidy, go shopping, or prepare proper meals; he hardly gave himself time to eat, wolfed his food (still does), and ate salad with his fingers, in spite of Jan's reproaches. His famous quiff of hair was a sore point with her. "Why don't you change your hairstyle?" she implored him time and again. "I can claim credit for getting rid of that," she said proudly in the end. She kept on at him about his appearance.

So hypnotic was David's effect on television that only his intimates noticed his failings. A well-known English woman columnist interviewed him for her series on men and their clothes: "He is influential in the same way as ... Jackie Kennedy in America," she wrote. "David's clothes, mannerisms, hair-do have been imitated by thousands of aspiring satirists."

David entered into the spirit of the interview: "Now, I have strong views on evening clothes," he pontificated.

When this solemn analysis of David's sartorial habits was published, it caused hilarity among his friends who knew of his attitude to clothes and the incident at the Riviera Twist-show taping, which was part of the growing Frost legend. He had not changed, and his suits were still something of a joke—or worse.

On one occasion when he turned up at the studio extremely ill-dressed, he asked the wardrobe mistress, sweetly as usual, to stitch his trousers. "Certainly not!" was the reply. His everyday clothes were not her responsibility. There was a row, one of the very few David was involved in.

"When I met David," Janette said, "he had been wearing the same shoes for four months." He wore his suits until they were threadbare. A reporter found out that he never sent a shirt to the laundry but simply bought new ones.

"I was neither interested nor disinterested in clothes," David said later. "It did not seem important. It was a matter of priorities."

Janette tried to keep his apartment tidy and his clothes in better shape. A succession of girl friends have since been brushing, pressing, and cleaning David's things and generally mothering him.

Even after he mended his ways, the reputation as a sloppy dresser was difficult to shed. Years later he was still no Beau Brummell, but he had more than two dozen Hardy Amies suits (one set in New York, another in London) when *Punch* published a cartoon showing a tramp in a shabby outfit being told by another tramp, "I did not know you were a friend of David Frost's tailor."

Whether it was Janette's influence or his vastly improved financial circumstances, his days as a poor dresser were left behind him, and he became a good customer of London's trendier men's shops. One day he breezed into Cecil Gee's, on Shaftesbury Avenue, which was popular with the younger set before Carnaby Street was discovered. Producer-director Bryan Forbes, taking a day off from directing *The L-Shaped Room*, was one of the customers in the shop. "David came in carrying three boxes of chocolates and pressed one of them into my hand," he recalled. He knew David as the star of *TW3*, but the two had never met before. "I did not like him much on the screen and thought he had an undergraduate bumptiousness, but we talked and I asked him to dinner and our friendship grew from there."

They have been friends ever since: "We found we had much in common. We were both interested in journalism and in show business, were both ambitious, driving characters—David perhaps more outwardly ambitious." Their conversations were serious. "David has a jackdaw quality for gleaning from other people's nests and then sitting on the eggs himself."

David was always late for dinner, so Bryan Forbes and his wife, Nanette, made the invitation "7:30 P.M. for 9 P.M., dinner at 9:30." "At nine forty-five P.M.," said Forbes, "when we are about to commit the dinner to the drain, he turns up laden with presents for the children and full of cheer, and three minutes later one has forgotten that one has waited two hours for him."

David is a voracious reader, and it so happens that Bryan

Forbes runs a bookshop near his home, a profitable hobby. "David's greatest delight is to get me to open the shop at midnight and fill up the boot of his car with books before he drives off."

With the end of the *TW3* series, David was off on a quick money-making tour of provincial cities and seaside resorts, where everyone was panting to see the televison idol in the flesh. Offers from people with a quick appreciation of the young satirist's popularity were the order of the day. One seemed to open up yet another promising career for David—as a movie star.

Anatole de Grunwald offered him and Lance Percival parts in the film he was producing for Metro-Goldwyn-Mayer in England, *The V.I.P.'s*, with a screenplay by Terence Rattigan. David's was not exactly a V.I.P. part, but he invested his few lines as a reporter with commendable verisimilitude. On the set he found himself in excellent company and made friends with the stars— Elizabeth Taylor, Richard Burton, and Orson Welles—all of whom, years later, when he was the star of his own talk show in New York, turned up as his guests.

It was not as a potential movie star but as host of *TW3* that the Americans were keeping an eye on David. *TW3*'s phenomenal progress on the English charts naturally raised the question of whether its success could not be repeated on the other side of the Atlantic. The answer was in the affirmative, and N.B.C. bought the rights. David was offered a guest spot on the show.

His friends and advisers did not think he ought to accept. They thought it would be wiser for him to wait until he could command top billing. Why risk his tremendous success by plunging into the strange American medium?

"I had splendid advisers," David recalled, "and very rarely questioned their judgment. You have to listen to all views, but in the final analysis the decision is your own. In this instance I disagreed with my friends. I thought there was a good opportunity of making a start in America—and I went."

Describing his impressions in the English Sunday newspaper *Observer*, he displayed some unexpected patriotism. The number of English shows in New York! Americans copying the English rather than vice versa. He, the arch-critic of his own country, seemed pleased to see it.

Although the *Beyond the Fringe* quartet and The Establishment group had make a breakthrough for satire in New York, David soon found that American television was not ready for the hard-hitting, ruthless political and social comment he purveyed at home. A less aggressive approach would be required. Anxious to acquaint himself as much as possible with the climate of American opinion, he read newspapers, devoured current literature, and talked to people, making mental notes of every new experience. He appeared on Johnny Carson's *Tonight* show and was impressed—why wasn't there a talk show of any sort in England?

Much of his time was spent with John Bird and Peter Cook, and while lurid reports about their quarrel were still abroad, he enjoyed a relaxed weekend at Peter Cook's house in Connecticut. No hint of animosity disturbed their pleasant afternoon by the side of the swimming pool as they talked about America and about television and engaged in their usual friendly banter. John Bird was there, too, snoozing in the sun. Suddenly, with his irrepressible joie de vivre, David jumped into the pool. He floundered, gasped for air, and went under. Peter Cook watched, greatly amused.

"I thought, 'Ho, ho, David is making a satirical attack on drowning,'" he said. It was some time before he realized that David was in trouble and went to his aid. "John Bird thought I had lost control of myself and was drowning David—thank God we saved him in time, or people would have said I pushed him in."

The narrow escape did not cure David. Some time later he repeated the performance in Hollywood when visiting his friend Bryan Forbes, who was at work on his film *King Rat.* He jumped into the deep end of the pool and nearly drowned. "That's the story of his life, isn't it?" Bryan Forbes commented. "David probably thought he could walk on water!"

Among those who introduced David to the New York scene was Clay Felker, now publisher of the successful *New York* magazine, an attractive weekly that concentrates on the foibles and problems of Manhattan. David's apartment at the Shoreham Hotel became a meeting place of his old and new friends. He visited all the right places where personalities are certain to be noticed.

With Leland Hayward producing, the American *TW3* was

being put together. Billy Taylor, a well-known jazz musician, prepared a musical score for the pilot show. "I saw the English show," he said, "and was very impressed with David Frost but did not meet him at the time." Billy did not continue with the project but a few years later became one of David's closest associates.

The resumption of hostilities—the beginning of a new *TW3* series in England—demanded David's presence in London. "Saturday is once again Satireday" was one of the slogans that heralded the return of David & Co. Preparations went ahead amid rumors that the B.B.C. was clamping down on the satirists, but opposition inside the corporation was largely centered in Tom Sloan, head of Entertainment, who was not happy that such an entertaining show remained outside his jurisdiction. He was thought to be one of David's few "enemies," although David himself would rather bite off his tongue than describe anybody as an enemy.

Whatever the countercurrents, David, Ned Sherrin, and the others went ahead without a trace of inhibition, but the first show of the new series, when it went on the air at the end of September, 1963, seemed to bear out the rumors. Harold Macmillan came in for the usual attention, and the late Pope Pius XII's "sympathies" for the Nazis were rudely aired. Some of David's jokes seemed preoccupied with sex, but on the whole it was a rather mild edition.

The gentler mood was quickly dispelled when Foreign Minister Sir Alec Douglas Home, the former Earl of Home, became the satirists' favorite butt. Appearing in the character of Benjamin Disraeli, David described him as "a pleasant man who has foreseen nothing and was qualified for nothing" and as "a pathetic victim of circumstance" who had been deprived of his title. Even partisans of the show thought the satirists were going too far.

Sex jokes creeping into the script roused the puritans—and some TV rivals. No other show was allowed such latitude, and Frankie Howerd contributed a typical comment on undergraduate—or rather, graduate—permissiveness: "These days you can't say 'f---!' on television unless you have a B.A. degree."

Criticism was growing harsher, and David came in for his share of the blame. He was now seen as a "basilisk-eyed grasshopper figure with bony features and a thin mouth made more for the grimace than the smile." He had little to smile about. Returning a football pitch in a charity match, he fell and fractured his left wrist. Driving to Beccles with his hand still in a cast, he was involved in a car crash. He was heading for a more serious crash, however.

TW3 probably speeded the mood of change in the country and the decline of the Tory administration. While reproaching the satirists for their ferocity, a majority of British people seemed to share their views on the Government. Fourteen years of Tory rule were coming to an end. New elections were in the offing.

For the B.B.C. it seemed an opportune moment to get rid of the offending show. It was announced that because of the impending election campaign, *TW3* would be taken off the air at the end of its current run. "They are tired," Hugh Carleton Greene said about the *TW3* team by way of explanation.

David retorted: "It is delightful for people to be so solicitous about our health. I would think we are remarkably fresh. We owe it all to Horlocks malted milk. We wake up refreshed after seven or eight minutes sleep."

"The B.B.C. has gone all clammy-handed and dry in the mouth" was one press comment. "Only idiots will cheer the murder of *TW3*" was another. *TW3* was doomed, but the B.B.C. hastened to announce that David Frost was staying on. Anyway, his contract—and his pay—were good for another few months, until April, 1964. Remuneration due to him for no work was estimated to be around five thousand pounds.

The show was not done yet, though. The news of John F. Kennedy's assassination roused the team to a last magnificent effort. The very people, both writers and performers, who had recently been accused of bad taste, vulgar tartness, and arrogant irreverence prepared a symposium, a requiem, for the American President which caught the true essence of the tragedy.

Sybil Thorndike, doyenne of the English stage, recited a poem, "To Jackie," which was tender and compassionate. Bernard Levin spoke a moving tribute. David's lines were dignified and allowed his deep emotional involvement to come through. Within days the tribute was shown on American television screens and created such an impression that it was given a second screening. American critics named it the year's best television documentary. A few weeks later the whole cast was flown to New York to stage their impressive lament for the late President at Madison Square Garden. Eighteen thousand people came to hear them.

There were another half-dozen vintage editions in London, and *TW3* received an accolade from British TV producers, who awarded the team a British-television equivalent of an Emmy. It was a deathbed honor. The end was near. Introducing the final edition of *TW3*, David looked grim-faced and angry, as he may well have been.

The precipitous conclusion of the amazing run enabled him to accept a standing invitation to appear on the American version, the only member of the original cast to be offered a contract. The agreement was for three shows, with an option for a much longer period. David applied for a work permit and was on his way to New York when the American Federation of Television and Radio Artists protested against the importation of another English artist, which, they claimed, "threatened to deprive an American performer of a job."

"David Frost is the kingpin of this new type of satire," producer Leland Hayward countered, but an added difficulty was that Frost's name, a household word in his own country, was virtually unknown in the United States. Noel Coward and Alec Guinness were appearing on Broadway; they were famous stars, but who was David Frost?

Prospects looked glum to all—except to David, who watched the battle from the sidelines. Leading American stage and television performers spoke up on his behalf, insisting that he was "one of a kind." The Department of Justice concurred and overrode AFTRA's protest.

The doors of the United States opened, and David entered, firing off a characteristic dart in the direction of his native country: "I really attribute this happy solution to the personal intervention of the former Lord Home," he said. "We have always got on splendidly, and I hope some time in the spring to help him, too, to get a working visa in America." Come spring and the British election, he implied, the Tory Prime Minister might well be out of a job.

Only a day or so remained to prepare for the taping of the first American *TW3* show, hosted by David Frost. Mellow as it was by

English standards, it bravely tried to startle American viewers with a few novelties, including a glimpse of Romy Schneider's naked behind. The political satire was less than acid. In reference to West German Chancellor Ludwig Erhard's visit to President Lyndon B. Johnson's ranch, David announced, "Erhard was so delighted with his reception that he has decided to rename Berlin's main thoroughfare Unter den Lyndon."

Among visiting firemen from London who watched the show was the B.B.C.'s Tom Sloan. He and David met on neutral ground. As with other members of the anti-Frost brigade, Sloan was captivated by the off-screen David. They dined and talked, and the old antagonism evaporated. Soon they were in deep discussion about a new television project. What emerged was a David Frost show for Tom Sloan's department under the general title "A Degree of Frost." The Beatles happened to be in the United States, and David persuaded Paul McCartney to join the show as a guest.

Though David was quickly settling down in New York, there was something missing in his life. The void was filled when Janette Scott arrived on a visit. They were seen together at opening nights and could not escape attention when they flew off to Hawaii for a brief holiday. "It was the first time that I experienced rain you could enjoy—rain on your skin. It was wonderful," David said.

Speculation about an impending marriage revived, and when Janette returned to London, she faced a barrage of questions. Had she not seen a lot of David in New York? "I saw many people in New York apart from David" was her defense. "I also saw the Beatles, but this does not mean that I am going to marry them."

She and David were forever flying to meet each other, even if only for a day. Janette went to Spain to make a film and was reported to be so popular with the matadors that they were not only dedicating the traditional bulls' ears to her but offering her a live bull as a present. For David this was the signal to join her in Madrid, but when asked why he had come to Spain, he answered—with his mind already on the American political scene dominated by Senator Barry Goldwater's disturbing campaign style—"I want to ask General Franco to persuade Barry Goldwater to modify his political campaign."

CHAPTER 6

Not So Much

AT THE B.B.C. the future of David Frost was a major subject of discussion, the planners deliberating how best to harness his tremendous drawing power. They were pondering what could be rescued from the ruins of the much-maligned *TW3* and rebuilt into a new show. Conversations among David, Donald Baverstock, Ned Sherrin, and Antony Jay went on for hours on end—Jay gave up his B.B.C. job but continued on a free-lance basis. Many of the writers who had put zip into *TW3* were drawn into the discussion, and David spent much of his time drafting scripts and formulating new ideas.

What emerged was a new vehicle for David Frost under the title *Not So Much a Programme, More a Way of Life,* Ned Sherrin producing. The difficulty was to avoid the lapses of taste which had marred *TW3*. The script-writers were advised to restrain their aggression. "There was a deliberate decision to take the heat out of the satire boom," Antony Jay said. "It was a step down. It could not hope to match *TW3*."

Three pretty singing stars were engaged to give more glamour to the show. The humor, while more subdued, was invested with social and political significance wherever possible, and among those who acted in some of the sketches were David's old university pals John Bird and the handsome Eleanor Bron, a superb comedienne. It so happened that the pilot show was being put together just when elections were about to be held in the United States as well as in Britain, ideal pegs for a historical review of heckling. David introduced brief sketches that reconstructed historical scenes. Two incidents in which Winston Churchill was involved were among the best examples:

Lady Heckler: "Mr. Churchill, you're drunk."

Churchill: "Madam, you're ugly—but I shall be sober in the morning."

Lady Heckler: "If I were your wife, I'd put poison in your tea."

Churchill: "If I were your husband, madam, I'd drink it."

Next, David took the part of a Labour member heckling Churchill in the House of Commons:

Churchill: "Czechoslovakia is in chains."

Heckler: "Rubbish!"

Churchill: 'Eastern European democracy lies in ruins."

Heckler: "Rubbish!"

Churchill: "The country of Masaryk is enslaved."

Heckler: "Rubbish!"

Churchill: "I fear the Honourable Member has little else in his head."

As the central character in a take-off of Christmas film clichés, David presided over the following exchange:

"We have followed a star to this stable. Tell us of the child within."

"It's a girl."

In another sketch a young wife was telling her husband breathlessly, "Darling, I saw the doctor today. And, oh, darling, the most wonderful news. I'm—I'm not going to have a baby."

By far the most important feature of the show was a discussion in which David was cast in the role of a sophisticated moderator raising stimulating topics with three or four experts, wits, and raconteurs. "His job is to midwife the talk," Ned Sherrin explained. "When it dries up, he throws them a bone and hopes one of the dogs will jump."

Among the early participants was Harvey Orkin, an American with a quiet offbeat humor who quickly became popular. Al Capp was frequently co-opted and was hugely entertaining. David's American associations were beginning to show. Another regular was Lord Glenavy, who under the name Patrick Campbell wrote humorous columns in the manner of Art Buchwald but whose conversation was less fluent than his prose. Far from allowing a speech impediment to inhibit his verbal clowning (few pukka aristocrats are without at least a hint of a stammer, anyway), Campbell made stuttering positively fashionable.

The emphasis was on topicality. When England's Parliamentary-lobby correspondents, as tightly knit a body as the White House press corps, were publicly criticized for keeping political secrets rather than exposing them, David chose the issue as a topic for the show. His guests on this occasion included Henry Fairlie, the political commentator, and Clive Irving, a first-class British communications expert. "As an ad-lib show," Irving said later, "it was unsurpassed. David was growing in stature every week and emerging as an excellent interviewer."

The discussion went on long after the end of the show. Irving came back for another appearance, and again he and David talked until the early hours. Going on to David's apartment, they continued to argue about television and interviewing techniques.

David smoked an occasional cigarette—someone else's, since he never bought any. When he drank, it was good wine but never a lot. Janette Scott often joined in these late-night sessions and encouraged David's growing interest in politics and current affairs. He wanted to put satire behind him and was thinking of a more serious way to project himself.

Prosperity did not change his style of life much. He was still without his own car. The circle around him grew with his success, though, and the number of people seeking his company became larger and larger. "Not all of them were true friends," Janette thought. Some just wanted to climb on the David Frost bandwagon as it gathered speed.

Others picked holes in his astonishing technique. One of the young writers who contributed humorous ideas and lines to the show was young Ian Davidson, who, like David, had gone straight from the university into television. In a long letter to a fellow writer in Canada he analyzed *Not So Much* . . . with youthful vigor, including strong and unflattering remarks on some weak spots in David's performance. Some weeks later David called him into his little office at Lime Grove. "What's all this about?" he asked quietly, showing Davidson an article in a Canadian newspaper which quoted part of the offending letter. It was a blistering attack. "This is a bit naughty," David said—"naughty" being the strongest term of condemnation he ever uses.

"I was shattered," Davidson recalled. "What could I say? I thought this was the end of me—there was nothing to do but resign on the spot."

David would not hear of it. He asked Ian to sit down and for three quarters of an hour defended himself against the criticism point by point. 'It was incredible," Davidson remembered years later, still puzzled: "It could only be his Christianity." (Or, as *Private Eye* said in a Frost profile: "Jesus Christ was the David Frost of his time.")

Occasionally, the writers of *Not So Much ...* tried to prove that there was still some fire in their bellies and reverted to (*TW3*) type. The result was renewed antagonism against Frost and his show. Satire had become tired and limp, and only tours de force could raise the viewers' blood pressure.

There was an outcry over a sketch involving the Duke and Duchess of Windsor. Discussing Prime Minister Sir Alec Douglas Home, Bernard Levin overstepped the mark and called him a cretin. There was shocked silence for a moment until David stepped in and made Levin modify his harsh remark. Still dissatisfied, David pressed on until Levin apologized. More than eight hundred viewers complained, and opposition to the new show inside the B.B.C. hardened.

The climate at the executive level finally changed when Donald Baverstock, guardian angel of the B.B.C. avant-garde, departed and was replaced by Michael Peacock, a solid Establishment figure. Harmony between producer and superiors gave way to strain and stresses, which communicated themselves to the performers, including David. "We were still a team," he said bravely.

Returning to London from his weekly flight to New York under the immediate impact of the assassination of Malcolm X, the Black Power leader, David found that the forthcoming show included a sketch featuring a dialogue between a white liberal and a black man, which Ned Sherrin thought particularly apposite to the situation. David did not think it was adequate. His suggestion was to make the assassination the subject of a whole program on the lines of the successful John F. Kennedy show. "I don't think the English public is sufficiently interested" was Ned Sherrin's reaction. David did not like to have his suggestion turned down but submitted to the producer's decision.

Without an open quarrel, he and Ned Sherrin were pulling in different directions. "David has a tendency to take over," a friend remarked.

Ned Sherrin thought so, too, but put it in these words: "When I produce a show, I produce it and nobody else." The professional clash did not end their friendship, but it was clear that once this show had run its course, they would not readily work together again; they never have.

Public reaction reflected the internal difficulties. Two thirds of *TW3*'s mammoth audience deserted *Not So Much* ... David had little time to ponder whether part of the blame was his. When asked point-blank, he did make his attitude clear: "We use satire," he said, "but we don't like to be called satirists. The word has come to mean a small group of people in a London club. We are not a coterie."

The tempo of his life increased. Having taped three shows in London during the weekend, he would rush to the London airport to catch a plane for New York, where *TW3* went on the air live on Tuesday. He made quite a performance of it. Three times out of four he arrived with only minutes to spare and could be seen rushing across the runway with a porter wheeling his luggage after him long after the other passengers were already in their seats. "He likes the privilege of his solo appearances," one of his critics thought. Sometimes the aircraft was kept waiting for the celebrated passenger after his secretary advised the airline that he was on his way.

Gaining five hours, the time difference between England and the United States (he still remembers the confusing sign on the plane, "It's the Cocktail Hour!," when he arrived in New York at dawn), David plunged into work. By Monday afternoon he was in the studio with notes and ideas for the following day's *TW3* show. The writer who worked with him on his monologues was Buck Henry, who later wrote the screenplays for *The Graduate* and *Catch-22*. It occupied them late into the night, and David rehearsed it all day Tuesday until the evening, when the show went on the air.

On Wednesday David was on his way back to England, a nerve-wracking weekly routine. Until the press remarked on his feat of stamina and versatility, viewers in London and New York were unaware that he was well on the way to establishing an all-time record as a transatlantic commuter. A British newspaper called him "A Male of Two Cities." He spent so much time in the air that he declared himself "a citizen of B.O.A.C." (British Overseas Aircraft Corporation). Others described him as "B.O.A.C.'s best customer," although the airline derived so much publicity from his patronage that they ought to have paid him rather than the other way around.

His shuttlecock existence produced odd situations. On one of his flights the air hostess approached him with the ultimate in apologies: "I'm very sorry, Mr. Frost," she said. "I'm afraid it is caviar again." It was getting a bit monotonous. David was never without an armful of English and American newspapers and magazines, and his bag bulged with books on every subject under the sun. His schedule was punishing. (As soon as he set foot on American soil, he dutifully pronounced it "skedule.")

With his insatiable appetite for work, he reviewed plays for *Punch* and contributed a weekly diary to the *Observer*. With Christopher Booker and Gerald Kaufman, a political journalist and friend of Harold Wilson, he started work on a political book *How to Live under Labour—or at Least Have As Much Chance As Anybody Else*. "On election night publisher Charles Pick and I were at a party together," David recalled. "Pick did not know what to think. A Tory victory was supposed to be better for business in general, but a Labour victory was better for the book he wanted me to write." By 1 A.M. Charles Pick had got his book.

What little time remained in London or New York was crowded with appointments, conferences, engagements, and rehearsals. Being a star involved David in a growing amount of correspondence, not to mention the fan mail, which was coming in at the rate of five hundred letters a week. Since he hoarded scripts, newspaper cuttings, and documents like a magpie and worked intuitively rather than methodically, it was too much for him to cope with alone.

As Diana Crawfurd was dealing with his contracts, which involved frequent visits to the Noel Gay agency, he decided to set up an office on its premises on Denmark Street. Advertising for a secretary, he stipulated that she ought to have "experience, efficiency, and beauty." The girl who qualified on all three counts was Hermione Parks. She took on the arduous job of looking after an unfailingly polite, extremely considerate, very generous, but somewhat disorganized boss.

Wherever he was, he telephoned his parents at least once a week and often kept a day clear to drive to Beccles to visit his father and mother at the manse. They were proud of their boy. "He accomplished what he set out to do," Mona Frost said. Many thought he had reached the peak of his career. How could he possibly go further?

"There are always new opportunities," David countered. "I never resist a challenge." Accepting challenges brought more opportunities.

He was still only twenty-five years old and refused to be divorced from his youth. The news from Cambridge that *Granta* was in financial difficulties brought an immediate response. Assuming the mantle of an impresario, David initiated a rescue operation, roping in old friends and new associates for a fund-raising performance, "David Frost's *Granta* All-Star Charity Night." Among the stars who supported him were Janette Scott and her mother, Thora Hird, a leading actress; Peter Cook; and Frankie Howerd; they raised three thousand pounds for the ailing university magazine.

Janette also appeared in public in another guise—or rather without any guise at all. When *Town,* a glossy magazine, came out with a series of *Playboy*-type photographs of her, the credit line read "Earl Wallerman," but it was difficult to persuade the gossip writers that this was not a pseudonym for David Frost. "It's a complete mystery to me," he said, denying any part in the affair.

The *Granta* fund-raising was not his only charitable effort. David was free with his time when his old Gillingham headmaster asked him to open a school fête. He was just as generous (some said extravagant) with his money when making a contribution to the school's funds or any other good cause.

The last of the *Not So Much* . . . shows was scheduled for the night of April 11, 1965. The show had never done as well as *TW3.* A small studio audience expecting a wake was treated to a highly entertaining prelude. In place of the usual off-screen warm-up with which Ned Sherrin usually put the audience in the right frame of mind, the cast staged a special farewell for Ned. It was a hilarious performance.

John Bird, impersonator extraordinary and scourge of politicians, parodied Harvey Orkin. An actor, Douglas Fisher, gave a highly animated impression of David Frost. Cleo Laine, the jazz-singer, presented the show's theme song with a twist: "Not so much a programme, more a kiss of death."

Among the mourners at the funeral of the B.B.C.'s finest hour of entertainment were Donald Baverstock, who bid farewell to his baby, and his successor, Michael Peacock, who was rightly or wrongly regarded as one of the grave-diggers. Many of the barbs in this burlesque, satirical version of the satire show were aimed in his direction.

Once the lights came on and the cameras turned, the show proper was listless and undistinguished. In a strained farewell after it was all over, Michael Peacock ranged himself firmly on the side of the angels: "This show was a remarkable achievement in television," he said. "Something else will follow in the autumn, but don't ask me what." That night David and the cast held a wake in Annie Ross's club in London's West End.

In the aftermath of the debacle, David found himself cast in the role of the scapegoat. *TW3* and *Not So Much* ... had brought fame and fortune to many of the performers, who were praised for all that was good in the shows. David was blamed for much that was wrong. Among his colleagues his reputation as "the television man" was undisputed, yet he was in danger of becoming the stereotype "man people love to hate."

In the *Daily Express* Robert Pitman, in his most acerbic mood, wrote David's professional obituary under the headline "DAVID FROST—A Short Life and a Sad Decline." David might well have answered with a variation of Mark Twain's famous reaction to the premature Associated Press report of his death: "The reports of my decline are greatly exaggerated."

"David Frost has been sunk without trace," Mrs. Malcolm Muggeridge said to her husband. "You mean he has risen without trace," Malcolm replied.

In the higher B.B.C. councils the possibility of reviving satire without David Frost was being ventilated, but the decision on whether or not to engage him for another series was not left to them. Disappointed as he was about the show's sorry fate, he was too shrewd and too sensitive to the public mood to cling to a worn-out formula.

The American run of *TW3* was also coming to an end. "I have had a most generous reception," he told his friends at a party. "I love this country, and one day I'm going to come back and really do a whole show my way."

In the meantime David made a decision of his own. It was to withdraw from the little screen. The drug of television was stimulating, but he was strong-minded enough to kick the habit for a while. It was a courageous decision and a great self-sacrifice. At this stage he had nothing else to go to. "He was uncertain which direction he should take," said Richard Armitage, his friend and agent.

"It was the best thing that could have happened to David" was the view of Ned Sherrin, who went on to produce yet another satire show—without David.

As often in such situations, David's personal life also reached a watershed. His association with Janette Scott was cooling. Friends of the couple thought they would either have to get married or part. David was certainly not ready for marriage: "Not for six or seven years" was his standard reply to questions about his matrimonial plans. (Six years later, though with less conviction, he was still saying exactly the same thing.)

Jan was waiting for him at Lime Grove one evening, when she was introduced to the American singer Mel Torme, who was at work in another studio. When David was late as usual, Mel asked her out to dinner. They met several times and were again dining together on the eve of her departure for South America. From South America she went to Los Angeles, where Mel proposed to her. David flew in to see her. They had long talks. "He wanted to make sure I wasn't round the bend," she said later. David seemed upset and was extremely concerned for her, but, Jan recalled, he never said, "Don't." Janette and Mel were married a few days later.

David was kept too busy to nurse regrets. While resolved to keep away from English television, he freely accepted engagements for guest spots on American shows, appeared on *Tonight*, went to Philadelphia for a week as cohost of the popular (Westinghouse) *Mike Douglas Show*, produced by Woody Fraser, and almost instinctively used the opportunity to experiment with slight variations on the established American talk-show formula. The conversations he conducted were a little different, a little more substantial, and longer sustained than those of other American hosts.

He saw Jan on one or two more occasions, and their meetings were free of recriminations. A gentle relationship developed between them. "It's rather a unique type of friendship," she explained. "Just because I happen to have fallen deeply in love with a rather marvelous American, it doesn't mean that my affection for David was switched off." There was no animosity between David and Mel, who has appeared as a guest on David Frost shows on several occasions.

The end of his love affair with Janette was a sore disappointment for David's mother, however. Would he ever get married? "When I find a girl with whom I want to share the rest of my life," he told her, "I shall get married."

"When it does happen," Mona Frost thinks, "it will be very sudden. He will just go off and get married."

For David there were many consolations. In his constant search for new material and personalities he became a regular of cabarets and late-night shows in New York and in London. In London his favorite was a nightclub run by Danny La Rue, the famous female impersonator, where he was often seen with a pretty girl by his side.

There would be no television for him for a year, but television occupied most of his thoughts. The man with whom he discussed it most intimately was Clive Irving, who was also changing the direction of his own career. "We decided to get away from it all," Irving said, "and flew to Ceylon for a change of atmosphere and a rest."

David resting? He was like a pregnant woman waiting for the birth of a new baby.

CHAPTER 7

Away from It All

FLYING AWAY FROM it all, David Frost—St. Batman, Malcolm Muggeridge called him—remained very much in his own orbit. He and Clive Irving made for Colombo, Ceylon's colorful capital, with its kaleidoscope of races: Sinhalese, Kandyan Sinhalese, Ceylon Tamils, Indian Tamils, Moors, Eurasians, Malays. They hired a car and toured the country, often staying overnight in primitive hotels. They were enchanted by the leisurely pace, the attractive landscape, the plantations. . . . It was the nearest thing to paradise, David thought.

Both were quick to strike up friendships, but some of their most revealing encounters were with old tea planters manning the last outposts of British colonial mentality. A patient listener, David was adept at making people talk—a technique that he has since developed to a fine art—letting them condemn themselves out of their own mouths. To each other the two trippers talked a lot about television: "But not obsessively so!" Clive Irving said.

David was evolving a set of rules to govern his approach.

"One must do things that are close to people's lives" was one conclusion he arrived at. "Whatever is done should be done so that viewers are involved." The best way to people's hearts was to identify with them, flatter them, and wherever possible, show them that you are on their side.

"I contemplated what I wanted to do next," David said. His first objective was to find a vehicle to take him out of the satire groove and to get rid of the undergraduate image. "There were

79

two things that needed to be done," he continued, "and within a year I did them both."

Some time earlier he and B.B.C. producer James Gilbert had talked about a new series but had not taken the matter very far. What was needed, David thought, was a faster, shorter, humorous show, contemporary rather than topical, social rather than political. This was one project he decided to tackle as quickly as possible.

"The second was the talk-show formula which I had seen on U.S. television. There was nothing in Britain comparable to Johnny Carson's *Tonight*. There was room for a talk show on British television fashioned to British needs."

Both projects were as yet in an embryonic state, but many of the ideas that crystalized during the vacation in Ceylon were reflected in what happened later. Which of the two should he concentrate on? For David there was only one answer: both. He got together with James Gilbert as soon as he returned to London and at the same time started conversations with Cyril Bennett, of Rediffusion. "I spent the next few months preparing both programs," he said.

That was not all he did. Over breakfast at the London Ritz Hotel, he disclosed that he and Clive Irving had formed a company, Paradine Limited (one of the directors was Mona Frost), to produce straight television interviews with prominent figures for an American network. His first guest would be Randolph Churchill, son of Winston, a stimulating and temperamental conversationalist.

David's own conversation retained an element of undergraduate humor. "I'll see you at the lovable and amazingly rotund Television Center," he would say to a friend. (One of his favorite responses to public acclaim was of a similar caliber: "Thank you for your support," he said, acknowledging a round of applause. "I'll always wear it.")

To eliminate the last traces of his reputation as an irreligious young satirist, he volunteered to do a series of five-minute religious broadcasts, which pleased the Reverend Paradine Frost. David spent many weekends at the manse in Beccles. "People stopped him in the streets and asked for his autograph," his mother said. "However much in a hurry, he was never too busy to talk. Everybody remarked that fame and fortune had not gone to his head."

Work was what he thrived on—not that he looked as if he was thriving. Rarely sleeping more than five hours, he had permanent bags under his eyes and his skin had an unhealthy gray pallor. His day started with a working breakfast in one of London's hotels (in New York it was frequently the Algonquin). Lack of sleep made him irritable, and he was rude to waiters until a friend remarked on it. It was obviously not deliberate, and he has since become a favorite customer in restaurants and hotels on either side of the Atlantic.

The first car he bought was a Mercedes. Not having passed the official driving test, he was by British law required to attach "L" ("Learner") plates to the car and not allowed to drive unaccompanied. When stopped by the police after a piece of erratic driving, he was not only alone in the car but also without "L" plates. He was summoned to appear before a magistrate but pleaded guilty by letter: "The plates were stolen by my fans" was his defense. He was fined fifty pounds.

Hard work did not stop play. The lure of cricket was as strong as ever, and David jumped at every chance of a game. At Edgbaston, Birmingham, he joined some of the finest English cricketers, popular heroes in their field as he was in his. A few weeks later cricket fans watched him batting at the famous Oval, in South London, another boyhood dream fulfilled.

When David, after a long interval, returned to television, it was not with a show of his own. He appeared as a guest on a show hosted by a potential rival, the amiable Irish ex-sports-broadcaster turned television personality, Eamonn Andrews. "David Frost!" one could almost hear a few million viewers exclaiming when the familiar face flashed across the screen in a brief guest appearance.

Not many months passed before David's name was on all lips again. For him the year 1966 started with a bang. On January 7, at 9:30 A.M. sharp, Prime Minister Harold Wilson, with two hours' work at his desk at Downing Street behind him, arrived at the Connaught Hotel, in Mayfair, and was conducted to the Regency Room, where David Frost was giving an intimate breakfast party for some of his friends in high places.

Already there were the Bishop of Woolwich ("David and I are in the same business"), novelist Len Deighton, philosopher Freddie Ayer, newspaper chiefs Cecil King, David Astor, and Charles Wintour. Others present were Methodist leader Lord Soper, Kenneth Adam, of the B.B.C., and Patrick Campbell. Three Frost intimates, Donald Baverstock, Cyril Bennett, and Clive Irving, completed the list of guests at the table. Beatle Paul McCartney was also invited but had a previous professional engagement.

Melon and grapefruit were served first. Over the eggs, bacon, and kidneys, some excellent talk developed. By the time coffee, toast, and marmalade arrived, the party was in full swing. It was still going on near lunchtime, when caviar and champagne were brought in.

The event caused a stir. News about the breakfast came from the Prime Minister's office in a routine announcement of his engagements for the day. "What I had in mind was a strictly private party," David said disingenuously. "I asked the Prime Minister because I wanted to return his hospitality."

The press devoted columns to the occasion. Reporters searched the history books and recalled that Samuel Rogers (1763–1855), who was a poet and very rich, had raised breakfast-giving to a social status-symbol. Lloyd George frequently gave political breakfasts, but in the recent past there had been nothing like it in England until David restored the ancient practice. "I think breakfast is a great institution," he declared.

It was too good a subject to escape the cartoonists. "He's a *real* V.I.P.—gets a 12-gun salute and breakfast with David Frost" was the tag line of a cartoon in the *Daily Sketch*. Some years later the significance of this breakfast in the television age was analyzed by Christopher Booker in his book *The Neophiliacs: A Study of the Revolution in English Life in the Fifties and Sixties*:

> To appreciate Frost's achievement in gathering together this assembly of notables one has to reflect how, until but a year or so before, the Prime Minister of the day and a similar cross-section of public figures would have dismissed such an invitation ... as an impertinent stunt.

What gave Frost the knowledge that his gamble would come off, was his intuitive sense of television's power to recreate the world on its own unreal terms—to reduce everything and everyone, politicians and pop singers, philosophers and journalists, bishops and entertainers, to the same level, as bit players in a universal dreamworld.

David was at the same time exercising his "intuitive sense" to create a novel formula for a television series. It was not an easy birth. When he and James Gilbert first talked about it, they thought in terms of presenting attractive nightclub shows in an original way. There was little David did not know about London nightclubs, but he and Jimmy Gilbert were thinking of some of the latest international attractions. "We went all round Europe to see shows," David recalled.

They were in Paris—or was it Brussels?—when they hit on a formula which had little in common with their original plan. Why not do a series with each show devoted to a different subject: high comedy with an edge; social and political problems sharply observed and well documented; telegenic sketches, monologues, and anecdotes. Their next step was to call in Antony Jay, whom David describes as "my guru." Jay was commissioned to write a number of essays, thirteen altogether, each on a different subject: travel, education, advertising, love, and so on, from which script- and gag-writers could develop a show.

"The problem," said Jay, "was to get thirty minutes of human and political material on one subject." To obtain this kind of concentrated humor, a large number of writers had to be recruited and—much more difficult—persuaded to collaborate. Copies of Antony Jay's essays were handed out to prospective candidates, who were asked to think about ways of turning them into items for the show. Not all of them accepted the invitation. Those who did were asked to join in a discussion.

At a bleak converted church hall in the Paddington district of London which was available for meetings and rehearsals, David greeted each new arrival—David Nobbs, Charlie Feldman, Dick Vosburgh, John Cleese, and others—with open arms: "How marvelous that you should have come!" Mass cooperation on this scale had never been attempted before. Comedy writers are notoriously secretive and reluctant to reveal their priceless thoughts in the presence of potential competitors.

"They were sitting round a table, rather reticent about their material," Antony Jay recalled.

David put the writers at ease. One of them said something and he responded, "What a marvelous idea!"

There was something about him that generated good material: "He appreciates it," Jay said. "His is a positive approach. People felt appreciated when he welcomed any tentative thought with acclamation. His maxim was, Why meet ideas with pursed lips? Whether it was used in the end or not, David never stepped on an idea and instead clutched at any slight possibility." It was very stimulating for the writers; it made them blossom out and enabled him to squeeze the maximum out of them. Years of success have not changed his approach.

The importance of his receptiveness, according to Jay, was that the encouragement he gave to others was particularly relevant for the new television era. Old comedians used the same jokes day after day, week after week, repeating them in another town and changing their routine perhaps only once or twice a year. Compared with the volume of good material needed to do two or three television shows a week, this was child's play.

"David managed to get twenty first-class people to write for him," said Jay, "and to think in terms of good lines for David Frost." Cross-fertilization of ideas by some of England's liveliest humorists produced excellent results. James Gilbert presided over the exchanges and made notes of the best of them. Much of the material for his own patter as host was written by David himself. He assiduously collected anecdotes, jokes, situations, analyzing each for quality, rewriting and polishing every sentence over and over again.

Exuberantly happy in his work, he was also enjoying the rich rewards of early success. Three years after arriving in London without a penny, he was earning around forty thousand pounds a year. His highly paid appearances on the B.B.C.'s *Not So Much . . .* and his American run on *TW3*, which had ended within a month of each other, had left him with a sizable bank balance. "I never do anything just for the money," he said. "That's also a

statement of my good fortune. I never have to. But once I decide
to do something, I make damn sure I get a good rate for the job."

Alert as he was to every opportunity to make money, he was as
quick to spend it. The Reverend Mr. Frost was retiring, which
meant handing over the manse to his successor. David bought a
bungalow for his parents, and buying his mother a car, encouraged her to take up driving at the age of fifty-seven.

He was generous to a fault. In his presence, a young actress
mentioned casually that she was furnishing her first apartment
but had run out of money before she could buy a mattress. A day
or so later a new mattress arrived at her home, ordered and paid
for by David Frost. The professional wits of course suggested at
once that he was probably planning to share it with the young
lady.

Cabarets were offering him rich contracts, and he returned to
Quaglino's for a week, reeling off his monologue, basking once
more in the limelight. He was noticed among the guests at a
party Prime Minister Harold Wilson gave at 10 Downing Street.

Out of the public view and at the end of the daily grind from
which the scripts of the first few *Frost Reports* emerged, he
worked with Cyril Bennett and Clive Irving on the details of his
talk-show plans, for which Rediffusion was the ideal channel.
Cyril Bennett was enthusiastic and sold it to John McMillan, who
forgot his vow not to allow David to darken his door again and
was as easily reconquered as many others before and after him.
The new series was planned for the autumn of 1966.

In the meantime, the *Frost Report* was taking on definite
shape. More writers were co-opted, some of them veterans of
TW3 and *Not So Much*. . . . One contributor was John Wells,
author of many acid remarks about David Frost in *Private Eye*.
"John Wells is a very talented writer," David said when people
wondered how he could work amicably with a man who had
attacked him so often.

A novel feature, methodically worked out for the *Frost Report*
and diligently rehearsed, was a series of quick-fire sketches performed in their own settings and largely designed for visual
impact, such as a tourist in khaki drill and tropical helmet, on the
verge of total exhaustion, staggering across the desert to a
table—to write a postcard.

These ten-second acts were entrusted to a cast of able but little-known performers like the brilliant Ronnie Barker and the diminutive Ronnie Corbett, a Chaplin in modern dress. Some of the best were submitted by a writer who called himself Gerrard Wiley. His spots were gladly accepted and promptly produced. It was some time before it occurred to producer and cast that nobody had ever set eyes on Wiley. The mystery of his identity was not solved until some time later, when Ronnie Barker, star of many Wiley quickies, admitted that he and Wiley were one and the same person.

David regularly watched rival shows and often laughed out loud when he heard a good gag. One that amused him highly—at this time there was criticism because the British Government was letting the Navy run down—was a takeoff of an Admiralty spokesman on the Barnard Braden show: "This year's naval review," he was saying, "will not be held in the English Channel but in the Serpentine"—the little lake in Hyde Park.

Noticing the credits, which included "Special material contributed by Neil Shand," David remembered meeting Neil some years earlier at Rediffusion and telephoned him. "Did you write this joke?" he asked.

When Neil said "Yes, I did," David invited him round to his apartment. A former Fleet Street journalist who had moved into television as a script-writer, Neil Shand combined an acute sense of topicality with a flair for presenting his subjects in show-business terms, a hybrid quality invaluable for David's program.

He accepted the invitation, and they found that they had much in common. For David's benefit he recited a few humorous ideas, among them some phony commercials, one of which went like this: "ZAPPO, the deodorant with new atomic power added—one puff and it blows off your arm." Another was: "Carter's Little Liver Pills—you buy the huge economy size and stand on the box."

Neil suggested an item about auditioning B.B.C. newscasters who, in marked contrast with the traditional poker face of the species, were breaking up and giggling. So enjoyable was Neil's little collection that David asked him to join his team of writers, and most of these gags turned up in the *Frost Report*. The association between them dating from these days is still going strong on both sides of the Atlantic.

In his search for undiscovered talent, David found one budding star literally on his doorstep. Julie Felix, the young Mexican-American folk singer who had sung her way across Europe, occupied the apartment below David's on the King's Road. They met in the elevator, David heard her sing, and he arranged for her to get a spot on the *Frost Report*.

Months of thinking, talking, planning, writing, pruning, recruiting, rehearsing, were coming to an end. The atmosphere among those involved was remarkably free from tension. After a couple hours' work in the old church hall David looked pointedly at his watch, then delved into his leather bag and from among the scripts, newspapers, and books extracted a battered old tennis ball he always carried around with him. "We tried to get through the morning's work as expediently as possible," Neil Shand said. "David was in a hurry to get us downstairs so that he could play football with the more athletic among us. Within minutes he was kicking the tennis ball around as if his life depended on scoring a quick goal."

The date for the unveiling of the first *Frost Report* was fixed for 9 P.M. on March 10, 1966, and the theme of the opening show was authority. Immediately there was a snag that might easily have hampered a less durable show. With a general election pending, political jokes on television were taboo under the regulations governing the medium in Britain. The *Frost Report* on authority could put policemen, judges, headmasters—and park-keepers—under the microscope and show up their pomposity, but for politicians it was closed season.

Or was it? Viewers who settled in their easy chairs and switched on their sets at the stroke of nine to observe David Frost's return to their screens were confronted by—Harold Wilson. For a moment it looked like one of those satire impersonations of yore. It was, in fact, the Prime Minister in person, using television prime-time to make an electoral broadcast, which all stations were required to carry. The *Frost Report* was delayed until the Prime Minister had said his piece.

While Harold Wilson occupied the little box, the studio audience were entertained—warmed up—by David Frost himself with a monologue in his best cabaret style. Among the "news items" he reported was the one about Ernst Finster, the phenomenal Finnish pole-vaulter who, at the Detroit Coliseum, pole-vaulted a height of 18 feet, 6 inches. Unfortunately, the roof of the Detroit Coliseum was only 16 feet, 3 inches, high. . . . So in one go Finster broke both the indoor and outdoor records—as well as three ribs, two collarbones, and one asbestos tile. It was one of David's favorite stories, which he had a lot of fun with in years to come.

When the show finally came on the air, authority was given a sound drubbing by the Frost crew. The bumbling actor-writer John Cleese became a star overnight. Ronnie Barker was in splendid form. The quickie sketches went over well. David sounded confident, more polished and professional than in his satire days. Putting his own gloss on the news, he often strayed into verbal burlesque. One he liked almost as much as the Finster story equally appealed to his audiences: "Four hundred and seventy yards of sausage are reported stolen from a factory in Reading. Police are looking for four men in a long, thin truck."

Another instant success was Julie Felix, strumming her guitar and singing with a captivating, sexy voice, her clear-cut Mexican features framed by long black hair. At the end of her act David, in full view of the camera, turned to her with the sweetest and most meaningful smile of his television career. It looked like a private signal and allowed of only one interpretation. "Is she your latest girl friend?" he was asked.

"Of course not," David protested, but thought to himself that this was not a bad idea at all. From that day, Julie was frequently seen in his company, and the English press often referred to her as "David Frost's girl friend."

The show was a great success, with David getting much of the praise. The satire days were finally behind him. His return to the screen, however, revived the old pastime of analyzing David Frost. The critics enumerated what he was not—not an original thinker, not a good writer, not this, and not that. It was working up to the catchphrase that still attaches to him like a leech: "David Frost does nothing, but he does it better than anybody else."

Peter Black, Britain's finest television critic, was less equivocal. "He has an awful lot of talent," he has written of David.

Frost Reports on holidays, sin, elections (topically, done on the day the British people went to the polls), news, education, love, and others followed at weekly intervals. One on nudism gave a characteristic definition of a nudist camp: "a place where men and women go to air their differences." The one on the armed forces included a typical quickie, enacted by little Ronnie Corbett as a private on his knees in a trench, tugging at the lapels of John Cleese as the kindly, soft-spoken chaplain.

Ronnie (desperately): "Please, padre, please! I can't do it."

John (kindly): "Of course you can, Foster. If you really try. Someone's got to get that message through to H.Q."

Ronnie: "Oh don't let me go, padre! Please!"

John (kindly): "Foster . . . it'll be all right, once you're out there. You'll find hidden reserves of strength and courage."

Ronnie: "I can't! I can't!"

John (savagely): "Look, Foster! It's you or me! Now you get the hell out there."

The *Frost Report* was set for a long run, and much of the acclamation was for the John Cleese–Ronnie Barker–Ronnie Corbett trio and their sketches. In television circles they became known as David Frost's Repertory Company, which did not remain an "in" joke for long. David was already looking beyond the *Frost Report*. The impresario in his soul wanted to exploit this success by turning it into something more permanent.

The obvious conclusion was for him to plan the television future of the three artists under the aegis of a Frost company. He formed David Paradine Productions to sign up artists, as he put it, "not as their agents but in terms of their exclusive services for television." His role in this company was executive producer rather than performer.

The first series of the *Frost Report* successfully completed and a second one booked, David spent much time and thought planning special shows for his three acquisitions, to start at the end of the second series. For Ronnie Barker he mounted the *Ronnie Barker Playhouse* and for Ronnie Corbett a series under the title *No, That's Me Over Here*, which was still going strong at the end of 1970. "They had star talent and quality," David said. "Paradine gave them their opportunity."

For John Cleese, David Paradine Productions devised a thirteen-week series on which Cleese himself and his friends Graham Chapman and Tim Brooke-Taylor collaborated. To complete a quartet, a veteran writer was persuaded to appear for the first time: Marty Feldman made his television debut. The show—*At Last the 1948 Show*—was offbeat, zany, upper cerebral, inconsequential humor. It was a big proposition, with a budget of over $500,000, and went so well that a second series of thirteen shows was contracted. In the end David's company had a project involving around $1,250,000 on its hands.

Publicity for *At Last the 1948 Show* was strictly within its spirit. "Why this title—what does it mean?" a reporter asked.

"It just tripped off the tongue" was the reply. "We wanted to call it *Spot*, but that might have alarmed thousands of dogs." And what was the underlying theme? "Ferrets, football, females—not to mention Frost." It was that kind of a show.

The *Frost Report* had an average audience of twelve million viewers, with a peak number of fifteen million. To celebrate the great run David gave a party for three hundred people at Battersea Fun Fair, London's Coney Island, which that other supershowman, the late Mike Todd, had also used for a similar occasion. In spite of a thunderstorm a host of celebrities joined performers and technical staff, enjoying themselves on the rides, all the while drinking to their host's health.

Actually, David was in the best of health, otherwise he could not have sustained a mode of living and working which grew more hectic every day—he was also hosting a record show on radio. Friends wondered why he engaged in such frantic activities. "I do not like to waste time and want to use what talents I have," he answered. "It's the Methodist in me."

CHAPTER 8

House and Heart

———

DAVID WAS FAST outgrowing his King's Road apartment and looking around for a house in a more entrepreneurial district. The one on which he settled was a big, pleasant Regency-style house in Egerton Crescent, a quietly elegant and therefore expensive backwater in Knightsbridge, not far from Harrods. His enthusiasm for the new place was only restricted by the lack of time to devote himself to the complicated business of setting up a home of his own. In a series of lightning forays he swept through some of London's best furniture stores, rapidly choosing pieces that appealed to him.

The outsize lounge on the first floor was his first consideration. It was bound to become the room where he would gather friends and business partners around him, and he aimed at making it comfortable and functional. A huge, well-designed modern desk that he selected was ideal for the big alcove at one end of the room. He bought a number of modern easy chairs (designed by Le Corbusier) and a Chesterfield settee covered with black leather. One of his extravagances—of taste rather than money—was a bulbous orange-colored chair in which he could completely lose himself, the kind of "fun furniture" that appeals to many young people these days. His soccer trophies were destined for the mantelpiece, soon to yield pride of place to a growing number of television awards and testimonials.

A large photomural of the New York skyline, which could be classified as pop art, a symbol of his transatlantic life, eventually came to dominate the room. The books that he transferred from the King's Road to the shelves in the sitting room reflected his variegated professional interests rather than his personal tastes, though these often coincided. (Later, visitors began to give detailed accounts of his books, which—the accounts and the books—changed from month to month. At one time Arthur Koestler's works dwelt peacefully by the side of *2,000 Insults for All Occasions*, and other combinations were even more incongruous.)

His approach to objets d'art was haphazard. In the passage of time he acquired paintings by John Bratby, an English modern, and for the staircase another set of modern drawings by Peter Sedgley. The basement had the makings of a game room, with ample space for a billiard table and an elaborate racing-car set that became a showpiece. With an occupant whose personal and professional lives were so intertwined, though, the house soon developed into David Frost's thought factory.

Long before he took up residence, his excitement about his latest piece of private enterprise sometimes erupted at unexpected moments. While dining at the Post Office Tower restaurant with his New York friend Clay Felker, who was on a visit to London, he decided to show off his new house. It was nearly midnight, but he drove Clay to Knightsbridge and took him on a conducted tour.

When he finally moved in, David bequeathed his King's Road apartment to Julie Felix, who owed her stardom to him and could now well afford grander surroundings. To look after the house David engaged a Spanish housekeeper, Luisa Carmo, a comfortable, chatty lady from Madrid who had previously worked at the Uruguayan Embassy in London. Her name crops up in conversation with television executives on both sides of the Atlantic, who commend her cooking. Luisa has attended David with sisterly devotion ever since—which is no easy task.

Good-humored and undemanding as he is, his interest in domestic matters is only marginal. "He never has time to talk to me" has become Luisa's perennial complaint. Whether he has had cause to or not, he has never rebuked her either.

It took Luisa a long time to get accustomed to David's habit of switching on all the lights in the house as soon as he entered. John Wells, the *Private Eye* Frost analyst, had an explanation: "It's insecurity," he diagnosed. It could also be that the habit of being in the limelight is difficult to shake off, and though David may be nocturnal, his nights are always full of bright lights.

The house soon became a meeting place for artists, writers, directors, producers, lawyers, and financial experts associated with the growing Frost empire. Even when surrounded by people, however, David would reach for the telephone every few minutes or answer the cascade of calls from far and near. When alone, he was rarely off the line. He seemed to need constant contact with someone somewhere. The moment a new thought struck him, he picked up the telephone and unburdened his mind. Discussing an urgent business matter, his face registered attentive concentration. A dreamy expression indicated a girl friend on the other end. Both kinds of conversation were punctuated by short, uninhibited bursts of laughter.

How he found time for girl friends was often a mystery, but two or three times a week the last entry in his diary, usually for 10:30 P.M., was a laconic, telltale "private dinner." To avoid complications he was, in fact, programming his love life as meticulously as a television network's schedules. Photographs in the following day's newspapers showing him with his companion of the previous evening often spoiled the game.

At this time, Otto Preminger was in London making a film, *Bunny Lake Is Missing,* and one of the American stars he brought over was the gorgeous Carol Lynley. She was soon "discovered" by David, who did the town with her and took her along to Whitby when his sister, Margaret Bull, persuaded him to speak at the annual dinner of the local Business and Professional Women's Club. After treating the ladies of Whitby to a brief version of the *Frost Report,* he went on his obligatory pilgrimage to Beccles to introduce Carol to his parents. In Mona Frost's memory she lives as one of the "young ladies" David brought home. Carol also graced the guest list of a second V.I.P. meal—a dinner—David gave at the Connaught Hotel.

On a visit to Danny La Rue's nightclub he was enchanted by Jenny Logan, the star of the new late-night show, and went backstage to congratulate her and the cast. "Let's go out for an hour or so," he said impulsively, although it was 3 A.M. "I couldn't think where one could take a lady respectably at this time of night," he recalled. They went for a drive and ended up at the London airport, where he took Jenny to the all-night bowling alley, not the most obvious place for an assignation. Not until much later did it occur to them what a funny way this was of starting a romance. They were too interested in each other and talked about their private lives: David told her about his family, and Jenny mentioned Martin, her little boy. The night at the bowling alley was the beginning of a love affair that lasted longer than any other in David's young life.

Women's attraction for David was not diminished by his youthfully categorical definition of his attitude. "When I am with a woman," he said, "I tell her what I expect of her. I never, never negotiate with her!" Actually, he rarely implemented his own prescription.

Neither had his success in this field much to do with his looks or even his television fame. "It's his manner, his total devotion, which make him irresistible," according to Nanette and Bryan Forbes, who have met most of his girl friends. "Our guest book is a Kinsey Report on David's amorous progress," said Bryan.

His wife added: "Only a woman can understand why he fascinates women. Having observed him so often, it is obvious that they are captivated by his total absorption with them. When he is with a girl, she is the only one in the world for him—or at least that is how he makes her feel."

The thought of marriage seldom entered into it, though. David had his doubts. "I don't know how you manage to be so very happy together," he told Bryan and Nanette a little enviously. "So many other married couples I know are desperately unhappy." He sounded as if he were afraid of marriage but quickly added, as if in self-defense: "What kind of life would it be for a woman married to me now?"

He had a point there. Even between television shows his pace was killing. Before breakfast, he wrote a column on the British press for the weekly *Spectator*. Lunchtime meant speaking engagements. Invitations to officiate at opening ceremonies—a foundry here, a supermarket there—took him on rapid excursions all over the country.

One day he was in Parkhurst, Britain's toughest prison for hard-core criminals, heading a variety show for the inmates and introducing Jenny Logan as one of the stars. It was, he said, "a stimulating and moving experience." He has been giving shows in prisons from time to time ever since.

The next day, at St. Martin-in-the-Fields, one of central London's finest churches, his address to the congregation was entitled "The Changing Face of Sin." "Sin is political," he asserted firmly. "The right wing says that everyone should have money, but if they haven't, it is sinful to try and get it; and the left-wing theory is that no one should have money, but if they have it, it's sinful to enjoy it."

On a B.B.C. religious program he joined the Reverend Billy Graham, the idol of his youth, in a round-table discussion. Graham's magic still worked on David, who (apart from a brief mention of *Lady Chatterley's Lover*) was on his best behavior and looked, one observer noted, as if he might "come forward," which in a way he had done a long time ago.

Not much later he accepted an engagement of a different order. It was to present six late-night shows—*An Evening With David Frost*—in Edinburgh, Scotland, during the annual festival. On the eve of the show, breezing into the Scottish capital with Neil Shand in tow, he found that no preparations whatsoever had been made. He had less than twenty-four hours to put the show together.

The scripts in his suitcase provided enough material, but there were no adequate stage props. Without much ado, he commandeered a truck and raced around Edinburgh grabbing what he could find—a lamp, a desk, other bits and pieces which he thought essential to convey the right atmosphere. The audience was already arriving while he was still organizing the stage-lighting to his own requirements.

Old pros were aghast at this kind of improvisation and were convinced that David was heading for disaster. The less iron-nerved among his colleagues were equally doubtful. David carried them with him in the best "It'll be all right on the night" spirit—and it was.

It was so good that he impressed Woody Fraser, of the *Mike Douglas Show*, who was in Edinburgh. He was full of admiration. "David Frost will be the first truly international TV personality," he told Neil Shand. It was a prophetic observation.

Woody Fraser was not the only American television man who thought highly of David Frost. Westinghouse Broadcasting executives who were in London for a conference to examine their company's problems from an international perspective asked David to give a show for them at the Savoy Hotel. Westinghouse President Donald H. McGannon congratulated him warmly. Altogether, the meeting, though neither party realized it, heralded a turning point in David's career, as we shall see.

Less attractive propositions came from manufacturers asking David to advertise their wares. One was for ten thousand pounds for a few words in praise of a brand of soap. David's answer was a firm "No!" Later a cigar company wanted him to endorse its products and offered forty thousand pounds. Again David said "No!" It was a matter of principle, he said; he could not recommend what he did not believe in.

A contract he did sign, once the intricate details had been ironed out with the help of his agent (Richard Armitage) and his lawyer (John Stutter), was for the first series of twenty-six shows for Rediffusion. It was worth twenty-five thousand pounds, but there was bound to be more than one series—and more money. Work on this show occupied most of his time and thought. To clear his own mind he defined his aims. "I shall not try to entertain or persuade," he said. "I want to stimulate. I want to raise the level of public debate."

Above all he was anxious to involve the viewers, wake them up. If they were dead tired when he came on, he hoped they would be wide awake at the end. "Television," he was convinced, "should make people feel alive and not be a sleeping pill. One might as well be a manufacturer of soporifics as host the average show."

Starting from the premise that the public was intelligent and should be treated accordingly, he dissected every aspect of television theory and practice in conversations with Antony Jay and Clive Irving, who were soon joined by the show's producer, Geoffrey Hughes. When the confrontations for which David was preparing himself eventually went on the air, viewers could not possibly guess how much thought had gone into the definition of his technique. What, in general terms, were good questions to ask? "The roots of our analysis went back to Donald Baverstock and the *Tonight* show," said Antony Jay, explaining some of the guidelines David had evolved for himself. "A good question was one that made the interviewee think while on the air. It should make him creative in front of the camera, induce him to give something of himself and disclose things no one else had heard about."

There were two kinds of television: art and life. Art, as they defined it, was craftsmanship that brought out available material in the most effective way. Life was when a situation developed on television which one could not anticipate. The aim was to create in an interview the kind of surprise element that attaches to a live broadcast of a sporting event like the World Football Cup or the Wimbledon Tournament or the World Series. To achieve this effect, it was up to David to make the interviewee reveal himself so that the viewer felt he was getting to know the real person and not the image.

Broadly, David and his associates separated interviews into categories: interviews intended to elucidate a complex situation, interviews that aimed at the revelation of a personality, interviews that served the examination of an idea (family, religion, race). Confronting a responsible man with his record and his action ("When you were in office, why did you do this or that?") fell into yet another category, and in a lighter vein there was the interview that gave an entertainer the opportunity, usually prearranged, to shine in conversation rather than entertain the viewer with a stand-up act. There were, of course, other variants, and frequently two, three, or more of the categories would have to be employed in the same interview.

David had to be clear in his own mind on what his role as an interviewer was, on how he could reconcile his task with his own opinions, which might be different from those of the interviewee. Without abandoning his principles, he would have to avoid the danger of becoming an arguer and of trying to dominate his subject to prove that he, David, was right. To be a good interviewer it was necessary for him to accept a situation in which his own views might be changed by a guest's arguments. It was essential to give the interviewee the chance to demonstrate that his views were right.

Some pitfalls had to be deftly avoided. Never, never ask a

double question that makes it easy to evade answering the one or the other point. Never formulate a long question that requires only a short answer or simply a "yes" or "no."

One of the skilled interviewer's most effective weapons is a pause. Those at the receiving end of his questions can rarely resist jumping in to fill the gap. Frequently, instead of challenging a man, it is better to let him condemn himself out of his own mouth. David resolved never to be harsh; it is not in his nature, anyway. He was fond of quoting Aesop's fable of the argument between the wind and the sun about who could get a man's coat off quicker. The wind blew sharply, and the man wrapped himself deeper in his coat and pulled his collar up; the sun shone warmly, and he took the coat off. By and by, David also learned that self-revelation in carefully judged doses encouraged others to respond in kind or better.

"Another problem we discussed was audience participation," Antony Jay recalled. "At the time we did not know, and nobody could tell us, how to measure audience attitudes and reactions. What was the best size of an audience to be homogeneous? One did not want too big a studio audience; neither did one want a clique whose reaction might well leave the home audience behind." The figure at which they arrived was between 200 and 250. Some experts felt strongly that it was a mistake to have a studio audience at all. David did not subscribe to this view. On the contrary—to a bigger extent than attempted before, he developed the trick of turning to the audience and asking individuals their views on points as they arose. Lights and microphones would be switched to people who could introduce a surprise element into the proceedings. It was not as easy as it looked on the screen but was by far the best way of reflecting, through the audience, the feelings of ordinary people, the viewers.

Interviews that David remembered with respect were John Freeman's *Face to Face* confrontations on B.B.C. television. Freeman, editor of a London political weekly who went on to become British High Commissioner in India, was a much more austere person than David, however, whose ebullience gave him a much wider range. Another example David had very much in mind was Edward R. Murrow, and it is no accident that many have come to regard him as Murrow's natural successor.

Important lessons could also be learned from the mistakes of other interviewers. It was vital to keep in mind what not to do. As an example David mentioned the lapse of an English host ("He shall be nameless," he said) who managed to get George Raft on his show. "There was a time," George was telling the interviewer, "when I was in trouble with the Internal Revenue Department; they said that if I didn't pay my taxes, I might go to jail. Then I had a phone call from Frank Sinatra, who said he could not bear to see his childhood hero, George Raft, in trouble, and promised to send over a check."

As David listened to the interview, a hundred questions presented themselves. How big was the check? Was the money ever repaid? What else did Sinatra say? Instead of asking any of these questions, the interviewer turned to another guest, an actress, and asked her, "Tell me, have you ever had any problems with money?"

David's reaction was significant: "I wanted to hurl something at the screen," he recalled. "I was so desperate to hear the rest of the Sinatra-Raft story." The lesson was so sharp that he resolved never to commit himself in advance to a definite line of questioning so as not to be caught unawares by a surprise answer. "You might ask a question," he said, warming to the subject, "and the guest might answer, 'I want to tell you about the most frightening thing that ever happened in my life,' but then you'd have to disregard the challenge and go on to ask, 'What are your hobbies?'" This was the ultimate sin.

As the beginning of his Rediffusion series approached, David was intellectually well prepared for his task. Considering that the talk show had never properly worked in England, however, it was still a venture into pastures new. The schedule was for David to host three shows a week, Wednesday, Thursday, and Friday at 10:30 P.M.

Each show would deal with three or four subjects, David talking to prominent people in the studio and also going out with a film unit to do interviews. There would be comedy items, most of them politically and socially oriented, and songs by pop stars. The interview, or as David preferred to call it, the conversation between him and his guests, would be the core of the program.

Much of David's time was spent at Television House. At ten

every morning, production staff and writers assembled in the big program-conference room and settled around an oval table. Present were three editors, two researchers, and the unit manager. Antony Jay and Clive Irving acted as advisers.

Conversation was subdued as the members of this small congregation studied the newspapers, making notes and formulating their ideas. Coffee, rolls, and croissants were wheeled in on a cart, and as everybody started nibbling and drinking the atmosphere was somewhat like that of a continental coffee house. Life was injected into the party with the arrival of producer Geoffrey Hughes, a big bustling man who always carried a pink folder ("Same color as his complexion," someone quipped). The scene was set for the entrance of the star of the show, David, with his familiar leather bag full of scripts. "I carry my work with me wherever I go," he said when challenged about his portable library. "It's worth more to me than money."

Prompted by David, ideas were thrown up—and shot down. Items in the newspapers were read aloud and discussed. Attempts at jokes were drowned in serious argument. The unit was groping to give shape and direction to the new show.

David made copious notes, jotting down random thoughts with big strokes of a felt-tip pen, encircling items, drawing strong lines that reflected his departmentalized mind. His doodles were rich, flowing, and symmetrical, and some words, underlined twice or three times, revealed his feelings. He quickly tore up the sheets of paper in tiny bits, though, as if loath to let others in on his secret thoughts.

There were occasions when the conversation flowed without seeming to touch him. David lost interest, got bored and fidgety, or left the table altogether. It was a sure sign that the subject did not appeal to him, and what did not interest him could not possibly be of interest to the viewers. Another subject would come up, and David was back in the discussion.

From the conference room he moved on to Cyril Bennett's office. With a burst of cordiality that other people reserve for special occasions, he greeted Joan Pugh, Bennett's tall, very attractive, and quietly efficient secretary. "I saw a lot of him in those days," Joan Pugh recalled. "He was very polite—extremely pleasant," she added, remarking on his natural good manners. "But one is slightly suspicious of celebrities, and I, for one, was greatly surprised that David was such a genuinely nice person."

In the nicest possible way David had his eye on Joan. "My secretary will be leaving to get married," he told her before long. "How would you like to work for me?" He was concentrating his private affairs in his new house, he explained. That's where she would be working if she agreed to join him. Joan promised to think it over.

Planning for the *Frost Programme* had gone as far as it could. Practical implementation of the plans was a different matter. Work on the script for a pilot show was progressing, and names of interesting guests were listed. The production staff went into action. When they approached the first few big names, they came up against a fearful, almost catastrophic snag. A large number of those invited to come on the show to be interviewed by David shied away, refused, or made excuses. Some who promised to appear wrote that they had changed their minds. The stigma of satire still clung to the star of *TW3* and *Not So Much*. . . . Public personalities seemed afraid to expose themselves in public to what they feared might well be the acid wit—well, yes, satire— that had been *TW3*'s stock in trade and had now turned into a double-edged sword.

Under these circumstances the pilot show did not go smoothly. The formula was too new, too indefinite in the minds of all but David and his brain trust, to inspire confidence. David himself seemed curiously lackadaisical and listless. It turned out to be a disastrous flop. There were a lot of nervous people at Rediffusion.

A second pilot show did not fare much better. Again, David seemed far below his best form. So great were the turnover of rehearsals, changes, and new plans formulated and abandoned that Denis Norden, one of the comedy-writers, went on stage and announced: "Let me introduce David Frost, the man who has made more pilots than a randy air hostess." For a second the executives stopped biting their nails and laughed.

"David is so acutely attuned to the public," says Richard Armitage, "that he cannot fully involve himself in the dress rehearsal. Unlike actors who give their best at rehearsal, David draws his strength from the immediacy. His dry runs are disappointing, his pilots absolutely dreadful. The adrenalin flows only for the real thing, when he confronts the public. But he has a way of turning disaster into triumph."

Few of the troubles and tribulations that beset the preparations were discernible on September 28, 1966, when David faced the cameras to introduce the first new *Frost Programme*, his return as a major television performer after a year's absence from the screen. Not a hair out of place, not a false step, not a misplaced word, as he announced the good things to come. Main guest of the evening was Robert Morley, the portly, sophisticated, and witty English actor and writer, whose presence suggested that David had opted for a serious subject treated with good humor as a curtain-raiser.

The subject was education. Stimulated by David's questions, Morley gave a hilarious account of his years in an English public (which means private) school which illuminated the quaint customs and practices of this peculiarly English system. As soon as he had finished, David asked for comments from the audience, which was liberally sprinkled with teachers. The result was a spirited exchange that made lively television.

Another guest on the same show was a famous English physician who presently found himself involved with a number of young doctors in the audience. Sandy Shaw, the pop singer who performs in her stockinged feet, supplied a touch of glamour to the show. If it was not sensational, it was solid and flawless. The new David Frost—David Frost, the interviewer and talk-show host—had made his bow. For him it was the beginning of a new era.

The next few shows offered lighter fare—rough play on the football pitch, a funny act by John Cleese. David introduced his "crossing" jokes, which were an instant success but could not be described as sophisticated:

"Cross a boiling kettle and the egg of a flea, and what do you get? . . . You get a steaming nit."

"Cross an American, some scribble, and a well-dressed man, and what do you get? . . . Yankee Doodle Dandy."

"Cross a kangaroo with a ball of wool, and what do you get? . . . A woolly jumper." (Jumper is a British term for a sweater.)

"And what," he asked, "is the technical name of a woman who refuses to practice birth control? . . . Mother."

Ned Sherrin was quoted as saying, "David's flair is a good deal more obvious than his taste," but the viewers loved it.

David talked to Laurence Harvey down the street at the Cambridge Theatre, but difficulties with suitable English personalities persisted, particularly since he would have no other but top people on the show. Suspicious minds still needed a lot of convincing. It was fortunate that two Americans who were very much in the news were in London and had no hesitation in confronting David Frost. The first was Mark Lane, lawyer and writer, who had strong and idiosyncratic views on the assassination of John F. Kennedy. David gave him wide range to expound his theories.

He was followed by Gore Vidal. Introducing him as the author of *Julian* and *Messiah*, David said: "Both have just come out as paperbacks, which could possibly explain why he is over here." The subject under discussion, however, was not Vidal's paperbacks but birching. Facing Vidal in the studio was Sir Cyril Osborne, Member of Parliament and strong supporter of corporal and capital punishment.

David promptly raised a highly controversial topic, the recent refusal by British Home Secretary Roy Jenkins to confirm a sentence of birching on two inmates of an English prison who were found guilty of violence while serving their original sentence. Calling Jenkins "a softy," Sir Cyril Osborne said that England needed a tough man at the Home Office, not an effeminate one.

"You are not saying that Mr. Jenkins is effeminate, are you?" David interjected.

"I am saying he is soft," Sir Cyril replied.

As Osborne propounded his arguments in favor of corporal punishment, Gore Vidal was getting angrier and angrier. "It's difficult to conduct an argument with the nineteenth century," he said. "You used to hang people. I am sure you were in favor of it. Hanging children for stealing a loaf of bread. It means brutalizing people!"

Now it was David's turn. "Sir Cyril," he asked, "how does brutalizing other people solve anything?"

"It doesn't brutalize them," Osborne replied. Calling opponents of corporal punishment nitwits, he insisted, "In both countries they've had their way since the war."

Osborne and Vidal then went for each other with little restraint. David needed all his skill to cool the ardor of the two contestants without depriving the viewers of a stimulating spectacle. The *Frost Programme* was beginning to do the job David wanted it to do. Viewers appreciated it, and informed opinion accepted the new forum of public debate as an essential ingredient of a democratic society.

"I'm speechless." David Frost **receives an Emmy.** *(David Frost Show)*

The Reverend W. J. Paradine Frost, David's father

Mona Frost, David's mother and confidante *(David Frost Show)*

Soccer: David making a goal *(Thomas Watson)*

Cricket: David could have been a professional
(London Weekend Television)

David and the original cast of *That Was the Week That Was* (B.B.C.)

David and his *TWTWTW* team, 1962 (B.B.C.)

Janette Scott, now Mrs. Mel Tormé, with David
(Syndication International)

At home in London: David in his mod chair *(David Frost Show)*

The Queen is an ardent Frost fan.

David's private team: outside his London house with Joan Pugh
and Bob Lambert *(David Frost Show)*

On the run: arriving in New York by helicopter *(David Frost Show)*

Doodles? No, notes for David's Hochhuth versus Churchill program, 1967 *(David Frost Show)*

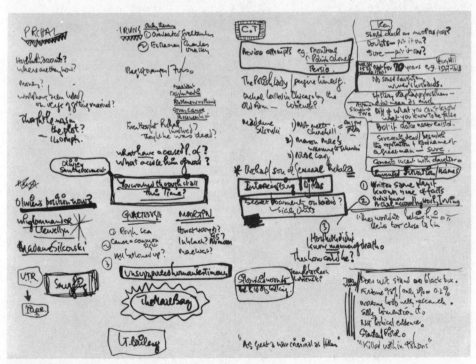

The Little Theatre, New York headquarters of the *David Frost Show*
(David Frost Show)

Billy Taylor, genial music director of the *David Frost Show*
(David Frost Show)

David Frost
and politics:

Vice-President
Spiro Agnew,

Mrs. Lyndon
Johnson,

Senator
Edmund Muskie,

and Mayor
John Lindsay
(*David Frost
Show*)

**David Frost
and the ladies:**

Maria Callas,

Sophia Loren,

Shirley MacLaine,

**and Coretta
Scott King**
*(David Frost
Show)*

David Frost
and some
laugh-makers:

Jack Benny,

Maurice
Chevalier,

Flip Wilson,

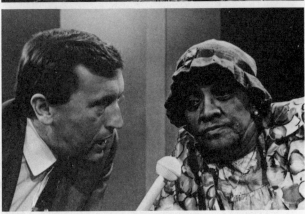

and
"Moms" Mabley
*(David Frost
Show)*

Typical
Frost shows:

Clare Boothe Luce
and Raquel Welch;

Sir John Gielgud
and Sir Ralph
Richardson;

Dennis Hopper,
Peter Fonda,
and Nancy Sinatra;

and Bernadette
Devlin, M.P.
(David Frost Show)

David Frost,
with friends:

Johnny Carson,

Louis Armstrong
and
Bing Crosby,

Richard Rodgers,

and Artur
Rubinstein
(*David Frost
Show*)

A Frost variety show: Adam Clayton Powell, Elizabeth Taylor and Richard Burton, Groucho Marx, and Lee Radziwill *(David Frost Show)*

**Frost favorites: Israeli Prime Minister Golda Meir
and Diahann Carroll** *(David Frost Show)*

Frost associates Neil Shand, Shelly Marshall, Peter Baker, Jack Reilly, and Chet Collier (seated) *(Wagner International Photos, Inc.)*

David Frost with Westinghouse board chairman Donald H. McGannon *(Wagner International Photos, Inc.)*

CHAPTER 9

Interviewer Extraordinary

IN ENGLAND, as elsewhere, there was no shortage of issues burning under the surface and demanding a public airing. These were the subjects David was most anxious to examine on the show. One that aroused deep emotions was the notorious John Christie–Timothy Evans murder case, which troubled the consciences of many people.

Years after several women were found murdered at Rillington Place, London (the name of the street has since been changed but survives as the title of a spine-chilling movie), the suspicion that the wrong man was hanged for the murders was strongly held by leading lawyers. The suggestion of an irreparable miscarriage of justice provided opponents of the death penalty with a strong argument. When a report on an official inquiry into the case was published, it offered a rich field of controversy, for which the *Frost Programme* was the perfect setting. David soon briefed himself on the complicated issues and explored new sources of information. Clive Irving enlisted the help of Peter Baker, a young journalist with a background of executive posts on the Beaverbrook papers and some television experience, who supplied a few telling points. A deceptively quiet and low-key operator, Peter Baker did his job so well that David asked him to join his team.

Baker's initial task was mainly journalistic: to instill greater topicality and urgency into the program and to balance the show-business influences. He has worked with David ever since. Like Neil Shand, Peter Baker ("two ex-Fleet Street ex-wonder boys," they were called by Beatles' biographer Hunter Davies) followed David to the United States, where he became producer of the *David Frost Show*.

The team behind David Frost was working well. More often than not the choice of subject and guest was the result of his putting his head together with Clive Irving. Once a decision was made, the researchers quickly prepared a dossier. David consulted Antony Jay about the most rewarding areas to explore and the most pointed questions to ask.

"David's great strength is to be able to take a brief and assimilate information," Tony Jay said. He was also able to isolate the characteristic and discard the unessential. Although readily accepting advice, he adapted prepared questions to suit his style and purpose. "I ask the questions the viewer would like to put," he said.

There was no longer much difficulty in recruiting prominent people as guests, and if one or another showed unwillingness, David intervened personally and almost always succeeded. "He is not easily rebuffed," said one of his aides. "He applies a mixture of charm and flattery which often does the trick." For one of his shows he managed to bring together more members of Sir Winston Churchill's family than had ever before been assembled in one spot.

Part of the Churchill show was a live broadcast from a literary luncheon for Randolph Churchill, who was carrying on his late father's historical writing. David talked to the grand old man's widow and her daughter Mary, Mrs. Christopher Soames. Young Winston Churchill, his grandfather's namesake, was also on the show. To get the whole clan before the cameras was a great accomplishment. Yet it was not wholly successful television because the interviews had to be edited and squeezed into half an hour's viewing time. This robbed them of the elusive effect of real-life immediacy.

While still preoccupied with the Churchills, David was already involved with his next subject, New York's Traffic Commissioner Henry Barnes. He ploughed through mountains of Barnes's own speeches and papers on New York's traffic problems, trying to relate them to conditions in London. Commissioner Barnes was taken on a drive round London, with the camera on him and the microphone in David's hand. The thickest traffic congestion they encountered was near the Bank of England, in London's "Wall Street." "Now, how would you deal with this?" David asked while they were stuck in a solid mass of traffic. The noise of the engines and the hooting of impatient motorists provided the background sound.

One suggestion Commissioner Barnes put forward was the possible payment of special taxes to pass through certain crowded areas, which might relieve the pressure there. Little boxes at the entrance to the streets would enable the tax to be collected. The conversation became so stimulating that David was unhappy to reach the end of the allotted time. He asked the commissioner to return to the show the following week.

The time trap threatened again a few weeks later when David's guest was Major Mike Hoare, commander of the white mercenaries in the Congo. As they settled before the cameras, a hint of disapproval, if not distaste, seemed to flash across David's features, but he controlled his emotions and came straight to the point: "Major Hoare," he said by way of introduction, "you are a unique figure in that you led this band of mercenaries. It was a curious thing for you to do, and for them to do. What led these men to go to a country that was not their own and fight for a cause that was not their own? Why did they do it?"

"There was only one reason," Major Hoare replied. "Money! The money was extremely good." He mentioned a thousand dollars a month for each man.

David next asked how he, Hoare, disciplined his men. Hoare said that it was a matter of personality and grip on the men and, he hoped, respect. Further down the line it could also be hard tactics, even fisticuffs.

Mentioning the case of one of his mercenaries who had raped a Congolese girl and then shot her in cold blood, the major said, "We decided to try him." The man was condemned, and all manner of punishment was contemplated—thirty-eight lashes with a whip, making him commit suicide, or executing him. When Major Hoare found out that the offender was a professional football-player, a suitable punishment suggested itself to him. "I decided," he recounted, "the best thing to be done was to pass a sentence that his big toes were to be blown off. . . . I took out my Colt revolver and shot his big toe off each foot."

"That's a frightening story" was David's horrified reaction. He pressed Hoare on the atmosphere of savagery, confronted him with stories of prisoners being executed. There was much more he wanted to extract from this man when the show's director signaled that the commercial break—the point at which the interview was scheduled to end—was only seconds away. Matt Munro, the singer, was standing in the wings to come on after the two-minute interval.

Instead of taking leave of his guest as he always did at the end of a conversation, David only said his customary, "We are taking a short break now." Geoffrey Hughes came down from the control box, and they talked rapidly. He could not possibly leave the subject, David told him, without exploring other aspects of this extraordinary story. Then and there—all within two minutes—he made the decision to cancel the other items and carry on with the interview until the end of the show.

"It was a landmark in the series," Geoffrey Hughes said. "It was the first time that we elected to go on talking to someone who was only intended to be there for part of the show." The interview with Hoare continued and brought out more terrifying incidents in the lives of the mercenaries. When it was over, David apologized to Matt Munro and offered him a bigger spot on a future program.

Escape from the straitjacket of a rigorous timetable had a liberating effect on the show. It proved to David that viewers were prepared to listen to an interview lasting three-quarters of an hour, a discovery as important in television terms as Onassis's decision to build his giant supertankers was in the oil business. Few other interviewers have had the strength and the authority to follow David's example.

Improvisation—though it did not look like that to uninitiated viewers—became the spice of David's talk show even when it was forced on him by circumstances. The series was moving into its third month when John Betjeman, one of the few genuinely popular poets in the world today, was invited to come on the show for ten to twelve minutes. The major part of the show was to be taken up by an entirely different subject, a studio discussion on premonitions, which arose in the wake of a disaster in the South Wales mining village of Aberfan, where a slag heap, washed away by torrential rain, had buried a school full of children.

Many people came forward and said they had had a premonition of the tragedy.

David's researchers sought out those all over the country who claimed to have had premonitions of this and other events. After talking to them on the telephone, they invited those with the most interesting experiences to tell their stories on the show. When David himself questioned them before putting them on the air, he found most of their claims too absurd for words. "They were fakers," he thought. Most of them seemed to be "fanatical believers in premonitions." He was not happy; the producer was not happy. With only an hour or so to go before the show, it was an embarrassing situation.

One thing was certain. David was not going to introduce these people on the air. He made a snap decision to devote the whole program to Betjeman. The prospect of a forty-five-minute solo appearance threatened to unnerve the poet, but David put him at ease, invited him to recite some of his poems, and discussed them with him. At his suggestion Betjeman turned to the audience and asked whether any of them had ever written a poem.

And lo and behold, oblivious of the lights, the cameras, the other people, a little lady in the audience stood up and recited, movingly, endearingly, some verses that she had penned under the impact of a deeply personal experience. The studio seemed to shrink into an intimate private room as others followed suit, revealing in verse some treasured mementos they harbored in their minds. It was totally unexpected. It was life on television, exactly what David and his friends had hoped to create. Viewers heard and saw what nobody else had heard or seen before, the basic ingredient of good television. Born out of failure, the show was turned into a tremendous popular success.

Yet failure, in a different shape, struck again before the year was out, when a whole program dissolved into thin air—before it could be put on the air. With only a couple of hours to go, David and his producer were frantically looking for something to fill the screen. In desperation they contacted three Members of Parliament, brought them to the studio, set them a theme, and let them talk. Although David helped the conversation along, it was less than inspiring.

An unhappy evening was saved—if that is the word—by a telephone call David put through to Louis Washkansky, one of Dr. Christiaan Barnard's first heart-transplant patients, in South Africa. The voice of this man who lived on borrowed time came across a distance of thousands of miles. The brief but poignant exchange made up for the tedium that had gone before. A short time later Washkansky's time ran out.

Undeterred by occasional failure, David reached out for the most elusive topics and personalities. More often than not his persistence was rewarded. Shortly after the abortive talks between Prime Minister Harold Wilson and Ian Smith, leader of rebellious British Rhodesia, on board the British warship *Tiger*, David invited Ian Smith to come to London and be interviewed on his show. Britain's conflict with the Rhodesian leader over the political rights of the black majority was an inflammatory issue, and the British Government refused to give the rebel a safe conduct for a visit to London.

David would not be gainsaid. If he could not introduce Ian Smith in person, he could talk to him on the telephone, for like the airplane, the telephone has become a natural extension of David's physical range. With only a short time to make the complicated arrangements, David proposed to employ a technique that Ed Murrow had used so effectively on *Small World*. It was for David to talk to Ian Smith on the telephone, with one camera team filming Smith in Salisbury and recording his voice while another was taping David and his questions in London.

This is how the interview was conducted, but the Ian Smith film and sound track mysteriously disappeared in transit in South Africa and was lost for a couple of vital days. "The news was so pulsatingly hot," said David, "that delay could spoil the whole enterprise. We had a discussion whether to go on with the interview or wait for the film and decided that we could not wait."

When the interview went on the air, David was seen and heard asking the questions as recorded in the studio. The voice of Ian Smith was transmitted to viewers as it came over in the original telephone conversation, crackling with atmospheric interference and in parts difficult to understand, while still photographs of him were shown on the screen. Viewers had to strain their ears, and the impact was all the greater.

David conducted the interview with skill and assurance. The

question everybody was asking was the first he put to Ian Smith. Did he plan to take Rhodesia out of the British orbit? Was his next step a U.D.I.—a Unilateral Declaration of Independence? Smith's reply was that he would seek a mandate from the people, meaning the white minority. Four million black Rhodesians were denied any share in the running of their country.

Another controversial subject David raised was the question of education. Rhodesia was spending sixteen times as much on the education of a white child as it devoted to a black child. The answer was vague. Pressed on democracy in Rhodesia, Ian Smith evaded a direct answer. He accused Africans sweepingly of intimidating and murdering people and burning their houses down, but when David asked for figures, he replied, "Offhand, this is asking rather much to give the exact figure."

"How many cases of little babies being burned?" David asked. Smith replied, "I am afraid I haven't got the exact figure."

Smith was equally evasive about the agreement proposed by Wilson, envisaging steady progress toward equality for black Rhodesians. He had initialed the agreement at the conclusion of the *Tiger* talks, but he retracted it as soon as he returned to Rhodesia. David wanted to know why. "I did not want to sign, but Wilson wanted a signed document of the memorable occasion."

The Frost-Smith telephone talk enabled millions of viewers to judge the rebel leader's ambiguities. What everybody had been saying about Ian Smith—that he said one thing at one moment and the other in the next sentence—became transparently obvious. Only once before (when the redoubtable Robin Day talked to Abdel Gamal Nasser while diplomatic relations between Britain and Egypt were suspended) had television put diplomacy in the making on the air. David's "diplomacy by television" was a big coup.

This intervention in world affairs was too tempting a subject for his friends to let pass without a few wisecracks. Chatting with Frankie Howerd, David casually said in the course of conversation, "Oh, God!"

Frankie pounced: "Stop this habit of talking about yourself!"

Joan Pugh, who by this time had joined David as his private secretary and was working in his house, stuck a little limerick in the same vein on the wall:

A general once lived named De Gaulle,
Five hundred years old, ten yards tall.
He thought he was God, which really was odd,
For God's David Frost—if at all.

The Smith interview was a turning point. David had established his capacity to deal with an intricate political subject. About the same time he visited Lambeth Palace, the residence of the Archbishop of Canterbury, Dr. Michael Ramsey, who had agreed to appear on his show. The Archbishop was delighted to meet the star of a popular medium who, unlike other idols of the television age, was also a religious person. They discussed the broad outline of the subjects to be raised, but the Archbishop was not told the specific questions he would be asked. The interview itself showed that David was now able to refer back to important aspects that had figured in some of his previous shows, a technique he employed more frequently as his experience grew.

He quoted John Allegro, the religious historian and student of the Dead Sea scrolls, who had said in his conversation with David that there was no historical evidence of Jesus Christ's existence. "Now, if I believe that Christ did not exist historically, as Allegro alleges," David asked the Archbishop, "can I be a Christian?" The Archbishop's answer was that there was so much and such diffuse evidence that he ruled out the hypothesis as not worth considering. David agreed but went on to ask whether one had to believe also in the Virgin Birth to be a Christian.

"The incarnation of Christ," the Archbishop replied, "is a supernatural fact, and the Virgin Birth is congruous with its supernatural character. That is to say, I would never believe in the divinity of Christ because of the Virgin Birth."

"We've got the point, Archbishop," David recapitulated. "On the one hand, one has to believe in Jesus Christ as a historical figure to be a Christian. On the other hand, one does not have to believe necessarily in the Virgin Birth." This interpretation of Christian doctrine had never before been stated so unequivocally and led to discussion in religious circles. Religion continued to figure in David's interviews, and he frequently probed his guests' beliefs: "Do you believe in God?" was one of the questions he put to many people.

His accomplishment in getting the Archbishop on the show provoked another fusillade from snipers who are fond of aiming their missiles at David. "Surely he calls the Archbishop Mike," one critic wrote. Without much evidence he asserted that David was trying to get Lyndon Johnson and Chou En-lai (surely he meant Mao Tse-tung) on the same show and had let it be known that he would also welcome Messrs. Kosygin and Breshnev. (That David would eventually end up in the House of Lords was a prediction that had often been made before.)

David would not quarrel with such fanciful comments. He does not quarrel at all, although he can be obstinate. "If there was a clash of opinion during a commercial break," producer Geoffrey Hughes recalled, "there were only two minutes to resolve it, and the person who felt most strongly prevailed." It was usually David.

Spontaneity became the show's most precious asset— spontaneity and intimacy. The atmosphere David created lulled even practiced politicians into a sense of privacy. At a time when he was much criticized for his free and easy manner, Labour Foreign Minister George Brown came on the show and was soon engrossed in the kind of exchanges one expects to overhear in a club rather than in a television studio. When David reminded him of his claim, reported a few days earlier, to have changed a good many things in his four months at the Foreign Office, Brown replied that he rather regretted that statement: "It was said, you know, rather loosely and friendly, as I often say many things. You know, a pleasant evening in a Labour club, and I didn't expect, I literally didn't expect, the newshounds to pick it up and take it out of context."

That was a real problem, David countered: "Nowhere's private anymore, is it?"

"Well, people have to be decent enough, sensible enough to know," George Brown replied, and made a little intrusion into David's privacy: "You were once kind enough to ask me to a little dinner party. You had a very pretty French actress if I remember. [David: "Did I? My turn to say, no comment."] In a very revealing dress. Now you asked me to that party. I came assuming you meant it was a party between friends. Well now, one has no difficulty in saying that's off the record, that's off limits. You and I know this. But you know these newshounds don't. Somebody who was at the party tells somebody else outside what was going on. He tells somebody else, and so it finds its way into print. I shouldn't have to answer for what I do when I am your private guest."

They continued to talk in this personal manner until George Brown exclaimed: "It's very odd to be discussing things as frankly as this with you in front of an audience and the cameras outside. It really is odd."

Another stimulating encounter was David's interview with Hugh Cudlipp, chairman of the International Publishing Corporation, a brilliant newspaperman who has put the stamp of his personality on the *Daily Mirror,* Britain's largest-circulation daily. Himself renowned for his quick wit and forceful repartee, Cudlipp obviously enjoyed the occasion. "The whole point about David's technique," he said later, "is that he does not approach his victim in the mocking and taunting spirit of a bear-baiter or with the steely determination of a matador, a method which immediately forces the interviewee on the defensive—and a man on the defensive, especially a politician, will never become expansive and anecdotal."

David Frost, Cudlipp thought, had the knack, not possessed by many TV interviewers, of giving his guest the opportunity of changing to a lighter vein after a portentous (or pompous) passage. After Cudlipp had pontificated about the more serious problems of newspaper-making (which the program was basically about), David suddenly asked, "What's the difference between the typical *Daily Mirror* reader and the typical *Daily Sketch* reader?" (At the time the *Daily Sketch* was Britain's only other national tabloid.)

"The *Mirror* reader," Cudlipp replied immediately, "has both feet firmly on the surface of the ground, and the *Sketch* reader has one foot in the grave."

Frost: "And what about the difference between the *Daily Mirror* reader and the *Daily Telegraph* reader?"

Cudlipp: "The *Daily Telegraph* reader is counting the gains he has lavishly accrued in the past, and the *Daily Mirror* reader is counting the gains he hopes to achieve in the future."

To make this sort of rapid dialogue possible was good television, Cudlipp said later. And David obviously did his homework, digging up the right—or embarrassing—quote and throwing it at his guest with a smile. He quoted Cecil King, at the time head of the company that owned the *Mirror*, as saying that if he were to fall under a bus, Hugh Cudlipp would succeed him. "Was that the first time you heard it?" David asked.

By now a relationship, an easy relationship, had been established between questioner and victim. They were working together. Cudlipp sensed that David wanted him to pull down the curtain with a quick reply. "It was the first time anybody had heard it," he answered. "But Cecil King is in remarkably good form. I would like to issue on your program a warning to all buses ... that I would strongly advise nothing less heavy than a three-decker to tackle that formidable target. And I would warn all single-deckers to keep a respectful distance."

David Frost had put Hugh Cudlipp in a relaxed mood in which he could reply, and wished to reply, without inhibition. "That's his secret weapon," Cudlipp said later. "The relaxed technique, in my view, produces the best television."

David's working day was growing even more intense if this was possible. He was rushing from Egerton Crescent to Rediffusion (except on days when he gathered his team around him in his drawing room), from Rediffusion to a business lunch, from lunch to rehearsals for one of his production company's "specials," from rehearsals to meetings with his bankers in the City (the financial district of London), from the City back to Rediffusion for the show. Even while driving from place to place, he was often on the two-way radio telephone in his car. One day he called Peter Baker and was carrying on a long conversation when Peter asked, "Where are you?"

"In the car," David replied.

"Well yes, but where?"

David looked up. "Outside my house," he answered, with some surprise. He had been too engrossed to notice.

Frequently after the show, when his weary colleagues wanted to go home at the end of a hard day, David persuaded one or two of them to stay behind for a few games of table tennis. His energy seemed inexhaustible. Before his own day ended there was more often than not a "private dinner," which could be pretty demanding. "I've got the body of an ox," he said, "but hopefully not the mind of one."

He looked paler and more baggy-eyed than ever. When he stepped across the invisible line and into the limelight, though, there was no hint of strain or effort. He was a picture of health and strength.

As if craving to take on additional burdens, he was constantly planning new ventures. What he lacked was time to sit down with his advisers and discuss at leisure the problems of his pro-liferating career—financing for new projects, allocation of funds, contracts, investments. The entertainer and television man in David were competing with the impresario and money man in him. In this enviably difficult situation he turned to Richard Armitage, for whom he had a much wider role in mind than that of an agent. "Couldn't we meet regularly to discuss matters?" David suggested.

"David asked me whether I would like to accept a retainer to take breakfast with him each Friday and contemplate his nonar-tistic activities." David being extremely generous with people whose services he wants, it was a substantial offer. Armitage was willing. Every Friday at 8 A.M. from then on, he presented him-self at Egerton Crescent. Luisa prepared an English breakfast, which both enjoyed: "It was so good," Armitage said, "I felt I ought to pay for it." Before long the weekly breakfast lasted the whole of Friday morning.

The talks brought out some of David's hitherto unsuspected qualities. He was not only surprisingly adept and inventive in business matters but also seemed to be as good with figures as with television cameras. His capacity for mental arithmetic with very big sums astounded Armitage. "David thinks huge," he said.

They arranged to fly together to the United States. "We can talk business during the flight," David said. Not long after they were airborne, he asked Armitage to start talking: "No, not yet about business—just talk about anything!" With that he got up and started to walk along the aisle. "Keep talking!" he told Armi-tage while he walked forward and backward. Armitage looked bewildered, and David explained: "I just want to check how far your voice carries and whether our conversation can be over-heard." He was still not satisfied and asked Armitage to walk up and down while he kept talking to determine the voice level at which they could not be overheard.

"He is rather security minded," Armitage explained.

On another occasion David was giving an interview on a flight between New York and Los Angeles. The newspaperman's voice carried a long way. "It could just be possible," David said with a straight face, "that the people behind us might also want to interview me. We wouldn't want them to hear your questions and my answers, would we?"

Reporters now pursued David—not that he made it difficult for them to catch up with him. "He has set more typewriters rattling in Fleet Street," said John Osborne, the playwright, "than anyone else who has ever broken and entered our homes from the little box of failed promises." Not only in Fleet Street. In New York, too, reporters sought him out. One asked him whether he thought that it was still possible for a young man to start from scratch and become a millionaire. There was no answer, but the reporter noticed a telltale smile on David's lips.

CHAPTER 10

The Grand Inquisitor

THE TELEVISION STUDIOS were besieged by angry crowds. Violence was in the air. There were shouts of "Lynch him! Lynch him!" and the police had their work cut out to keep the peace. In the studio the atmosphere was as tense. At times it looked as if the audience might storm the platform to get at the man David was interviewing.

The man in the dock—the expression comes naturally to mind—was one Dr. Emil Savundra, a chubby, bland Anglo-Indian financier who had relinquished control of a firm, Fire, Auto and Marine Insurance Company, eight months before it had crashed with debts of one million pounds. Savundra's business methods were harshly criticized in the British press, but he agreed to come on the *Frost Programme* and answer David's questions. Emotions ran high because in the studio and in the street were many victims of the insurance company's failure, bereaved people who had paid premiums but who had never received compensation.

There were strong suspicions that the company's assets had been spirited abroad by means of ingenious manipulations and that any remaining funds would end up in Savundra's pocket. David probed deeply into the complex situation and asked Savundra about doubtful stock deals and a highly controversial loan of £300,000 he was said to have received from the company. "It never reached me," Savundra protested.

The manner in which he answered questions was unrepentant, even provocative. When people in the audience said that their insurance claims had not been met, Savundra turned on them: "I will not cross swords with peasants!" There was an uproar. He was, he added, quite prepared to cross swords with David Frost, "England's bravest swordsman."

David was not mollified. "These peasants have made you the millionaire you are today," he told Savundra sharply.

A widow with the spotlight on her wagged an accusing finger; she had lost her husband in a car crash, and it had taken her attorneys two years to arrange a settlement for five hundred pounds. "It seems improbable," Savundra interjected. "There must have been some material nondisclosure," he added, and laughed.

Another widow claimed that her husband had been killed in a car crash in 1965: "I was supposed to get seven thousand pounds, but the company's check bounced." Savundra was still laughing.

David Frost, who had kept his voice low so far, reacted angrily. "You try to make this into a great laugh," he hissed.

The audience rose to him: "Good old Frostie! Well done, Frostie!"

"This and other heartbreak stories," was Savundra's callous rejoinder, "have made me realize only too well that selling out was the best thing I ever did."

"What do you mean?" Frost challenged him.

Savundra: "By selling out, I have no legal or moral responsibility."

Frost (with mounting anger): "You have no moral responsibility?"

Savundra: "I have not!"

For once, at the end of the show, David could hardly contain himself. "I have never seem him so livid," Neil Shand recalled. "It was bloody anger, not righteous indignation. For a moment I thought David would hit the man." He strode off without giving Savundra another look.

The confrontation brought the full measure and the tragic human implications of the scandal home to millions of viewers. The repercussions were considerable. A few days later, when proceedings against Dr. Savundra started in the courts, the counsel for the defense complained that his client had already been subjected to "trial by television." Without mentioning the name of

David Frost, he stated that "action for contempt of court would be taken against a TV personality"—in English law public discussion of matters that are sub judice constitutes contempt of court. No such action was, in fact, taken against David Frost, nor could it be taken, because the case against Savundra was only brought to trial after the television show, and it was not then known that police inquiries into Savundra's affairs had been going on for some time.

This key factor was missed in the ensuing controversy about "trials by television"—one commentator described it as "lynch TV." David was reproached for assuming the role of prosecutor, judge, and jury and for denying Savundra the safeguards that protect an accused man in an English court: No leading questions are permitted, and the accused has legal representatives to tell him what to say and what not to. Discussion of Savundra's affairs on television, it was said, might prejudice him in the future.

There were demands to ban "trials by television." In a House of Commons debate, one M.P. praised David for his contribution to television but thought he ought not to entertain viewers in this manner. Other M.P.s spoke in his defense. Conflicting interpretations were put on a statement by a government spokesman who said that in his view statutory safeguards against such shows were neither necessary nor desirable. He added that he had discussed the matter with the television authorities: "I know that some sort of voluntary code of conduct will emerge." It was quite wrongly assumed that trials by television would be officially discouraged.

Still, it was said that David had been tough and hostile when talking to Savundra. "I am not tough," he answered. "I am never against anyone. This whole 'trial by TV' is a phrase made up by newspapers. It's a load of cobblers. People come of their own free will, and they are free to say what they like."

Paying him a handsome compliment, Ned Sherrin said that David had the air of a quiet counsel for the prosecution, disguising shrewdness under a human and deceptively casual manner. "He is the grand inquisitor of religion, morals, and politics."

In the courts the case against Savundra dragged on for some time until he was found guilty of fraudulent practices and sent to prison for eight years. He appealed, claiming that the Frost interview had prejudiced his trial. On the day the appeal was heard, some eighteen months later, David was playing cricket with great abandon. "I've had a great day," he said at the end of the match. "I scored twenty-five runs and made a catch behind the wicket."

While he was playing, Lord Justice Salmon heard Savundra's appeal. Summing up, the judge had some harsh things to say about the Frost-Savundra confrontation. "Trial by television cannot be tolerated in a civilized country," he pronounced. Savundra, who had no experience in television, was faced with a skilled interviewer whose clear object was to establish his guilt before millions of people. Still, the judge ruled that the interview was not sufficient grounds for quashing the conviction.

David was angry. That evening he penned a letter to the *Times*, Britain's traditional forum for public controversy, saying that the judge should have checked his facts. Careful inquiries were made, but no one on the *Frost Programme* had any reason to think that prosecution of Savundra was imminent.

The *Frost Programme* continued to examine problems over a wide range of human endeavor. *Playback, Talking with Frost*, a verbatim record of David's outstanding interviews, listed the show's subjects:

MONEY Cruelty EXECUTIONS Marriage ADULTERY Revenge MORALITY Poetry DEMOCRACY Religion SEX Politics CENSORSHIP Hero Worship HITLER Wilson CRITICS Pornography COMEDY Contraception RHODESIA Punishment HUMANISM Vietnam JESUS Press UNEMPLOYMENT Wages PRAYER Smoking JAMES BOND Retirement LAW Charity HUMOUR Death AMBITION Privacy DANGER Civil Service FRIENDSHIP Leadership PRIDE Segregation PROFIT God ROMANCE Philology TRUTH Theology EXHIBITIONISM Celibacy BIRCHING Hanging ASTROLOGY Children WAR Climbing ATROCITIES Teachers AGGRESSION Devotion RESIGNATION Elections TEMPTATION Africa CRIME Harmony RESURRECTION Sin HEADLINES The Pope SOPHISTICATION.

Hours grew longer at both ends of the day. David was up and about before 6 A.M. on more than one occasion, once to rush to the London airport—not to take a plane himself this time but to tape an interview with a passenger in transit, the Maharishi Yogi, an Indian mystic at whose shrine the Beatles worshiped. Edward

Heath, leader of the (Tory) opposition, later came on the show. David had just time to say, "Tonight we have the privilege——" when the television technicians stopped work. Power was cut off, and a strike notice was put on his desk. "I know it's Friday the thirteenth," David said, "but this is ridiculous!" When work was resumed, there was just enough time to tape a fifteen-minute interview with Mr. Heath.

King Hussein of Jordan, Sir Oswald Mosley, onetime leader of the British Fascists, Simon Wiesenthal, the indefatigable hunter of surviving Nazi war criminals, John Osborne, and Dick Gregory were among those David interviewed in the next few weeks. Not all his guests were such weighty personalities. He had a number of children on the show, and his gentle questioning elicited some charmingly frank answers. Once, failing conspicuously to get a response from a talking mynah bird, he carried the noninterview off with practiced panache. (But David was better, obviously, in getting a response from other birds on and off his show!) When he tried again on his American show with the mynah, he was equally frustrated.

Refusing to commit himself to any set of views, Right or Left, David appeared as a humane progressive with some contradictions in his political thinking. He was against corporal and capital punishment but not particularly against blood sports, a big issue in England; he was quick to condemn man's cruelty to man and was aghast at the insensitivity of people who advocated the defoliation of a country (Vietnam). He was not so progressive as to accept that everything new was better than what had gone before. A favorite target was pomposity: "There are always new pomposities to explore," he said.

According to an opinion poll he was known to 96 per cent of the population, rivaling the percentage of the Queen and the Prime Minister. He was the young people's second choice as the Prime Minister they would most like to see in office (Enoch Powell, the antiblack Tory politician, headed their list). Rare for a television performer, especially one so young (he was still only twenty-eight), he was admitted to the hallowed pages of the British Who's Who. Withal, he remained curiously unaffected by his fame. His private life changed little except that less and less of it remained private.

One evening, as reported in the polite phrase, he escorted

Jenny Logan; the next he attended a first night, of which Julie Felix was the star. The usual speculations about an imminent marriage were swiftly followed by the usual denials. His friends chuckled about his arrangements—one who overheard his telephone conversations was puzzled when David asked a girl he was due to meet on Saturday to make it Sunday and the girl with whom he had a rendezvous for Sunday to meet him on Saturday. Why the switch? He refused to explain.

Things became even more complicated when a new star appeared in his orbit, Anne de Vigier, daughter of a wealthy manufacturer. Anne talked freely about David and his unpunctuality. "When I have a date with David," she sighed, "I always take a book." She did an awful lot of reading.

Not all his girl friends were so philosophical. One morning the bell rang at Egerton Crescent, and a girl stormed in and smashed the glass of one of his paintings. David would not say what had provoked this violent gesture, but it was no secret that another girl was staying in the house at the time. Because the pictures were abstract images of a certain shape, friends read a Freudian motive into the girl's violence.

Numerous hurried trips to the United States played more havoc with David's social life at this time. Bryan and Nanette Forbes asked him and Jenny Logan to see a show on a day he was due back from New York. As they were setting out for the theater, they had a call that David's plane was still in the air. They went ahead with Jenny, who could hardly disguise her disappointment. During the intermission there was another message that David had just landed at the London airport. He never saw the show but caught up with the party at a nightclub. By New York time a new day was already dawning, but David was as high-spirited as ever. Perhaps the candy he carried with him and munched in prodigious quantities helped to restore his energy. Jenny and the Forbeses might well have been angry, but David threw himself with such verve into what remained of the evening that they enjoyed themselves hugely. "With David," said Nanette Forbes, "you may have spent quite an ordinary evening, but you go home feeling that you have done something extraordinary and fabulous."

In April, 1967, he flew to Montreux, Switzerland, where a selection from the *Frost Report* ("Frost over England") was the British entry at the international television festival. It was a big triumph and won the highest award, the Golden Rose of Montreux. Returning to London, a big surprise awaited David at his own house. His colleagues of the *Frost Report,* all twenty-three of them, were waiting to toast him with champagne.

The press went completely overboard for David. "FROST ALL OVER THE WORLD" was a London evening paper's triumphant banner headline. Others were no less extravagant: "MR. FROST STRIKES A GOLDEN BLOW FOR BRITAIN," "ALL EUROPE BIDS FOR TV GOLDEN BOY FROST," "TOP OF THE WORLD FROST WINS TV AWARD," and to make it nice and simple, "FROST OVER WORLD." As we shall see, it could not have happened at a more opportune moment.

Almost en passant, he was also still supervising the production of the television series *At Last the 1948 Show.* As a light relief he gave another of his "intimate" parties for a few hundred people, this time at the White City Sports Stadium, where on other nights some twenty thousand spectators watch dogs racing or athletes competing. Whenever he stood still for a moment, John Bratby tried to complete a portrait of him.

It was difficult because David was also crisscrossing England to perform in provincial cities. During his tours he did not waste much time either and carried a big pad with him wherever he went, noting down ideas and phrases. Slowly they were building up to a book he was writing in collaboration with Antony Jay. It was an overall assessment of English morals, English prejudices, English peculiarities.

Many of the sentiments were reminiscent of the *Frost Report,* but it was impossible to say where Frost began and Jay ended. The more consistent and methodical work was obviously done by the less peripatetic Antony Jay, whereas many flashes of wit and the construction of many phrases were unmistakably David Frost. Later in 1967 the book was published under the title *To England with Love* and was well, if not uncritically, received.

Though so much of David's time was taken up with extraneous activities, nothing stimulated him as much as the four or five hours he spent before the television cameras every week. One innovation in his interview technique was to do away with the sprawling desk that puts distance between the hosts of most talk shows and their guests. To give the interviews an air of casual conversation David literally pulled his chair close to his partners.

The impression of spontaneous, unscripted conversations—which is what they were—was heightened by his refusal to stick to any predetermined pattern of questioning. What elevates his technique above that of most other interviewers is what has been called his overlapping mind, his ability to listen to an answer, and while listening, frame the next question arising from the answer. He rarely asked the same question twice until he began to interview two or three people a day for six days a week, when repetition became unavoidable. Sitting almost sideways to the audience and facing his guest straight on, David kept a folder with relevant documents on his knees. Marked with bold strokes of his felt-tip pen, the cover was his prompt sheet, which noted the areas he intended to discuss. Later a clipboard replaced the folder. There are reminders of items that struck him while reading up on his subjects and points that his researchers have dug up. Some entries are encircled or framed with squarish patterns. Question marks abound. Few better examples of his proliferating curiosity exist than the prompt sheet he used during his show devoted to *The Soldiers*, a play by Rolf Hochhuth, a German writer who specializes in the dramatized demolition of historical reputations.

Having previously accused Pope Pius XII of condoning Nazi crimes (in a play called *The Deputy*), Hochhuth wrote *The Soldiers*, an involved and inordinately long stage opus, with Sir Winston Churchill as the central figure. It represented Churchill as the instigator of the murder of his friend and wartime ally General Wladislaw Sikorsky, the Polish exile leader who was supposed to have opposed Churchill's political strategy. The murder theory suggested that an airplane crash in which General Sikorsky lost his life was the result of sabotage by the infamous British Secret Service, acting on Churchill's orders or at least with Churchill's connivance.

Hochhuth's play was first shown in Berlin in 1967. English public opinion was outraged. David Frost invited Winston Churchill's son Randolph to defend his father's name. Hochhuth, who speaks no English, seemed reluctant to be interviewed through an interpreter but later agreed to be available on the telephone.

Although the play was ill-constructed and tedious, it generated considerable heat. So great was the interest in the arguments for and against and the desire to have the monstrous accusation effectively refuted that David devoted three shows to the subject, one in 1967 and two in 1968. On the show with Randolph Churchill was Kenneth Tynan, of the English National Theatre, who wanted to put the play on in London; his management turned it down. Because living people were involved, the censor prevented the play being staged by independent theaters. Another guest was David Irving, a young English historian, Hochhuth's friend and adviser, who had touched on the subject, if not conclusively, in one of his books. The discussion was fierce, and tempers erupted even more violently on the second show, which coincided with the abolition of theater censorship in England, clearing the way for an English stage production of *The Soldiers*.

By this time David's researchers had gone even more deeply into the subject. Instead of Randolph Churchill, who had died earlier in the year, his young son Winston took up the cudgels in defense of his grandfather. He was joined by a surprise witness who was personally involved in the Sikorsky tragedy, Edward Prchal, the pilot of the plane. (Hochhuth had asserted that the pilot had died in Canada years earlier.)

"Are you dead?" David asked him.

"This is my astral body," Prchal replied. He described the murder accusation as "the biggest slander of the century."

A third newcomer on the show was the film actor Carlos Thompson, author of a book that closely examined Hochhuth's work and found it wanting. Hochhuth's case was again represented by David Irving. Kenneth Tynan also returned to the fray.

As the tale unfolded like a historical detective story with a hundred tiny clues, David Frost took the unusual step of calling on his chief researcher, Peter Baker, to bring before the cameras some critical points that figured in an official inquiry into the air disaster. Irving and Thompson argued violently; accusations and counteraccusations were made until David had difficulty in keeping the discussion within bounds.

Whenever the camera turned away from David, he studied his prompt sheet. "Prchal" was the first name he had jotted down, followed by a pertinent query: "Hochhuth's documents—where are they now?" (Hochhuth claimed that documentary evidence proving his murder theory was deposited in a Swiss bank but would not be released for fifty years.) "Thought he was in the plot," read another reminder.

"Olivier's position now" referred to Sir Laurence Olivier, director of the National Theatre, which had rejected the play. "Madame Sikorsky" suggested another line—the late general's widow was too fragile to come on the show but indicated through a friend that she did not share Hochhuth's view. "Unsupported human testimony" (as distinct from technical findings), "Sikorsky's word," "The starter's pistol," and "Killed within 48 hours" were among David's other notes. At one stage he wrote "perjure himself" but was far too cautious to attach a name to this note. Yet another one, which said "As great a war criminal as Hitler," referred to an odious comparison of Churchill and the Nazi führer which could be read into the play.

Along the whole length of David's folder ran a list of items he was anxious to examine with his guests. Altogether there were more than fifty jottings on the double page. There was no hope of getting through more than half of this formidable agenda.

Indeed, looking up, David saw the studio floor-manager signaling that time was running out. The acrimonious debate was still in full swing when David had to bring it to an end. "We will return to the subject tomorrow night," he announced, which was news to producer Geoffrey Hughes. "May I ask everybody to come back tomorrow night? Winston? Kenneth? Mr. Prchal? Carlos Thompson? David Irving?" They all nodded agreement.

Forgotten in the verbal melee was Rolf Hochhuth, who was standing by on the telephone in Zurich. "Oh, my apologies," David exclaimed when his attention was drawn to it. "My apologies to Herr Hochhuth. Is he still there on the phone?—because I will go and apologize to him now. We will return to this subject and the huge question mark . . . tomorrow night."

What actually happened was that after a short pause David resumed the discussion then and there, while the glint of battle was still in his guests' eyes. The new session was recorded for transmission the following day. It turned out to be another riveting session.

The Hochhuth version of the tragic incident was discredited

and Sir Winston Churchill's reputation vindicated. Newspapers all over the world reported every facet of the dramatic reconstruction of history on television. Some of the contestants carried their arguments further—into a court of law—but David Frost was not involved.

For him controversy usually ended when the lights were dimmed at the end of the evening's show, and few of his guests were inclined to carry it further. A rare exception was Dr. Christiaan Barnard, the South African heart surgeon, whom David questioned about the complaint that he, Barnard, had failed to consult the dependents of the "donor" of a heart before removing and transplanting it. Barnard did not come out of the interview very well and was so angry he called David "a nasty little man," but the facts, public opinion, and the press supported David's case.

More frequently David's interviews developed into private conversations, personal friendships, business associations, or all three. At the time when the English currency was under pressure and "the gnomes of Zurich," those Swiss bankers, were selling sterling short, David mounted a show with a strong team of financial experts, among them David Montagu, a leading British merchant banker. He and David became business partners before long.

"Not everybody takes kindly to David Frost," a television critic wrote, stating the obvious. What was less obvious was that David Frost took kindly to everybody. Trying to find out what made him really angry, his associates agreed on one subject: drugs.

Yet he sounded almost brotherly when Dr. John Petro, an English doctor, came on the show. Without introducing Petro by name—because British doctors are not allowed to advertise themselves—David explained that "the doctor" had been accused of overprescribing drugs and attending his patients in teashops and subway stations, where he handed out prescriptions entitling them to buy drugs legally.

"Do you feel, Doctor," David asked very quietly, "that you have ever overprescribed heroin or cocaine?"

"Unwillingly, on possibly rare occasions," Dr. Petro replied.

Taking it from there, David extracted some reluctant admissions of irregularities from the doctor, who explained that he had had no time to consult the Home Office about new patients (to establish whether they were registered addicts), which he was legally obliged to do. Though prompted by David, Dr. Petro refused to answer questions from a doctor in the audience. When asked about a patient who had been peddling drugs prescribed by him, Dr. Petro answered that this was the only way in which the patient could raise money to pay him.

David asked whether he accepted at face value what he was told by people who wanted drugs—addicts are notoriously inventive and cunning when trying to obtain prescriptions. "I go into their history very fully," Petro replied. "I encourage them to come off the drug and give them every help." Few believed what he said.

Squirming and twisting under the impact of the questions, Dr. Petro was such a miserable figure that David seemed almost relieved when the interview ended. "There we must leave the subject," he said. "Doctor, thank you. Goodnight."

Too many unanswered questions remained, however. After a hurried conversation with the producer David decided to invite Dr. Petro to return to the show the following day. Introducing the second session, David seemed strangely tense. He briefly recapitulated what had already been said about the doctor and tackled him about the unorthodox places where he treated patients and the fees he demanded.

With some ex-patients taking up the sordid tale from the floor, the charge of overprescribing and demanding high fees from impecunious young addicts came up again, and David asked Petro point-blank whether he was not, in fact, encouraging some of his patients to commit desperate acts in order to obtain money for drug prescriptions. The pathetic figure facing him on the platform had no adequate answer. David looked almost as unhappy. This was the note on which the show came to an end.

Dr. Petro rose and walked wearily off the stage—and straight into the arms of two waiting detectives, who arrested him and took him to a police station. Now it was David's turn to be asked a searching question. Did he know that Dr. Petro was going to be arrested? "Certainly not," David replied. "While he was on, we did not know what was going to happen to him!"

"The suggestion that we knew was certainly not true," said

Geoffrey Hughes. "We had a big inquest on the program," he recalled, "and it turned out that Scotland Yard were actually trying to arrest Petro that morning"—the morning after his first appearance on the *Frost Programme*—"but could not find him." While Scotland Yard was looking for him, Petro was in the Rediffusion offices, negotiating his second appearance. "It was the decision of the police to wait until the program was over," said Hughes.

Once more the cry of "trial by television" went up. Petro himself did not think his interview with David had precipitated his arrest or prejudiced his case. He was charged under the Drugs Offences Act (his name was subsequently dropped from the Medical Register), but while out on trial, he contacted Geoffrey Hughes and asked to be put on the show for a third time. Under British law once a charge had been brought this could not be done. Said Hughes: "The fact that Petro wanted to come back shows he didn't think he'd been treated unfairly."

To ask or not to ask certain people to come on the show, that was the question. David's inclination was to give a person a chance to speak on his or her own behalf even if it was liable to leave the show open to criticism.

Not much later another borderline case arose when the *News of the World*, an English Sunday newspaper, revived memories of the Profumo scandal, the case of the cabinet minister who became involved with Christine Keeler and resigned from the Government. The serialization of Christine Keeler's memoirs started a nationwide controversy, and *News of the World* owner Rupert Murdoch was reproached in some quarters and accused of sensationalism. David asked him to come on the show. What had to be decided was whether Christine Keeler should also be invited.

"We had a long discussion about it," Antony Jay remembered. "One group took the view that she was highly relevant and should be there. The question arose—if she was asked to appear on the show, was this not the same as publishing her memoirs?"

They discussed compromises. How about interviewing her without a previous announcement that she would appear? David thought she was relevant, although he recognized that if she was invited, he would be criticized and his motives questioned. Nevertheless he felt she had a right to be there when her story was the subject of the show.

The discussion between David and his team went on for an hour and a half. "It was thrashed out until a joint decision was reached," Antony Jay said. "The case against was slightly stronger." David accepted the verdict as the right one on balance. Christine Keeler did not appear on the *Frost Programme*.

CHAPTER 11

Television Tycoon

By 1967 THERE was not much in the area of public performance that David Frost had not done. The flow of invitations to appear on television, stage, cabaret, and at an infinite variety of functions continued faster than he could decline. Yet when an alert B.B.C. radio producer asked him to come on his program, David felt a tinge of nostalgia and pride. The program was *Any Questions?* which roused memories of his boyhood and student days.

Canceling all other engagements for the day, he traveled to Woolaston, a godforsaken little place in Gloucestershire, to take part in the broadcast. For *Any Questions?* he would have gone anywhere, any time. He proved it some time later when he was again asked to join an *Any Questions?* team, this time at the Guildhall in Axminster, a small town in Devonshire. He would be there, he promised, although he already had another date for the same day penciled in on his crowded diary—to present prizes at the school of his young niece, Alison Pearson, at Bury St. Edmunds, in Suffolk, some two hundred miles from Axminster as the crow flies.

By the time David was shaking hands with Alison and ninety of her schoolmates and exchanging pleasantries with the headmistress, another David—David Jacobs, host of *Any Questions?*—and three members of his team of four were already at Axminster. The program, due to be taped in front of a big audience, could not be postponed, and at the appointed hour Jacobs introduced poet John Betjeman, Alastair Burnet, editor of the

Economist, and Sylvia Sims, the actress. "You may have wondered," he said, "why I've only introduced three members of the team tonight. I was hoping to introduce to you that television man extraordinary, David Frost, who has an engagement in the north of England and is flying to our program, and we hope he's on his way. . . . Until he arrives, we can do nothing but get on without him."

David was indeed on his way. To join *Any Questions?* (maximum fee twenty-five pounds) he had hired a private plane at a cost of several times that amount. Two speakers had already tackled the first question—about men on the moon—and John Betjeman was just beginning to speak when the audience broke into loud applause. David Frost had arrived.

He explained that the plane had taken longer than he had expected and the roads from the airport were slightly worse. He made his apologies and cheerfully added: "If the proprietor of the Bell Inn is listening: Keep the chef in the kitchen. I want to eat after the program!"

He was given a copy of the questions. "Is this number one? Oh, fantastic!" he said breathlessly. He quoted Ted Kennedy as saying that the moon program ought to be slowed down and priorities redistributed a little. This was also his view.

The next question seemed specifically directed at David. "Are you aware," he was asked, "of having an image, and if so, do you make a conscious effort to cultivate it?"

To worry about an image was a terribly unrewarding enterprise, David answered. People had a tendency to simplify and remember only a part: "If a poor girl gets pushed into a goldfish pond at the age of four," he said, "forty years later, when she marries, the papers will say 'Goldfish-pond girl to wed,' and the poor soul is lumbered for life."

What price fame? David recalled going into a large store at the time of *TW3* and the salesman saying, "Oh, Mr. Frost, oh, I never miss your program, never miss it at all, and oh, yes, my wife likes you too." But when David handed him a check, he asked, "Have you any means of identification?" A little less inhibited, a little less ponderous than the others, David kept audience and team amused right to the end of the show. He was obviously enjoying himself.

His Rediffusion shows were going strong, but toward the end of the series the British television scene as a whole was in an unsettled state. Only a year or so remained before the licenses of the independent—that is, commercial—television companies would come up for renewal. The structure of the industry was likely to be changed. The record of each company would be closely examined by the I.T.A. (Independent Television Authority), which was responsible for giving out the new licenses.

In the light of past experience there seemed to be a case for redrawing some of the geographical boundaries within which companies operated. Granada, for example, the highly prestigious company that dominated the north of England, would probably be required to yield some of its territory to a new company that would cater mainly to Yorkshire, England's biggest county. One or another organization might disappear altogether; some might well be asked to amalgamate, among them Rediffusion, which was unlikely to survive in its current form. Performers were bound to view the prospect of such major changes with apprehension. New companies, new executives, new program directors—where would all this leave them? They saw danger ahead.

Not David. Changes? Changes, surely, offered opportunities. With Clive Irving, Richard Armitage, and other friends and advisers he discussed the prospects of each company, the possibility of new groupings, the future of well-known executives. Whereas his friends were thinking of this in relation to David Frost the performer, David Frost was nursing an entirely different vision.

If, as there was good reason to assume, Yorkshire (about six thousand square miles) would get its own television company, was it not worth trying to get control of it? Let's put in a bid for the franchise, David suggested. The people around him threw up their hands in horror. Why on earth should David Frost want to descend from his pinnacle as a television star into the jungle of politics, finance, and vested television interests that were taking up battle stations to fight for new licenses?

All except Clive Irving were strongly against it. "It's impossible anyway!" they said. "Why waste your time?" He had so much else to do—his shows, his production companies.

"I listened carefully," David said a few years later, "and

weighed the chances, as I saw them, against their advice. They said it could not be done. I thought it could. It was only the second time that I went against their advice on any major issue and decided to do my own thing."

His original plan was to stake a claim for Yorkshire television, but even as the thought was conceived, the target seemed to him too modest. At a Rediffusion party he heard some of the television people joking about Yorkshire. "Wouldn't London be better?" he asked himself.

Taking Clive Irving into his confidence, he began to toy with a novel idea that could greatly enhance his chances of success. Hitherto, commercial television had been a matter of business-men investing capital much as in the manufacture of shoes or soap, and almost as an afterthought, hiring television people to run the shows. David wanted to do it the other way round—start out with the creative people, with the television experts, and then find the financing to enable them to operate.

On January 11, 1967, he was at the Rediffusion studios, hosting a show that could not have been further removed from the prob-lems that occupied his mind. His subject for the evening was the housing shortage in England and the dreadful conditions under which some people lived. It was a matter of deep social concern, and when the clock demanded that the discussion be brought to an end, it was far from exhausted. As so often happened when a topic absorbed David, supplementary items on the show were abandoned, and guests waiting to come on were left to cool their heels in the wings.

David was most apologetic. Three people had been waiting in vain to come before the cameras, among them Leslie Caron's ex-husband, Peter Hall, the young and able managing director of the Royal Shakespeare Company at Stratford on Avon. He and David went out to dinner, and before long the conversation turned on David's television plans. Peter Hall listened, was impressed, and said, "Count me in!"

If there was still a lingering doubt in David's mind, Peter Hall's reaction dispelled it. This, he said, was the moment when he finally made up his mind to go ahead. The first thing he did was to compile a list of people he would want to associate with his project, people whose positions and reputations would make them acceptable to the I.T.A. One name much in his mind was that of

John Freeman, whose term as British high commissioner in India was coming to an end and who ideally combined television experience with personal authority. Cyril Bennett, with whom David was working, was another obvious candidate.

To obtain financial backing David next applied himself to the commercial aspects. He approached David Montagu, the merchant banker, who was quickly persuaded of the venture's potential. The makers of television sets, David argued, were natural partners of television performers, and he looked to one of them to come in on his scheme.

At the top level of public life, David's natural habitat, names are so familiar that formal introductions are unnecessary. Though he had never met Sir Arnold Weinstock, managing director of the multimillion-dollar British General Electric Company (which made television sets, among other electrical equipment), David picked up the telephone and asked to speak to him. In a few sentences he gave the industrialist an outline of his plans and suggested they go more deeply into the matter over lunch. "Arnold's reaction was delightful," David told Wallace Rayburn, to whom he gave the first detailed account of his operation. Anything that improved the standard of television, Weinstock thought, could only help a manufacturer of television sets. Yes, he was prepared to come in.

Other leaders of finance, industry, commerce, and television received similar treatment. Not all responded as readily. Two or three did not think David had much hope of winning out. He did not complain but kept the rebuffs to himself. "Those who were prepared to back me," he said, "were, after all, on a thousand-to-one chance."

His most spectacular "failure" followed his most determined effort. To bring John Freeman into the group David took the first airplane to Delhi. He and Freeman discussed the matter at the high commissioner's residence and even went into details of the kind of contribution Freeman could make. He would be appointed deputy chairman and would provide guidance on current affairs. John Freeman was enthusiastic. It was only when the British Government, rather than let him return to private life at the end of his tour of duty in Delhi, offered him the post of British ambassador in Washington that he reluctantly withdrew.

David talked to Sir Donald Stokes and to the London Cooperative Society. He also made contact with Humphrey Burton, at the B.B.C. One important figure he thought of was Aidan Crawley, Tory M.P. for Derbyshire West, who had an impressive career in television behind him. Crawley was already contemplating a future in commercial television and was in close touch with Michael Peacock, who had made his name (and unmade David's satire program) with the B.B.C. Both had been thinking, at first, of Yorkshire but soon teamed up with David.

At the beginning of February David's current Rediffusion series ended, and another edition of the *Frost Report* was due to begin. One compartment of his mind, though, was totally devoted to the big project of the franchise. Because of the intense competition for the licenses and for the services of the small number of acknowledged experts, the conversations were conducted in the strictest confidence.

The chief protagonists met almost furtively at David's house or Aidan Crawley's home. Other meetings were held in Weinstock's or Montagu's board rooms. Their secret was well kept until Michael Peacock resigned from the B.B.C. "to take up an appointment with commercial television." The announcement brought it all out into the open.

The financial arrangements of which David Montagu took charge involved considerable amounts. To give the application for a London franchise a chance of success a capital of at least £6,000,000 was required. In accordance with David's original concept it was decided that a substantial share of the equity should go to the creative people involved. As the structure was built up brick by brick, million by million, a third of the £1,500,000 equity was reserved for them.

David Frost and Aidan Crawley, with 5 per cent (£75,000) each, became the biggest individual stockholders, but under I.T.A. rules David was debarred not only from the chairmanship or managing directorship but also from taking a seat on the board. If this "impossible dream" were to come true, others like Crawley, Peacock, and Dr. Tom Margerison (a scientific journalist with great organizing flair who soon came into the picture) would have to be entrusted with the task of making it a reality on a day-to-day basis. They were a strong team.

Financial interests provided the other £1,000,000 and undertook to put up a further £3,000,000 if necessary. Arrangements for a bank overdraft of £2,000,000 brought the total stake up to £6,500,000, nearly $15,000,000. It was half a million pounds more than the essental minimum. The Imperial Tobacco Pension Fund, Lombard Banking, Pearl Assurance, London Cooperative Society, Magdalen College, Oxford, the publishing firm of Weidenfeld and Nicolson, and Bowater's, a big paper group, made up the hard core of the backers; newspaper and magazine interests were later co-opted at the request of the I.T.A.

The lineup of executives was also nearing completion. Michael Peacock was the designated managing director; Clive Irving and Tom Margerison were getting seats on the board. Cyril Bennett would be controller of programs.

David's mind was commuting between the financial and the creative wings of the new and as yet unnamed organization. The chance to start this project from scratch, the laying of the foundations, appealed to David. (Richard Armitage calls him "the great initiator.")

The document the group prepared for submission to the I.T.A. listed five main objectives. In eighty pages David and his friends described how they intended to improve the weekend ratings of London television, revitalize it with new shows, widen the range of programs, exploit the considerable talents they were gathering around them, and create a healthy commercial basis.

Introducing themselves as London Television Consortium, the Crawley-Frost group submitted their formal application in mid-April. A few weeks later they—Aidan Crawley, David Frost, Michael Peacock, Clive Irving, Tom Margerison, and David Montagu, attended by their accountant—were invited to meet the top brass of the I.T.A., Chairman Lord Hill and the twelve members of his board. They answered searching questions and elucidated many points of their voluminous document. It was a weird experience for these substantial people, eminently successful in their careers, to be subjected to this kind of inquiry. Though they would not admit it at the time, they felt like schoolboys taking an entrance examination.

Each in turn put the best possible construction on the aspects that immediately concerned him. David Montagu stressed the solidity of the financial arrangements, Tom Margerison explained the technical provisions, Clive Irving was most strongly committed to current affairs (this part of the application was his brainchild), and Michael Peacock gave an overall view. The "hearing" was concluded with set pieces by Aidan Crawley and David Frost.

Lord Hill and his twelve apostles gave no hint of their reaction. Other applicants remained to be tested in the crossfire of their questions; the relative merits of each proposer had to be weighed. David and his consortium went off to lunch at the Hyde Park Hotel, only a stone's throw from I.T.A. headquarters; they analyzed the questions put to them and chewed over their answers. There was nothing but to wait for the decision.

So as not to influence the stock market, where shares of the companies under scrutiny were quoted, the I.T.A was tight-lipped, and no hints of their thinking leaked out. The Crawley-Frost proposition was believed to be the most interesting and original, though. "Some exciting ideas" was the phrase circulating. If speculation in the press was anything to go by, David and his friends were sure to make the grade.

A month remained before the decision was due to be announced, but David did not let the uncertainty distract him unduly. The *Frost Report,* which kept him busy, was consistently entertaining, and he continued to give his one-man shows in provincial cities—surprisingly but prophetically, one local critic remarked that David was in danger of getting too nice and clamored for more of the old rough stuff.

What little time remained he gave to deserving causes. He opened a Salvation Army exhibition and drew a big crowd. He also helped the Society for the Prevention of Cruelty to Children to get substantial donations from some of his millionaire friends. A big gathering assembled when he opened a Methodist church fête at Gillingham and again when he played in a charity cricket match and appeared on the football field.

He was not without honor among his professional colleagues: He was named Show-Business Personality of the Year, which earned him a silver medal to put next to the Golden Rose of Montreux. The extravagant press notices about his string of awards could not but enhance the chances of his consortium. A well-wisher sent him a telegram: "You are a so-and-so genius and seriously you are doing a jand job." ("Post Office spelling not so good," David commented.)

Then came the sad news from Beccles, where the Reverend W. J. Paradine Frost's health was failing. David left everything to get to his father's bedside in time to meet a medical specialist and was caught speeding on the way. Only his astonishing faculty for keeping his feelings to himself disguised his deep anxiety about his father's deterioration. On Saturday, June 10, he drove again to Beccles, stopping off at David Montagu's country house on the way. They talked about their application. "He was rather pessimistic," David Frost recalled.

The days of waiting—if what he was doing could be described as waiting—were coming to an end, and even as practiced an artist as David experienced the pangs of "performer's limbo," the period between a show's taping and its screening when nothing can be done or undone. That evening messages from Lord Hill reached the consortium and the heads of other television contractors, asking them to present themselves at I.T.A. headquarters on Sunday morning. The die was cast.

At the appointed hour Messrs. Frost, Crawley, Montagu, and Margerison (Michael Peacock was away on vacation) were at the I.T.A., where they were kept waiting while Lord Derby, head of Wales and West of England Television, was in conference with Lord Hill. Paul Adorian, managing director of Rediffusion, arrived to take his place in the line behind Frost & Co. ("A somewhat brutal procession," David thought). Lord Derby emerged from his interview somber-faced and thoughtful. His company, as it turned out, lost its franchise, and the territory went to a new group that included Richard Burton and Elizabeth Taylor. The shake-up of the commercial companies was considerable. Rediffusion was told to merge with another company to serve London during the week, Granadaland was split, and a new company for Yorkshire was approved.

As they filed into Lord Hill's room David Frost and friends knew as yet nothing of all this but were not left guessing about their own fate for long. Reading from a document, the chairman of the I.T.A. told them in a few crisp sentences that they had been awarded the franchise as the sole contractors to provide commercial television for London's thirteen million viewers during weekends (7 P.M. Friday to the end of transmission on Sunday). Among a few minor stipulations, the I.T.A. instructed them to give certain newspaper and magazine interests a share of the equity.

David obviously felt like throwing his hat in the air but maintained a dignified reserve in keeping with his new status as a television tycoon. The grant of the franchise automatically multiplied the value of his share in the equity. At the lowest estimate it was worth a million dollars now. They went on to the Ritz for a celebration lunch. "We were dazed," David recalled, though this was not the impression he gave at the time.

The lunch was hardly over when, to quote David, "Another of my various lives took over." Leaving everybody behind, he went to catch a train for Eastbourne, the seaside resort, where he was scheduled to give a one-man show at the Congress Theatre. Followed by a posse of reporters and photographers, he settled in his compartment and held an impromptu press conference, which continued while the train went on its way.

"The British public," he pronounced gravely and a little self-consciously as the cameras clicked, "is more intelligent, better informed, and has better taste than it is given credit for." This was the credo on which the consortium built their plans. They had no intention, he said, of doing away with the old programs altogether—the plays, the series, and so on. "But there is going to be less Variety with a capital 'V' and more variety with a small 'v.' We hope to give people what they will grow to want." He was tremendously thrilled, he confessed: "Everybody said it was impossible, but we have done it."

An hour out of London, the journalists left the train to get their stories and photographs back to Fleet Street. David went on to Eastbourne, where the audience gave him a friendly reception. They knew nothing of the drama in which David Frost, entrepreneur and impresario, was playing the leading role, but they cheered a competent performer who was going through his amusing routine with perhaps even greater panache than usual.

Congratulations poured into David's house. Friends came to wish him well. "How on earth did you do it?" one of them asked.

"How? I'm jolly shrewd—that's how." It was a good answer, but he was sorry as soon as he said it because it sounded like a boast.

"It was a joke," he explained. "You know, I never make claims on my own behalf."

Others made the claims for him. "His trick is starting at the top," Tom Sloan remarked.

Frankie Howerd had a word for this occasion, too: "David started by attacking the Establishment and has ended up owning it!"

John Freeman enumerated the ingredients of David's success: "High intelligence, energy, driving ambition, unspoilt simplicity, a religious conscience—in that order."

Malcolm Muggeridge, a television rival whose technique is to smother his guests with his own talk and his own personality, chose this moment to write a profile of David Frost for the left-wing *New Statesman,* calling him "a man for all ratings" whose range comprises Sherrin and the Archbishop of Canterbury, the Establishment and the anti-Establishment, show and every other sort of business. "His very lack of talent makes him king of the telly," Muggeridge opined. "In Frost the viewer sees himself—glorified but still recognisable."

For a man without talent David Frost was not doing badly. His Rediffusion shows, resumed in September, consistently caught the headlines. From one day to another one never knew who or what would turn up on the *Frost Programme,* which was precisely its attraction. One day it might be the ephemeral Twiggy, the next the Bishop of Southwark, a personal friend, who spoke about ghosts. Another guest was Danny La Rue, whose nightclub David was still visiting regularly.

Frequently when his work on the show and the preparations for the debut of London Weekend Television left him a spare day or two, David nipped across the Atlantic. And these quick visits to the United States were becoming of greater import for him than anything he did in England.

CHAPTER 12

Channel 5 Calling

IN THE SUMMER of 1967 Westinghouse Broadcasting inquired whether David Frost could accept an engagement at the end of October. Known as Group W, Westinghouse Broadcasting runs television stations in Boston, Baltimore, Pittsburgh, Philadelphia, and San Francisco, in addition to seven radio stations. The invitation that reached David was not to appear on one of their television shows, though. They wanted him to address some 150 Westinghouse executives during their annual conference in London. They were coming for a week's talks, interviews, functions, and addresses by English public figures, enabling them to look toward the future and see "The World in Perspective," the conference slogan. David's address would come during a lunch at a London hotel.

He was happy to oblige. There was a fee, of course, but it was the prestige of being asked that really attracted him. That it was a major American television organization was a good omen, but gratifying as it was, he could not by any stretch of imagination have then regarded the lunch assignment as an important event in his professional life. Yet it turned out to be the birth of David Frost as an American television star.

Not that American television was passing him by altogether. Paradine Productions was already producing a sixty-minute "special" for the A.B.C. *Stage 67* series, "David Frost's Night Out in London," a spectacular with Laurence Olivier, Albert Finney, and David in a number of sketches with Peter Sellers. This

161

assignment, however, valuable as it was, paled into insignificance compared with the events the Westinghouse lunch set in motion.

David had no hint of them when well before noon on Sunday, October 29, 1967, he presented himself at the new Royal Garden Hotel on the northern edge of Hyde Park, only a short ride from his own house. He was greeted by Westinghouse president Don McGannon and two of his top executives, Chet Collier and Dick Pack. On the printed schedule of the conference he was listed as "David Frost, Author, Producer, Columnist and Television personality." His subject was "To England—and America with Love."

It fell to Dick Pack to introduce the guest speaker. "One of the things you have probably already discovered," he said, "is that Great Britain represents tremendous achievement and accomplishment by using young people in the popular arts and pop arts and in communications. Today we are privileged to have with us a young man who represents that to its fullest, a very uncommon young man who at twenty-eight is jack-of-all-trades and master of quite a few of them. He is undoubtedly Britain's number-one television personality." David would talk on any subject that interested them.

"What a superb toastmaster, Mr. Pack," David responded. How different, he said, from another who recently, instead of saying, "Pray, silence for Mr. David Frost," announced him with a solemn: "Pray for the silence of Mr. David Frost."

David treated his audience to some lighthearted stories of his transatlantic commuting, recalling an exhausted Lufthansa stewardess who had opened her mouth only once during the flight to say, "Mr. Frost, it is quite interesting zat because of zee difference of zee pressure inside zee cabin and outside zee cabin, if zat window beside you vas to break now, you vould be forced out like a tube of toothpaste."

When asked about Lyndon Johnson, David, neatly sidestepping a political answer, sought refuge in a couple of jokes. One was about Harold Wilson phoning President Johnson all the time and the President saying, "I don't mind you always phoning me, but I do wish you'd stop reversing the charges." The other was about Harold Wilson assuring the President, "The drain on Britain's gold reserves has finally stopped—they have all gone."

He was more serious on the subject of British television. "The future of British television, thanks to the reforms made in the last few months, is fantastic!" He was not happy about the quality of television at this time, however, he said, and ended his peroration with his favorite quote from Ed Murrow (vintage 1959): " 'Television can entertain, and of course it must, and it can inform, and it must, and it can even inspire, but what television is or what it is going to become as a mass medium depends on the will of the humans who operate it; otherwise it is just coils and lights in a box.' " Added David: "To me that is television at the moment."

After his speech the delighted executives gathered around David, among them Chet Collier, who recalled first seeing David on television in 1961, when watching *TW3* in his room at the Dorchester Hotel during a visit to London, and the roly-poly Dick Pack ("Folksy, not roly-poly," says David), who suggested that he might do a few "specials" for Westinghouse. The subject was brought up again by Chet Collier, who was thinking in terms of major television programs. David was eager.

"We had lunch at David's house in Egerton Crescent," says Chet Collier, reveling in the memory. "Luisa served lunch—I remember we had lamb chops." Over the lamb chops the project took on a more concrete form. Chet suggested that David should produce four one-hour "specials" a year for Westinghouse, primarily in England. They went to a studio to view a number of David's English shows. "His interview with an insurance swindler stood out—that man called Savundra," Chet said.

In the following weeks David and Chet met again several times. One dinner in San Francisco sticks in Chet Collier's mind. They met at Ernie's, one of the best restaurants in the world—superb cooking, excellent service.

Chet handled David the wine list and asked him to choose. A connoisseur of good wine with a delicate palate, David chose a Chateau d'Essen, 1916, which Chet ordered. The bottle cost fifty-four dollars. Perhaps it was David's way of saying that he was not going cheaply.

When it came to talking money, agreement was quickly reached. Chet offered David $40,000 per show, escalating to $45,000. In terms of a four-year contract, the deal was worth $1,000,000. With the Presidential campaign in the United States getting under way, it occurred to them that they ought to devote the first "specials" to typical Frost interviews with the Presidential candidates.

Conferences about business deals of such magnitude had to be fitted neatly into David's timetable, which was dominated by his Rediffusion shows. He was in his place at the studio, conducting the proceedings as if nothing had happened since he last faced the cameras the previous week. And the cameras, often so revealing, gave no hint of his preoccupation with the debut of London Weekend Television, the official name of the successful consortium: the recruiting of staff and heads of departments, the examination of ideas and scripts, the technical arrangements and accommodations—a thousand pies, in each of which David had a finger.

Neither did he allow a personal tragedy to affect his public persona, although friends were aware of his deep anxiety about his father's condition. The Reverend Paradine Frost was ill beyond recovery. A good man to whom David owed his spiritual values, his equable temperament, and altogether much more than was apparent, he bore his fate without complaint. On Friday, November 24, 1967, David was called to Beccles and was on his way immediately after the evening's show. The end was near. The Reverend Frost died on Sunday morning.

That same day a "Hunger Lunch" in support of a Christmas charity appeal was scheduled. David had agreed to preside. "Father would not have wished me to let them down," he said. He traveled to London to keep his appointment, not in the theater tradition of "the show must go on" but in the spirit of his father's lifework. Looking drawn—almost exhausted—he chaired the lunch, which consisted of Indian bread made of two penny's worth of wheat grain; milk; and fish-protein biscuits. With a reference to the recent sterling devaluation, he asked people to increase their donations by 14 per cent. The slogan he coined was: "I am staking a child's life on you this Christmas."

Up and down the country the newspapers of Monday, November 27, paid tribute to the Reverend Mr. Frost. David confirmed that he would keep an engagement for that evening which also served a cause close to his late father's work. "He is more religious than many of my clergy," the Bishop of Southwark said. To others it may not be so obvious, because David does not go to church often on Sundays and does not boast of his Christian deeds and charity as well as his other work. He is Christian by stealth.

Finally, just before Christmas David had time to relax. He gave a party for the team of the *Frost Programme*—"a small party for a hundred people or so." It was a first-class production. John Cleese played Father Christmas, and David was in great form as himself (although it was said that only the one who appeared on the screen was "the real David Frost").

For Christmas Eve he invited a few personal friends, Jenny Logan, the Forbeses, and the Maudlings (Reginald Maudling, the current Tory home secretary, and his wife) among them. They were sitting down for dinner when David appeared with a tray of expensive trinkets from Asprey's, on Bond Street, a present for each of his guests. "He is the most generous of men," Nanette Forbes said. "Mine was a golden thimble—lovely, except that I cannot sew."

On Christmas day David and Jenny were expected at the Forbeses' country house. They were greeted joyfully when they arrived almost on time, but for a moment their hosts' faces dropped when they saw Jenny's son, Martin, whom David had brought along unexpectedly. Bryan and Nanette were embarrassed because they had no present for the little surprise visitor. They need not have worried. David's car disgorged a store of presents. "You must have cleared the shelves of a sizable shop," Bryan Forbes said. Among them was one package carefully wrapped and labeled: "For Martin, from Bryan and Nanette Forbes." David had anticipated the little complication.

As usual, he was the life and soul of the party. "When David enjoys himself, everybody enjoys himself," said Bryan. As always, he spent much time with the children, his games assuming an air of fantasy, which appealed to them.

After the seasonal interlude it was back to reality. Indeed, the Christmas spirit was sadly lacking when three days before the end of the year David became the central figure in another television row. British Defense Minister Denis Healey arrived at the studio with the glint of battle in his bright eyes. The battle was joined when David's questioning touched on some delicate topics.

He mentioned a report that the defense minister was in favor of selling arms to South Africa—as hot an issue in 1967 as in 1971—while other members of the cabinet opposed such a deal. "That's a shocking allegation!" Healey retorted angrily. Was David revealing cabinet secrets? Was he publicizing a story that was untrue?

There was an acid exchange in which David did not always get the better of the skilled politician. The audience was drawn into the argument, which swayed to and fro. The defense minister was still angry when he left the studio long after midnight. "He came spoiling for a fight," David said afterward.

Discussion about the Healey interview went on into the new year. Ten Downing Street—the Prime Minister's office—and the Government's legal experts were looking into the matter and studying transcripts. Party politics intervened and magnified the row, which flickered on intermittently before it finally subsided.

Only one more month, a dozen shows, of David's Rediffusion series remained before the company would become part of a new outfit, Thames Television. By that time David would be sailing forth under his own banner—or rather under the auspices of the new London Weekend Television. Even so, while tied to London for three nights, he often spent the rest of the week in the United States. Paradine Productions was working on the Frankie Howerd "special," and David himself was beginning to put his mind to the Presidential interviews, which required a good deal of mental preparation.

At Egerton Crescent his constant excursions into new and bigger ventures created more and more work. A serene and unflappable supersecretary, Joan Pugh kept the machine running smoothly, dealing with David's voluminous mail, the innumerable telephone calls that linked Knightsbridge with the four corners of the United States, and visitors David had no time or inclination to see. Outwardly, at least, Joan's temperament seemed not unlike David's. However great the pressure, she thought he was wonderful to work for. "Never a reproach, never a rebuke," she said.

If she slipped up, he did not get angry. "It's done" was all he would say.

"It makes one feel all the more guilty," Joan said, sighing.

One of her most arduous chores was (and still is) to get him out of the house in time to catch his planes. There was always one more telephone call to make, one more set of instructions to dictate, one more document/script/letter/book to be extracted from his portable filing cabinet so it could be dealt with before he carried it away with him. Invariably, a mountain of work remained behind as he sped off in his car, stretching the speed limit to the very edge of police tolerance. "Even if we travel together," Richard Armitage said, "I will not go to the airport with him in his car. I do not like driving on two wheels." (David had to be dissuaded from asking Transport Minister Barbara Castle on the show to tackle her about the "restrictive" seventy-mile speed limit.)

"He is no Stirling Moss," remarked one of his aides who went on some of these nightmarish drives with him. The Mercedes caused David embarrassment when, with Britain's perennial economic crisis in mind, he prepared a show on the theme of backing Britain, and it occurred to him that he ought not to drive a foreign car. The Mercedes was exchanged for that prince of British cars, a Bentley (sky-blue). There was more trouble in store. David was driving down Bond Street when a taxi went through a red light, and David, in swerving to avoid it, ended up in the window of a well-known store. The accident was not David's fault, and Bernard Levin sent him a cable: "I've heard all about shopping early for Christmas, but this is ridiculous."

The volume of work involved in David's business affairs burst the confines of his private residence. To bring the various Paradine Productions enterprises—films, documentaries, television advisers, and others in the pipeline—under one roof he took a suite of elegant offices on Davies Street, Mayfair, next door to Claridge's. At the same time, Richard Armitage became in name what he had been in fact for some time—managing director of all David Frost companies.

By the end of January the Rediffusion series ended, with a friendly confrontation that hindsight invested with a certain piquancy. David's principal guest was the American comedian Bob Newhart, who a few months later became one of the contenders for the hot seat of the big Westinghouse show that David conquered for himself. The first move toward this conquest—though the objective was as yet not clearly defined—was David's pursuit of the American Presidential candidates. The names on his working schedule were Vice-President Hubert H. Humphrey, Senator Robert F. Kennedy, Senator Eugene McCarthy, Governor Nelson Rockefeller, Governor Ronald Reagan, Mayor John V. Lindsay, Richard M. Nixon, Harold Stassen, and George Wallace.

For an English television host, however prominent in his own country, to tackle nine men of such caliber in the middle of a tense election campaign was a daunting prospect. The primaries were in progress, which complicated geographical arrangements: The timing and coordinating of the interviews was a problem. To fix up the appointments necessitated a good deal of travel across the width and length of the United States.

David's first priority was to concentrate on the structure of the interviews, in which he hoped to explore the personalities of the Presidential contenders at the moment of their great political tests and to show them to their own compatriots in a fresh and revealing light. Even with this mammoth task ahead of him, David would not have been true to himself if he had not devoted some time and energy to fringe activities—except that to him they were pretty important, too. The American edition of his book was due to be published (by Stein and Day, New York) under the title *The English*, and he was determined to plug it for all it was worth. On the *Merv Griffin Show* he told one of his many stories about the English—it was about an Englishman he met who was so snobbish he would not ride in the same car with his chauffeur. David and Merv got on well together. Later it was said that David literally talked his book into being a best seller (it stayed on *The New York Times* best-seller list for a month), but it would have made the grade with less-expert publicizing. It sold around one hundred thousand copies in its hard-cover edition.

Set for an extended stay in the United States, David accepted Clay Felker's invitation to move into his palatial duplex on East Fifty-seventh Street. It was there that a few weeks later Chet Collier telephoned David early one morning. "Merv Griffin is ill," Chet told him. "Could you take over the show tonight?"

The ninety-minute show, which went out every evening on Channel 5, was due to be taped at 6:30 P.M. David reached The Little Theatre, at 240 West 44th Street, at eleven in the morning to meet producer Bob Shanks. Two or three more guests were required, and in a swift conference David and Bob discussed potential candidates before David went off to keep a prior appointment. He returned to the studio at four.

Looking unruffled and relaxed, he took up his position as guest host of the show, one of the fixtures of American television. Singer Fran Jeffries and comedian Pat Cooper supplied the light entertainment. They were followed by three weightier personalities: Susan Strasberg, the young actress "Method"-trained in her father's Actors Studio, the way-out poet Allen Ginsberg, and William Attwood, editor of *Look* magazine.

Instead of engaging in a lighthearted showbiz chat with Susan, in the style of Merv Griffin, David steered the conversation round to her experiences with psychiatry. She talked more frankly on the subject than she had ever before done on television. His interview with Allen Ginsberg turned on marijuana and developed into a fierce duel when Ginsberg suggested that the smoking of pot should be legalized. David, who had done his homework, countered effectively by confronting Ginsberg with some of his own arguments against the practice. William Attwood had come on the show to talk about his interviews with Prince Sihanouk, which were currently appearing in *Look*, but David discovered that he had also talked to President Nasser, which seemed of greater interest. They talked mainly about Nasser. Experts thought that the show had gone extremely well and remarked on the high level of the conversations. It was a hint of what David could do—and would be doing before long.

Clay Felker, David's host, was preparing to launch a new magazine, *New York*, which has since become increasingly successful. His apartment was a meeting place of well-known American writers and journalists with whom David felt a strong affinity. At Clay's cocktail parties and other get-togethers he exchanged thoughts with columnist Jimmy Breslin, an original mind; Peter Maas, a confidant of Robert Kennedy; Joseph Kraft; and others. Subtly questioning these knowledgeable insiders and extracting information from them, he began to acquire an intimate insight into American affairs.

His curiosity extended beyond politics, and the circle of his friends soon included Wall Street bankers and financial experts who kept him abreast of stock-market intricacies, take-over bids, company launchings. David did not hide his fascination with high finance and big business. Tycoons submitted themselves to his probings as willingly as did the writers and politicians. "His questions made a lot of sense," Clay Felker remarked.

It was not all work. Anne de Vigier came to the United States on a visit, and there was no shortage of American girls who took an interest in the young visitor from London. Always with a pretty woman by his side, David did the town untiringly. The Rainbow Room, "21," the Plaza, Le Pavillon, La Côte Basque, were some of the stations on his progress through New York's night life.

He saw a good deal of Antony Armstrong-Jones—the Earl of Snowdon, Princess Margaret of England's husband—who was in New York on a television assignment. When they went to The Running Footman, a restaurant on East Sixty-first Street, in their casual clothes—turtleneck sweaters instead of shirts and ties—they were refused admittance and went round the corner to an Italian restaurant to eat scampi. David's friends thought that his voracious appetite helped to sustain his energy. Every meal he ate was "fantastic." His stamina was astounding. He went to bed late, rose early. Even after a sleepless night he seemed to thrive on work.

On a visit to San Francisco he was again lunching at Ernie's with a friend. Seeing a man at a nearby table, David asked, "Who's that?"

"That's Kenny Hyman, head of Warner Studios," was the reply.

A few minutes later David excused himself and walked over to Hyman's table. "Hello, Kenny—I'm David Frost," he said. Hyman asked him to sit down, and they were soon engrossed in conversation. They had breakfast together the following morning. Within less than twelve hours of meeting him, David had made a friend of Hyman. Another hour or so, and a major business transaction was emerging from their talks.

David told Hyman of his idea for a film about opinion polls, a wonderfully hilarious subject, he thought. He had the writers to write the script for it and the actors to star in it. Would Warner Brothers be interested in financing the project? Kenny Hyman, as shrewd a film executive as they come, was infected by David's enthusiasm. He agreed then and there to put a million dollars into the deal.

Almost overnight David had become a film producer under the comforting Warner Brothers umbrella. "He has that feeling for an opportunity, this tremendous perception," said Richard Armitage, to whom it fell to develop the projects David had initiated. "A chance conversation—and he builds on it." A new Frost company, David Paradine Films, came into being. It was up to Armitage now—and John Stutter, the lawyer—to set the wheels in motion under David's remote control.

He was already up to his eyeballs in the preparation and production of the Presidential interviews. To assist him he engaged one of his London producer-scriptwriters, the talented Ian Davidson, who was familiar with his approach. In long conversations, using Davidson as a sounding board and idea man, David developed his technique for this complicated assignment. Because what politicians say is usually so predictable, he was anxious to devise questions that might throw them off balance and get them out of their ruts.

The target was four "specials" under the collective title "The Next President?" Talking to the men from among whom Americans were about to choose their head of state was more than a job to David. It was a way of discovering the country for himself. His trick had always been to start at the top. Now he was starting his dialogue with America there.

CHAPTER 13

The Next President

THE BASIC AIM of the Presidential interviews, as David saw it, was to give viewers an opportunity to compare the candidates—their differences and their similarities. Some questions he fashioned were tailored to each man; others were identical questions, the answers to which would show where they agreed and where their views clashed. One question David decided to ask most of them was: "What would you like the first sentence of your obituary to say?" Another "communal" question aimed at a wider perspective: "Who is your favorite historical figure?" And what, he proposed to find out from the candidates, was their idea of a typical American place or characteristic? He was anxious to clarify the candidates' attitudes to "the great malaise in America" everybody was talking about and what they thought was at the root of it. And, finally, what were people on earth for? Few interviewers had raised such topics with politicians before.

Much spadework had to be done contacting aides, writing letters, fixing appointments, making technical arrangements, finding studios or other suitable accommodation in each locality. While still flying between Europe and the United States to keep up with his diverse interests, David started out on his Presidential assault course in earnest in the first week of March, 1968. He arranged for himself and Ian Davidson to take a plane from London to New York on March 7, but on the eve of their departure a mountain of mail and other paperwork remained to be dealt with at Egerton Crescent. Joan Pugh pleaded with him but could not pin him down for even a couple of hours: "You come with us to New

York," David said in the end, "and we'll have seven hours in the air to get through all these letters." They flew off together, and throughout the flight David dictated answers to letters that had been accumulating for weeks and months. Joan filled three notebooks, spent the night in New York, and took an early plane back to London the following day.

By that time David and Ian Davidson were at work on the complicated interviewing schedule. With luck, it would be possible to catch up with Senator Eugene McCarthy in Manchester, New Hampshire, the following week while the New Hampshire primary was in progress. Again with luck, Harold Stassen might be available in the same place at the same time. There was a hotel in Manchester where a suite could be rigged up as a studio. An appointment with Mayor Lindsay was fixed more easily on the spot in New York City, and Governor Reagan agreed to be available in Sacramento, California, the following week.

Richard Nixon proved to be rather elusive. Not only was he constantly flip-flopping between New York and California, but perhaps remembering his disastrous television appearances in 1960, seemed not too eager to put his six-o'clock shadow on show. Westinghouse pulled all possible strings. David approached friends who were close to Nixon until the candidate's resistance broke down, and a meeting with David was arranged for March 23 in New York.

George Wallace was prepared to face the cameras in Montgomery, Alabama, a day later, and the meeting with Robert Kennedy was arranged for the day after that in Portland, Oregon. Governor Rockefeller would be available at the State House in Albany, New York, on March 29—if his time permitted. The Humphrey interview could take place in Washington any time after that.

On March 12 David and his team were in Manchester, glad to be making a start. Senator McCarthy was extremely courteous, and a brief preliminary talk gave an inkling of his original thinking and his simple dignity, which inspired so many young people. David started the interview by asking one of his set questions— what would the senator like the first sentence of his obituary to be? The answer came promptly: "He died."

Anxious to get something more specific, David quickly put a supplementary question: "Now, the second sentence?"

"If you become President of the United States," McCarthy replied, "you ought to be indifferent to what your biographers might say about you. . . . That was true about Harry Truman, a great President, really, about Pope John the Twenty-third." The senator did not rise to David's bait.

The historical character he most admired was a composite: "I've kind of got me hitched to Thomas More." He also admired Edmund Burke—Burke was the great liberal orator and philosopher who defended Warren Hastings, first governor of India, who was impeached for oppression of the natives. Senator McCarthy added another tribute to Harry Truman.

David raised the subjects of the youth of America, of dictatorships, and then asked what he called "a very big question"—"What are people on earth for?"

"Some questions you've asked have been reasonably large already," Senator McCarthy said, before replying: "It's a triple sort of thing—the idea of coming to know as much as you can and of reflecting it somehow and transmitting it to other people."

"Not to waste one's time or talents, in effect," David summed up. This was his own philosophy.

Senator McCarthy amplified: "That's it really, though it doesn't mean that you can't be somewhat selfish and kind of turn in upon yourself. I don't have the idea of full public service. I think there is a place for some private life."

The series of interviews had got off to a most gratifying start. The talk with Harold Stassen in the same setting was on a lower key. It showed the seasoned campaigner as a strong supporter of the United Nations but revealed little that was new.

Two days later David was in New York, facing Mayor Lindsay with "a very wide question—what is your ideal for America?"

America, in Lindsay's view, was a young country with constantly changing conditions and people, a dynamic, fast-moving, high-pressure nation that is competitive yet preserves values and traditions, a country of vast expanse and diversity. The typical, real America was "almost any suburban community."

When Lindsay mentioned Great Britain going through a malaise during the turbulent period of its election, David interjected: "Oh, we've enjoyed a perpetual malaise."

Lindsay: "Your people preserve a wonderful sense of humor."

Frost: "We find we need it more and more."

They talked about leadership—Eisenhower's in dealing with the problems of Europe and Asia, Kennedy's in the area of civil rights. No, there wasn't any decision in his political life that he, Lindsay, regretted. Patriotism? People did the most outrageous things in the name of patriotism; Tacitus described patriotism as a healthy competition with one's ancestors.

Frost: "That's a great definition."

The first line of Lindsay's obituary: "Thanks so much."

There were five days to go before the next interview. David flew to London for an extended weekend to attend to details of his forthcoming work for London Weekend Television. He was back in the United States and in his place at the State House in Sacramento on Wednesday, March 20, to be received by Governor Ronald Reagan.

More political than usual, David raised the issue of violence—the rising problem of crime in the cities, the muggers, the demonstrators. It was shocking, Reagan said, how one could suddenly look out of the window and there was a parade with picket signs and they were ready to push the policeman out of the way. The demonstrators did not want to present their case to the Government. What they were saying was, "If such and such a thing happens, we'll kill so and so." Revolution was in the air.

Almost gently, as so often when he worked up to a crucial point, David said it was a violent country in many ways. Then he asked innocently, "I read somewhere that you collect guns yourself, don't you?"

Governor Reagan was almost thrown off his balance. "Well, not from the standpoint of wanting to attack anyone," he said uncertainly, "but as a collector." Contradicting himself in the same breath, he added, "I am not a serious collector," but confessed, "I've always had them. I've had a ranch. . . . I'm not a hunter to any extent. . . . I like target shooting."

Frost: "In a country, though, where everyone realizes there may be riots or violence or whatever, guns are incredibly available, aren't they?"

Reagan: "Yes, although I am not one who believes in overdoing the restriction on that, because the wrong person can always get the gun, so perhaps it's proper that the right person should have them at least available."

With regard to the principle "My country, right or wrong," the governor thought people must support their country, even if they disagree with their Government, until they can persuade the Government to change its course. His favorite historical character was the Prince of Peace, the Man of Galilee. He wanted his obituary to say nothing more than "He tried and did his best."

Afterward there was a brief internal crisis in the David Frost camp during the drive to the San Francisco airport with David at the wheel. "Slow down!" his colleagues implored him. They thought he was driving dangerously. "That's the last time we shall drive with you!" they protested. David was too absorbed with the job to argue.

Three days separated them from the next assignment, the interview with Richard Nixon in New York. On the appointed day they were directed to the building on Fifth Avenue which was to become Nixon's headquarters. It was still empty and deserted. The lights were rigged up and the cameras were put in readiness for the occasion, which David regarded as the highlight of his confrontations.

Nixon was relaxed and confident when he arrived to face his questioner. He looked fit and tanned, without a shadow—six o'clock or otherwise—over his features. They went to work without delay.

It was impossible, he thought, to pick out one place as representing the real, typical America. What made America was its diversity. One outstanding American characteristic was a rather hopeless idealism, he said. "Americans really believe their mission is to work for a world in which everybody could choose." He wanted America to move from Franklin Roosevelt's four "freedoms from . . . " (fear, want, etc.) to "freedoms to . . . "—to travel, to choose, to expand one's view. He did not believe in the principle "My country, right or wrong."

They talked about dictatorships, Communist and Fascist, about democracy, about the British Constitution—the model, David suggested, for constitutions that half the independent nations of Africa had overthrown. The conversation flowed as if they were in a private living room. "I am not one of those," Richard Nixon said, "who believe that colonialism was an unmixed evil. Let's take British colonialism—and I don't say this because you happen to be British," he went on, with the kind of personal response

David's questions often generate. "British colonialism left a great legacy for good in Asia and Africa and in the United States."

Reviewing his political past, he said he liked to think that his work as Vice-President had been of value in the international field. Referring to "your people in Britain who like to take a little wager," he added that he would have taken a bet of a million-to-one that he would never be running for public office again. Of course, there were many episodes in his life he would like to rewrite: "I suppose the answer which first comes to mind is the campaign of 1960. Should I or should I not have debated with John Kennedy on television? And if I did, then perhaps I should have had, as some people said, a better makeup man and the rest. . . . Mistakes were made. I prefer to look to the future."

The rest of the talk was about press criticism, Bobby Kennedy, excesses in political campaigning. Nixon mentioned "that disgraceful sign": "Hey, Hey, LBJ, How Many Kids Did You Kill Today?" He thought people were on earth for greater vision, for a greater purpose. He would like the first line of his obituary in *The New York Times* to say, "He made a great contribution to the peace of the world."

Offstage—out of camera range, that is—David was feeling the strain, and his entourage was not free from tension either. The Nixon interview was barely committed to tape when they had to catch a plane for Montgomery, Alabama, but David would not be put off a million other things he was involved in at the same time. He was still on the telephone in the airport building when his flight was called. The engines were already running when he was rushed to the airplane. Seconds later the doors were slammed. The same thing happened during a brief stopover at Charlottesville, Virginia—the plane was ready to take off, but David was again on the telephone.

"Welcome to Dixie," the sign read at Montgomery. In the heart of anti-civil-rights country David's men—well, Ian Davidson for one, by his own account—felt uneasy. "I had long hair," Davidson recalled, "and clothes that looked outlandish. I must have looked like a civil-rights man. At times I nearly died of fright."

Once David settled down to the interview with George Wallace, all cares, his and his crew's, disappeared. His concentration was total. David posed his questions crisply.

"Which place, in your view, is the real America?"

"No sector has a monopoly."

"What is a distinguishing American characteristic?"

"By and large, we are nationalistic."

"What is the root of the American malaise?" David asked. Wallace's answer was a tirade against centralized government and a forceful assertion of states' rights. When Wallace claimed that he had never made a statement in his life that reflected on anybody because of race or color, David countered that whenever he, Wallace, had taken issue on race questions with the Federal Government, it had been because he wanted the Negro to have fewer rights written into the various acts or bills. Wallace's book, *Hear Me Out*, bore out this contention. Then David sprung a surprise: "Let me then ask the age-old question that's asked on the race issue," he said. "Would you let your daughter marry a Negro?"

There was a terrible silence. It was some time before Wallace wriggled out of this one. "I don't even want to get into a discussion of that business," he said at last. "In fact, I don't want to discuss the matter of race, really, because the most important thing in our country is maintaining law and order."

David next asked whether Wallace supported the Ku Klux Klan. "I made the strongest speech against the Ku Klux Klan ever made in this state over statewide television in 'fifty-eight," Wallace answered.

Frost: "What one sentence from that would you quote?"

Wallace: "I don't remember. . . . It's not important, either!"

The interview was more acerbic than any that had gone before, but when it was over, Wallace was amiable enough. David's other subjects had been so busy that they had hardly finished their last sentence when they were off and gone. Wallace apparently had plenty of time. He stayed on while David repeated some of the questions for the camera and the sound track.

From Montgomery, Alabama, David went to Portland, Oregon, where Senator Robert Kennedy was contesting the primary. David was at once captivated by Bobby's charisma, and so were Ian Davidson and the camera crew. Little time was wasted. To the question about "the real America" Senator Kennedy replied that it was in the smaller communities—upstate New York or perhaps Iowa.

And the American malaise? Was it the cities, the attitudes to the war or the race question, or something deeper? "I think it involves the national purpose," Kennedy answered, "almost the soul of the country, the tremendous material wealth in the United States and how it's going to be utilized, the great military power —we don't quite know what to make of it."

He praised young people who went and served and those who fought against discrimination by doing things on behalf of their neighbor and community. He felt that politics was an honorable profession.

In reply to David's questions he said his approach was not necessarily similar to President Kennedy's: "We are living in a different time." He was looking to the future. His greatest achievement, he thought, was his role in the Cuban missile crisis, the ideas he was able to contribute to President Kennedy's decision when the question was whether the world was going to be blown up or not. "A miscalculation in a major way," he said, "and that's the last miscalculation you make."

Episodes in his career he would like to rewrite? There were things out of one's hands that one would rather had never occurred. "But I don't know that there's anything that I think I would have changed," he added. He defined leadership as the capacity "to inspire people to exercise their best qualities." [Frost: "That's a pretty good definition."] There was a story about a French general who yelled out of the window, "There go my people. I must follow them. I am their leader!" Leadership, he thought, was the opposite of that.

The kind of America he wanted to see? "We have to cut down in the reliance on nuclear weapons, get a system along with other nations to help the underdeveloped countries, and establish a system within our country so that people, even the very poor, can educate their children so that they in turn can find decent jobs and live a decent life and not be hopeless and not be filled with despair. That's what I would like to see in the future."

There was no future for Bobby Kennedy. His talk with David was the last personal interview he ever gave for television. In Los Angeles on June 5, 1968, only a few weeks after meeting David, the senator was struck down by an assassin's bullet. The interview was not screened until a year later, on the anniversary of the tragedy. For a poignant half hour it brought Bobby Kennedy to life again and was a dramatic reminder of what the United States had lost. Ethel Kennedy herself told friends that it was the best interview her husband had ever done.

After the Nixon-Wallace-Kennedy interviews (and nearly six thousand miles of travel) on three successive days, a foretaste of the pace David Frost was going to set for himself, it was back to New York. Chet Collier was among the guests at a small party at Felker's apartment. The Westinghouse man was curious about how things were going, and David reported on his progress. He was so enthusiastic that he told Chet, "It is impossible to squeeze these conversations into sixty minutes. I must have at least ninety!"

They were still talking when the party ended. David walked Chet down Fifty-seventh Street. They strolled into a bar and continued to discuss the matter while munching sandwiches. Chet Collier was soon persuaded. "OK, let's do ninety minutes," he said. He worked out the additional cost in his head. "It was over twenty-thousand dollars," he said later, "but it was worth it."

In terms of time, the Rockefeller interview turned out to be a difficult proposition. Quite apart from the election campaign, the governor of New York was in the throes of a big budget battle, and David was kept waiting some time at the State Legislature building. When Governor Rockefeller finally emerged, he did a David Frost on David Frost: "Hello, Dave!" he said, greeting his interviewer before David could produce his own welcoming routine.

The interview itself started by David saying that in an election year everyone behaved a little bit like a doctor trying to analyze what's wrong with the patient, America. Governor Rockefeller replied: "You need to be a psychiatrist now!" He thought the American people were beginning to lose confidence in themselves and in their country. "I don't personally think it's justified." The problems were Vietnam, the cities and the explosions from their ghetto areas, fiscal and monetary difficulties that were not being faced.

The achievement of which Rockefeller was most proud was getting elected governor. His worst moment—when he had taken a stand on extremism at the Republican Convention in 1964 and had been roundly booed for fifteen minutes. The best way people could get satisfaction and enjoy happiness (this in answer to the question of what they were on earth for) was by contributing to the full realization of opportunity for people within their country, within the world. Among historical figures he had tremendous admiration for Mahatma Gandhi, with whom he had enjoyed lengthy conversations in 1930 or 1931.

Obliquely referring to the wealth of the Rockefellers, David asked whether there was anything he had wanted and had been unable to get. Yes, was the reply, he remembered bidding at an auction for a Modigliani painting once and losing to the Museum of Modern Art, but he had got one fourteen years later, which showed that patience and persistence were rewarded. Governor Rockefeller hoped that his obituary would say "A few people were better off as a result of my having lived."

Before March was out, David conducted the last interview of the series, with Vice-President Humphrey, who was full of praise for President Lyndon B. Johnson, "a great man." There was no malaise in America, he said. There were concern, ferment, change, difficulties, and troubles but no basic sickness: "I think it's a nation that is growing up, maturing." The Vice-President, in answer to the obituary question, said that he wanted to be remembered as a sort of healer.

Frost: "Healing demands medicine. What is the basic medicine?"

"I think," Humphrey said, "when people begin to balance it out, that every right brings with it a responsibility, every privilege carries with it a duty, every luxury a burden. They will understand that they are not put on this earth just for their own self-indulgence, that they are here for the purpose of building a society, a great society, a good society, a society of free men!"

"Offbeat and incisive questions" was a typical American press comment when the interviews were shown a couple of months later. "Satirist Frost is one of those interviewers who sometimes makes his subjects squirm," said the Boston *Herald Traveler,* "but he also has the knack of drawing them out in his wry English manner." For David it was a famous success. Stein and Day published the interviews as a book (*The Presidential Debate, 1968*), which was well received. David was beginning to identify with his American viewers; he was less aggressive than on his English shows, but then, Americans did not have the background of acid satire on which the English had been feeding for years. As time went on, though he insisted that his approach was the same in London and New York, he could not altogether escape the American influence. Yet his Englishness, which some thought of as a handicap, proved a strong asset.

Almost immediately he was offered another major assign- ment—to guest-host Johnny Carson's *Tonight* show on July 4 and 5. Independence Day was not the most auspicious time to make an impact, but David accepted without hesitation. What tempted him was not the money—the standard fee of one thousand dollars a day was not among the biggest rewards he could com- mand—but the opportunity to prove himself as host of a show.

While *Tonight* producer Rudi Tellez and his team went to Cal- ifornia to prepare the following week's show, David came under the wing of coproducer John Carsey. Neil Shand was there to lend a hand. The guests invited for the two shows were very much after David's heart. One was Jimmy Breslin; another was Richard Goodwin, speech-writer for Robert Kennedy and Eugene McCarthy, for whom he mapped out a thirty-minute interview. The third was Bill Moyers, President Johnson's erstwhile press secretary.

The topics one could discuss with these men were not the ones habitually offered to viewers of the *Tonight* show. What David aimed at was to produce a preview of political developments in the United States. Fishing in the deep waters of America's future, he exercised his natural curiosity. The conversations were lively, and his guests came up with many original ideas.

David was so absorbed in his subject that he was totally una- ware of what went on behind the scenes. The taping of the show was only a few minutes old when Rudi Tellez called John Carsey from California to find out how it was going. He called again half an hour later—and a third time. Tellez was worried lest David was bringing on his guests too early. Was he not in danger, Tellez asked, of leaving a blank at the end?

Carsey reassured the producer that things were running smoothly and that David had the show well under control. As a matter of fact, watching the proceedings on the screen, Tellez could see for himself that there was nothing to worry about. Next day's show went as well. There was not a single call from California. No greater compliment could be paid to the ambitious stand-in for the great Johnny Carson.

Later in the year David was asked to host yet another *Tonight* show. After conducting his own Sunday late-night program in London, he took off on Monday morning for New York, where he was due to appear that same evening. This time he introduced a performer who had impressed him on one of his London shows, Holley Gray, the world-record plate-spinner who could spin thirty-six plates all at once. On *Tonight*, spurred on by David, Gray broke his own record and twirled thirty-seven plates simultaneously. The evening's principal guest was another English friend of David's, actor-writer Robert Shaw, whose remarks about the Pope caused a storm.

To celebrate David's performance his American agent, Gerry Leider, of Ashley Famous (now International Famous), threw a party. "We did not know it at the time," David said, "but we had a good deal to celebrate."

CHAPTER 14

David Frost, U.S.A.

EARLY IN JULY, 1968, around the time when David Frost appeared on the *Tonight* show and cut his teeth as an American talk-show host, Chet Collier, now president of Westinghouse Broadcasting, was in charge of the company's production subsidiary. He was in his New York office at 90 Park Avenue when the telephone rang. His secretary put the call straight through to him.

"Hello, Merv!" Chet greeted the star of his *Merv Griffin Show*, a household name and Westinghouse breadwinner. In his four years with Westinghouse, occupying peak time in New York—8:30 to 10 P.M.—on Channel 5, the popular talk-show host had garnered 140 stations as regular customers. The tapes of his program were shown five days a week. With a big financial stake in the success of the show across the country, he was pulling in close to a million dollars a year for himself.

Merv's voice sounded forebodingly somber. In a few words, he told Collier he was quitting. Of course, he would complete his contract with Westinghouse, which had another eleven months to run. After that he would be joining the rival C.B.S. Chet Collier was shocked. He asked Merv to come and talk things over. Griffin replied that the C.B.S. offer was too good to refuse and that his deal with them was in fact already signed and sealed. "It was a big blow to the company," Chet Collier says, "but there was nothing I could do."

This was a matter for the highest authority. Don McGannon, Westinghouse's top executive, called his principal aides together and formed a committee of four—Chet Collier, Tad Reeves, Jim Allan, and Dick Pack—to find a man capable of stepping into Merv Griffin's shoes. It was an unenviable task, and there was no time to lose. Surveying the familiar talk-show scene, they saw an arid desert with very few bright spots. Most serious subjects were shunned, there was much inconsequential chatter, controversy was nonexistent. Apart from the *Merv Griffin Show*, Westing-house was running the *Mike Douglas Show*, with a record number of fifteen million viewers for the five-day daytime pro-gram, most of which was devoted to variety acts and showbiz talk.

Merv Griffin's biggest competition was the late-night show over which the amiable, talented Johnny Carson presided. Undisputed king of the talk-show hosts, Johnny, who had succeeded Jack Paar, managed to get the best out of his show-business guests but was not as strong on other subjects. A loyal flock of some eleven million viewers earned him 15¢ per head, or about $1,500,000 a year. Another TV talker was A.B.C.'s Joey Bishop, very funny and first-class in situation comedy but not so good at interviewing or sustaining a lengthy conversation on camera. His show was already doomed, and he was soon to be replaced by Dick Cavett, another good stand-up comedian, quick-witted and clever, who has developed considerably recently.

There was obviously no hope of luring Johnny Carson to West-inghouse to take over from Merv Griffin. Who could do the job? The problem was acute. Only a few months remained to find a replacement or face a severe loss of revenue.

"We began at once to consider people," said Chet Collier. As soon as the news got about, agents started bombarding the com-mittee with names, photographs, films, and tapes. "We listened to scores of them." Each of the committee members came up with suggestions. Dick Cavett seemed a distinct possibility, but he was under contract to A.B.C. Bob Newhart, the comedian, came under consideration. The names of satirist-comedian Henry Morgan and singer-performer Steve Lawrence cropped up. An Englishman, Dave Allan, though little known in the United States, was highly recommended.

"We even looked at unknown talent," Chet added. Tapes of newscasters John Barber and Dennis Wholey were scrutinized, but none of these faces fitted. The situation was getting desperate. At this stage Chet Collier received another telephone call. This time it was David Frost on the line to discuss a business matter. Almost as a throw-away he added at the end of the conversation: "What are you going to do about Griffin leaving you?" He did not have to say more.

It was a very long shot, but Collier's reaction suggested at once that he would be seriously considered and stood a very good chance. With the Presidential interviews already on tape, Westinghouse had a vested interest in David Frost and was watching his progress with hawkeyes. He had shown what he could do as a talk-show host on *Tonight* and as Merv Griffin's stand-in. Come to think of it, David Frost might be a very good solution.

Chet Collier had no hesitation in putting his name forward as a candidate to succeed Merv Griffin. The big question, of course, was whether an Englishman could pull such a thing off in America over a long period. "We did want something different in the way of talk shows," Chet said. "The committee felt there was a need in U.S. television for a more intelligent, more sophisticated show doing things that were not done elsewhere, permitting conversations with non–show-business people. . . . We thought audiences were ready for such a change. We liked what we had seen of David and were convinced that he could provide something exciting. . . . Still, there was this gnawing feeling that his accent might be in the way."

In the meantime David had to fulfill his commitments in London, where his accent was certainly not in the way. He returned to English television under a shadow that was not of his making. It darkened into total blackout. Labor trouble spoiled the debut of the newly licensed commercial companies. London Weekend Television was due to start operations at 7 P.M. on Friday, August 2, 1968, but studio technicians were going slow or "working to rule" (taking job action).

Instead of carefully planned hilarity with the opening show, which threatened, "We Have Ways of Making You Laugh," viewers were treated to apologies for an "unnatural break." There was no show. Of David Frost, scheduled to follow later (at 9:15), they saw no more than a brief announcement of his impending appearance and—an empty screen. Backstage negotiations went on, and the evening hung in the balance until matters were resolved just before David's show. It was up to him to rescue the first night.

For the grand occasion he was appearing as "Actuality Frost," the interviewer-inquisitor, the first of his three guises specially designed for the new company. (Saturdays he would be "The People's Frost" in a lighter vein, and Sundays "Funny Frost," host to comedians and other showbiz personalities.) Standing by in the wings were Cyril Bennett, the program director, and Clive Irving, head of current affairs, with a personal stake in the serious Friday show. All the big brass of London Weekend was watching with fingers crossed.

As the lights went up at long last, David introduced his guests: John Braine, writer and lifelong socialist, Paul Johnson, the highly articulate editor of the left-wing weekly *New Statesman,* and more to the right of the political spectrum, Kingsley Amis, the novelist, author of *Lucky Jim.*

One of Braine's previous television appearances had nearly been spoiled by a bout of stage fright, but David was confident that he could create an atmosphere to soothe raw nerves. He was quite right. Totally oblivious of the cameras, Braine launched into a highly provocative tirade against the erosion of freedom under socialism and against socialist tyranny—a change of mind first revealed on this show.

Paul Johnson countered with a fierce attack on the Tory rat race, and Kingsley Amis paraded his anti-Labour views in support of Braine. With David stoking the embers, the argument spread to the audience and escalated into a good old-fashioned political row. It was, to quote Peter Black, the *Daily Mail's* respected television critic, "a showpiece demonstration of the planned-collision type of discussion."

Next evening David presented Bob Hope (in a prerecorded interview). If the audience expected the familiar Hope patter and well-delivered script-writers' jokes, they were in for a surprise. Instead, they were introduced to Bob Hope's little-known other persona, a serious man with strong views on, among other things, Vietnam—"a struggle between right and wrong, between our system and theirs."

On Sunday the technicians were still on the warpath when David was due to go on the air with his third show of the weekend. Their place was taken by executives, led by Michael Peacock, Cyril Bennett, and Clive Irving. They manned the cameras, operated the lights, and shifted the props.

This is how Peter Black, of the *Daily Mail*, summed up the first Frost weekend: "There is something exasperating about such an overpowering success as Frost has had (is having, will have). . . . The fact is that he is a master populariser who does better than anyone else the highly important job of leaving a mass audience more alert than when he found it." Another critic called David "the first hero of Independent Television reborn."

To some people David's success may have been exasperating. To others he was a hero. His impact on ordinary people produced odd incidents. At one of London's smaller airports, a hundred vacationers bound for Italy and Yugoslavia were kept waiting for hours while their airplane was undergoing repairs. Angry and frustrated, they shouted in chorus, "Send for David Frost!" They could not think of anyone more likely to help them in their predicament.

A few days later a stunned nation, listening to B.B.C. Radio, heard a solemn announcement: "We record with deep regret the death of Mr. David Frost at his home in Hampton Court Palace" (a royal residence). Frost fans, missing the joke in the shock of the moment, telephoned the B.B.C. and the newspapers and asked, "Is it true?" No, it was not true. It was a quotation from a mock obituary on David Frost which had appeared in *Punch*. "It was a joke," the B.B.C. explained.

David was very much alive and was seen to be as he attended theater and motion-picture first nights (mostly with Jenny Logan). When he was not at London Weekend, business conferences at home and board meetings at the Davies Street offices of his production companies kept him busier than ever. Somehow he also squeezed in two charity shows, one in aid of Biafra and one for old people. In charity circles it was said, "Frost never refuses."

His film project was a very personal affair. The subject for which he had secured financing from Warner Brothers was a skit on opinion polls, the story of a young man who becomes Prime

Minister. Frost-watchers concluded that it was his ambition to be Prime Minister one day, and the suggestion turned up in scores of newspaper and magazine articles about him.

To write the film script David engaged John Cleese and Graham Chapman. "Go and shut yourselves away somewhere," he told them, "and do not come back without a finished script!" Chapman and Cleese flew to Spain, where they wrote *The Rise and Rise of Michael Rimmer*. The satirical flavor was much in the David Frost mold. Spiced with in jokes, it was a very funny story. He recruited his old sparring partner Peter Cook to play the title role.

Whenever he could, David dashed to Beccles to see his mother, though he increasingly asked her to come and stay with him in London because he could not spare the time to travel north. His household was joined by Bob Lambert, a jovial, efficient Londoner who had seen service in Korea and had driven him in his Rediffusion days. Engaged as a chauffeur, Bob soon began to make himself useful in many other departments of David's life.

The kaleidoscope of celebrities who went on the *Frost Programme* was bewildering. Self-confessed revolutionaries were followed by solid Establishment figures. Foreign affairs competed for attention with domestic issues. A cardinal (Heenan of England) and a king (Hussein of Jordan) appeared with David. "The Pill," bigotry, jerry-building, corporal punishment, the economic crisis, race, the space program, were some of the subjects he discussed on other occasions.

Rolling Stone Mick Jagger came on the show to talk about himself, singer Marianne Faithfull, and marriage—or rather nonmarriage. Following the publication in the large-circulation *Daily Express* of sensational photographs showing the Queen in bed, David raised the subject with *Express* editor Derek Marks, one of Britain's outstanding journalists, who made a good case for their publication. "They were charming pictures," Marks said. Buckingham Palace knew in advance that they would be published, and the Queen did not say she objected. Naturally, if she fell flat on her back at Euston Station, she would rather that picture was not used: "There was no question of bad taste."

David had to bone up on a mind-boggling variety of topics. Noel Coward and Muhammad Ali have little in common except that they both appeared on the *Frost Programme* in quick succession. One Friday it was General Moshe Dayan, the Israeli defense minister; the next it was Baldur von Schirach, onetime Hitler Youth leader and gauleiter of Vienna, who had served most of his twenty-year sentence as a Nazi war criminal in Spandau Prison, Berlin.

Before traveling to meet Schirach at his home in Trossingen, West Germany, David studied his history and gave much thought to the most effective approach. "I can't try him all over again, can I?" he said to himself. Though he prefers to meet his guests "cold"—without prior personal contact—he decided to talk to Schirach before the interview to explore his attitude and came to the conclusion that there was no point in saying something spectacular, like, "I name you Rat of the Week," because the only response he could expect would be a routine, "Yes, we were wrong." "I thought that the most chilling, interesting thing would be to draw him out so as to show that he was not sorry, that he was almost yearning for those days again," David said afterward.

Early in the interview, thinking of the six million Jews murdered by Hitler and incinerated in gas ovens, David asked Schirach: "If there was one thing that future generations could know about Adolf Hitler, what would you want this to be?"

"The wonderful way that he dealt with unemployment in the thirties!" Schirach calmly replied.

When David asked about his years in Spandau, Schirach talked about—tomatoes. "We grew tomatoes," he said. "And do you know what happened to those tomatoes, Mr. Frost? We were not allowed to give them to the old people because they had been grown by war criminals. So do you know what happened to the tomatoes, Mr. Frost? They were taken out and burned. . . . Mr. Frost, do you know what it can do to a man to have his tomatoes burned?"

For David it was a terrifying experience. "This sort of insensitivity and incomprehension of what the Nazis did was frightening," he said. He thought Schirach had condemned himself out of his own mouth, but he overestimated his viewers, some of whom did not get the point. There was criticism because David had not been as stern as they hoped he would be.

With the American Presidential-election campaign moving

toward a climax, the *Frost Programme* imported some of David's Presidential interviews to England. David chaired a discussion between partisans of the two contending parties. When Chet Collier and his merry Westinghouse men saw the impact of these very same shows on the American viewers, they became sold on David for the Merv Griffin job. Chet Collier called Gary Nardino, of Ashley Famous, who was David's agent. Tad Reeves came into the negotiations; Carl Trunk, a Westinghouse lawyer, was summoned. David had the assistance of Richard Armitage, John Stutter, his London lawyer, and Paul Marshall, an American attorney. In December, 1968, news leaked out that David was "on a short list of three to take over from Merv Griffin."

David himself was not optimistic. "I had hopes, of course," he said, "but as I looked at my London Weekend contract and what the Westinghouse offer entailed, it seemed mutually exclusive in terms of time ... hopeless!" It may have looked hopeless, but it was by no means impossible. David's aim in the ensuing negotiations was to get Westinghouse to agree to terms that would enable him to honor the London Weekend contract for the next season. "The mills of God grind slowly," he said, "and it took a lot of talking with Chet Collier, Tad Reeves, and above all, Don McGannon to give me a sporting chance."

They were talking in terms of a five-year contract for 250 shows a year, which would be worth at least $2,500,000 to David. For Westinghouse it meant a commitment of well over $15,000,000 over the same period. For David it was a tremendous opportunity. For Westinghouse it was a tremendous risk. A hundred details remained to be hammered out as agents and lawyers combed through the complex paragraphs of the big proposition. Timetables, reruns, credits, staff questions, artistic details—one item at a time, the ground was cleared.

There remained the obstacle of David's London commitments, which threatened to obstruct agreement. In the United States David was a newcomer to the highest echelon of television personalities. In England he was not only the outstanding personality, biggest individual shareholder, and major asset of London Weekend Television but also a star performer under contract for a major series. There was no question of David defaulting on this obligation.

He was confident he could do three shows in England over the weekend and turn up at the New York studio on Monday morning, ready to tape five ninety-minute shows before departing for London on Thursday night. Chet Collier was wrestling with his own doubts. "Is this physically possible?" he asked. "Can any man stand the strain and the pressure of constantly commuting between England and America and doing eight shows week after week?" He was inclined to answer in the negative.

Besides, it was a hard nut to swallow for Westinghouse to have their new talk-show host, anchorman of a multimillion-dollar operation, committed to such a heavy overseas program. Would David reconsider? "I would not dream of reneging on my London obligation!" he repeated.

Don McGannon and Chet Collier were in Fort Lauderdale, Florida, on business when the point at which the matter had to be resolved one way or another arrived. They called David in London and asked him to come over. He reached Fort Lauderdale on Saturday morning. That evening the three men dined together at the Hilton Hotel and talked deep into the night. They talked all through Sunday. At the end of the weary road the Westinghouse men agreed to accept David's position. The tentative terms of agreement incorporated Westinghouse's recognition of David's contractual obligation to London Weekend.

David had made it. Or had he? He was on top of the world. The money was fabulous, but it was not only the money. It was the prestige of being the first Englishman ever to be offered a show like this on American television. It was the challenge. Could he impose his technique and his approach on the established American pattern? Could he put guts into the talk-show business? Would he be allowed to conduct shows like his Savundra interview in London? Would he be permitted to probe and examine Americans and American institutions?

In television terms it was an enormous undertaking, almost an impertinence: the new milieu, the mountain of information to be absorbed, the traveling involved, the problem of turning his mind from one country to another. David was gratified that the Americans were prepared to entrust him with this formidable responsibility. He was confident that his associates at London Weekend would share his pride and his joy.

Back in London he asked Richard Armitage, the quick-thinking, fast-moving agent who had first introduced him to show business and who had become his closest adviser, to inform London Weekend of the American proposition. As far as London was concerned, there would be no immediate change in his operation. As a major shareholder and star performer, London Weekend could rely on his services.

On the morning of the Friday following the Fort Lauderdale talks, Richard Armitage called on Michael Peacock, the ex-B.B.C. executive then in charge of London Weekend Television. By the evening of that day Armitage—and David Frost—had Peacock's reply. It was simply, "No!" Peacock rejected David's arrangement outright.

To David this reaction came as a complete surprise. He was shattered. Over the transatlantic telephone he warned Chet Collier of the difficulties ahead. "He sounded pretty depressed," Chet Collier remembered. For David a battle loomed in which he had a stake on both sides.

Even in the face of Peacock's categorical rejection, Richard Armitage skillfully managed to keep the talks going. Peacock seemed to be behaving more like a program controller than a managing director. "We invited him to look at the situation in a wider context" is how Armitage politely put it. Surely this was not a question of a performer for hire. The problem ought to be judged in terms of London Weekend Television as a whole. The American deal could only raise the prestige and the economic value of their man.

With Jenny Logan by his side, David spent Friday and the best part of Saturday at Egerton Crescent, hugging the telephone. He was like the spider in the center of the web. Although keeping aloof from the talks, except for one meeting on Saturday morning, he was in touch at every stage of the proceedings, but recently he said, "Richard did it all."

On Saturday night Armitage telephoned, but David was out. Where was he? Joan Pugh, who shares most of his secrets, could not say. Nobody knew. For three hours David was missing. He had, in fact, escaped to a cinema with Jenny Logan to see *Rosemary's Baby*, perhaps not the most enjoyable film in the circumstances. That the film took place in America only aggravated

David's despondency about the last-minute hitch. "The thought that there should be something in the way of my American plans was almost unbearable," he confessed.

Sunday brought no relief from the pressure. For David the only satisfaction was that the talks were going on. Armitage went to Peacock's house in Barnes, a London suburb. Peacock kept harping on the point that there was no guarantee that David would be on time for his show—the vagaries of air travel! Armitage countered that it was not a matter of permitting an artist to arrive a little late. He implored Peacock to take the wider view.

A total breakdown was a menacing possibility. There was little time for contingency planning, but David naturally pondered whether the Americans could possibly be persuaded to agree to him taping three shows per day so as to give him a wider margin for his London timetable. A private jet was hired, and the pilot was asked to stand by. The plan was that if Peacock could not be made to yield, David and his lawyer would fly to the United States to talk to Westinghouse and seek a way out.

David was not throwing in the sponge, however; he never does. "David," said Ned Sherrin, "learns from his mistakes without admitting that he had made them." David also overcomes every crisis without admitting that it ever existed. One by one, he telephoned the men who had secured the London Weekend franchise—by virtue of his initiative, acumen, and hard work if the truth be told. One by one, they came around to his point of view. They told Peacock in effect, "You can't deny David such an opportunity and expect unbounded enthusiasm from him," and asked him to renegotiate.

The pressure was on Peacock now, and the gloom began to lift from the Frost headquarters in Knightsbridge. Assured of the support of his friends, David questioned whether Peacock actually had the power to stop him from appearing in the United States. Surely not! What had to be achieved was an arrangement acceptable to both sides.

On Monday Richard Armitage had breakfast with London Weekend chairman Aidan Crawley and gave him a detailed account of the two conflicting positions. What mattered was that David knew he could manage the two jobs both physically and intellectually. Late in the afternoon the two negotiating sides faced each other at the London Weekend offices. John Stutter joined Richard Armitage; Michael Peacock had the counsel of Cyril Bennett, controller of programs, and other executives.

After that meeting Armitage and Peacock adjourned once more to Barnes to continue the talks in the privacy of Peacock's study. The tide was clearly turning, and Frost could sniff the sweet smell of victory in the air. Peacock finally withdrew his objections, and there remained only the chore of discussing details and developing a few points of principle (options, compensation in case of cancellations, and similar items), enough work to keep the lawyers busy for weeks completing the bulky contract.

Richard Armitage drove back to Egerton Crescent. As he stepped into the big drawing room on the first floor, David's eyes, those quizzical, searching, steady, confident eyes, were on him. "Well," Armitage said, "we tried—and we succeeded!"

"Champagne!" said David.

The problem was resolved, the passage across the Atlantic clear. Had David made the right decision? In the hour of triumph a hundred conflicting thoughts raced through his mind. The new situation required a profound readjustment.

He looked tense and tired, quite unlike his smooth and cheerful self as seen on a million television screens. Emerging from his house, he climbed into the big blue Bentley. Bob Lambert, as much a companion as a chauffeur, took the wheel. "Just drive," David said. They had gone some way before he was more specific. He wanted to go to Westminster Abbey's little Saint Faith Chapel, which is reserved for private prayer. The chapel, just off Poet's Corner—the part of the abbey with Chaucer's tomb and Shakespeare's bust—was closed, however, and he returned to the car.

On the way back they passed the Scottish Presbyterian St. Columba's Church on Pont Street, and David asked his driver to stop. This was not the first time he was seeking solitude in a church. "I wanted to meditate," David recalled.

"He went to pray!" his mother said firmly.

Praying and meditating went very much together. At this moment, though, there was pandemonium in the House of God in which he had hoped to find guidance and clear his mind. Looking back on a major turning point in his career, David smiled: "It was a Monday morning, and the cleaners were sweeping the floors and chattering, the organ was being repaired—there was not much peace in that church."

Nonetheless, he achieved his meditation. "You can think anywhere," he said. And pray. The prayer settled David's destiny for years ahead. He committed half his professional life to the United States of America and turned himself into a complete transatlantic man.

In the turmoil of these fateful days Jenny's company was reassuring and soothing. "You have been a great source of strength during this weekend," he told her.

"Yes," Jenny replied with a melancholy air. "I am helping you towards something that is going to take you away from me." Perceptive and unselfish, it was a remark typical of the girl who had shared David's life for so long—on and off for four years, during which they had parted but returned to each other several times. Was this the end?

CHAPTER 15

Mounting a Talk Show

To MOUNT A SHOW such as David visualized and Westing-house expected was a formidable undertaking. David started from scratch, and the first thing he needed was a secretary. In the early stage of preparations his U.S. agent, Gary Nardino, gave him office space and also lend-leased him his clever secretary, Cate Ryan, who soon joined David full time and has been Joan Pugh's opposite number in New York ever since.

As a base David chose the Commodore Hotel, establishing temporary offices in a suite of rooms. He asked his two London cronies, Peter Baker and Neil Shand, to come to New York to help him launch the *David Frost Show*, Peter as producer and Neil as "creative consultant." The show was beginning to take shape.

David reveled in the work. As Richard Armitage often says, "He loves setting up things, launching new projects." Another hotel, the Lombardy, on East Fifty-sixth Street, became his private residence; he lived there in a seventh-floor three-room apartment with the slightly disorganized atmosphere of a bachelor pad until he moved into the Plaza Hotel in June, 1971.

By March, 1969, the operation was in full swing. Don McGannon was assigning some top executives to the show. Over the telephone he told David Henderson, who was running the Westinghouse television station in Baltimore, Maryland, that David Frost would be taking over from Merv Griffin. Henderson was doubtful. "I don't think Frost can make it" was his first reaction. Don McGannon was unperturbed. He appointed Henderson executive vice-president of Group W Productions (he has since become president), which would administer the show, and told him, "David Frost is your baby now."

David, Chet, Peter, and Neil were looking for an associate producer to deal with light entertainment when it became known that Bob Carman, an experienced television man, was casting round for a new assignment. Carman, who had been associated with Jack Paar and Joey Bishop, was planning to settle in California, where a call reached him to come to New York for a talk. "Though I had seen David Frost briefly on *TW3* in 1965 when I was with Jack Paar," Carman said, "I had never met him. I liked what I had seen of him, but frankly, it seemed problematic to me whether an Englishman would last in a job like this." After discussing the matter with Chet Collier, he met David for the first time: "I found he was a man of great warmth—open, well-balanced, enthusiastic." Carman signed on as associate producer but was still not sure whether it would work. "I moved to New York but left my family in California," he said.

Although interviews with people of substance would be the hard core of the *David Frost Show*, music would be an important ingredient. David remembered the music Billy Taylor had written for the American *TW3* pilot show four years earlier. Where was he now? Billy was program director of WLIB radio station and was doing a radio show, broadcasting for some seven hours a day. "I received a call to meet David Frost," he said. The meeting took place at Paul Marshall's offices. "David asked me whether I would be interested in forming a group for the show," said Taylor.

Plans seemed as yet to be fluid, and David told him, "I am not knowledgeable about music at all—in fact, I am to music what Noel Coward is to prizefighting. But when I listen to music, certain things register."

They talked about opera singers, pop stars, all kinds of personalities from the world of music who might appear on the show. The group would have to be capable of playing many different styles. "I was attracted by the thought of the tremendous variety of a show like this," Billy recalled, "but I had a good job with ample scope." Still, in principle, he was interested.

By the third week of March "Operation David Frost" entered

another phase. Westinghouse arranged for David to introduce himself to the National Association of Broadcasters with a special show at the Shoreham Hotel, Washington. David Henderson remembers their first encounter, when they were introduced on the steps of the hotel. "I found David very gracious, very out-going," he recalls. Although they did not have a chance for a long talk, the Frost charm was beginning to work on Henderson.

That evening British Ambassador John Freeman gave a recep-tion for David at the Embassy. From there it was back to the Shoreham Hotel, where David entertained an expert audience with a brisk routine in the style of his nightclub acts. It was a big success.

Next morning at a special breakfast David gave a number of Westinghouse executives his thoughts on the show and explained that it was his intention to conduct it much as he ran his London program—interviews with top people from every sector of Ameri-can life: top politicians, top performers, top personalities in the news. "On that morning I realized there was more to that man than I had assumed," Henderson confessed. "Frost seemed to have all the characteristics of a first-class talk-show host, a much greater dimension than *TW3* suggested. He was not a one-line comic and had more to offer than I thought a host could bring. I was much happier."

The next stage in David's promotion was a series of presenta-tions around the country. In ballrooms all over America broad-casters, show-business personalities, civic officials, were enter-tained by him. He repeated his Washington performance in Chi-cago, Dallas, San Francisco, and New York and talked to adver-tising people at a series of breakfasts.

"The warmth with which he was received was the first clue to his future success," Henderson said. "During that time we came to the conclusion that all Englishmen were not stuffy, did not wear top hats, and did not drink tea in the afternoon." The doubting Henderson was converted into a firm believer in David Frost.

At the New York party at the Royal Box of the Americana Hotel Billy Taylor, who had just joined Frost, and his newly formed band of eleven played their own version of David's theme song (composed by George Martin). In the passage of time the musical director of the *David Frost Show* has rendered the tune in many different styles.

In the meantime David was assembling his team. Walter Kempley, thousand-dollar-a-week writer on Johnny Carson's *Tonight* show, was recruited at a substantially higher rate; the figure mentioned was thirteen hundred dollars. (He has since gone on to other pastures.) Jonathan Reynolds, former assistant to Senator Eugene McCarthy, John Berendt, ex-*Esquire* and *Holiday* editor, and Jeanne Vanderbilt, a knowledgeable "society" insider, were among those who joined David. Altogether there were four talent-bookers and three writers. Peter Baker and Neil Shand were expected to inject journalistic realism, which was sorely lacking in American talk shows.

In a parallel endeavor Westinghouse canvassed American television stations, offering tapes of the *David Frost Show* at rates ranging from five hundred dollars a week for small stations to fifteen thousand dollars or more for bigger outfits like KTTV in Los Angeles and WNEW in New York. By the time the show went on the air, it was being syndicated to thirty-seven stations, but their number increased rapidly and soon included almost all the fifty key stations that are the industry's yardstick of success. A three-year projection that Westinghouse mapped out envisaged the show equaling, if not exceeding, the syndication figure of the departing *Merv Griffin Show*. By the end of 1970 they were well on the way to achieving this target.

The technical arrangements were for the show to be taped in New York a few days ahead of the screening date, the master tape to be flown to the Westinghouse television station in Pittsburgh, and the duplicates made there to be distributed nationwide. Metromedia's *Allen Ludden Gallery* staked a rival claim for the 8:30 to 10 P.M. peak time in New York, but it was soon warded off. This was the slot allocated to David's show, other stations to run it at their own convenience.

The advent of "The Great Briton" was widely advertised, but his name was not given. David's identity was only revealed when he appeared as a guest on the *Merv Griffin Show* on July 1 and again, three days later, on Merv's last day as a Westinghouse host. As Merv vacated The Little Theatre on Forty-fourth Street and took over the Cort Theatre four blocks away, the *David Frost*

Show moved in. David's office was on the third floor, and the staff was installed in the rather cramped premises on the second floor, mostly small cubicles along narrow passages up and down dark stairs. The big staircase leading down to the studio bore the footprints of long lines of slim chorus girls who used to trip down from their dressing rooms to the stage below when the building still served the living theater.

The stage, at ground level, was designed to David's own specifications. The low perch on which he insisted enabled him to get close to the studio audience if not actually to join it. He likes to think of himself as host and audience in one. He refused to have a sidekick—"No second banana," he said, pronouncing it the English way before correcting himself—like Ed McMahon (with Johnny Carson) or Arthur Treacher (then with Merv Griffin).

The only stage props were two swivel chairs, more if there was more than one guest. David quickly did away with the big desk, stock-in-trade of other talk-show hosts, and also dispensed with the traditional sofa on which they seat their guests side by side. A movable backdrop was installed to hide Billy Taylor's band from view. There was room for an audience of 450, some of them invited because of their special interest in the topic of the day.

The date for the unveiling of the *David Frost Show* was set for the beginning of July. David and his team started to prepare a stockpile of interviews and, so as to leave nothing to chance, decided to tape some shows on familiar English home ground. Westinghouse did not know for sure what they were getting while David worked without his employers looking over his shoulder. It did not turn out as smoothly as he had hoped.

In May, with his eyes fixed firmly on his debut, David flew to Britain for an appointment with Prince Charles. To bring the heir to the British throne to American screens would be a rare attraction, and Charles's investiture as Prince of Wales—the first since that of his predecessor, now the Duke of Windsor—fortuitously coincided with the inauguration of the *David Frost Show*. The Prince was booked for an interview with David.

The enterprise was mounted as a full-length color film, eventually to be shown all over the world. To meet the Prince David traveled to Newbridge-on-the-Wye, in the heart of Wales. In Llysdinam Hall, the suitably aristocratic home of Brigadier Sir

Michael Venables-Llewellyn, Lord Lieutenant of Radnorshire, a
drawing room had been turned into a studio. Big film cameras
were in position, strong lights installed.

Prince and interviewer settled down in front of the fireplace,
Charles on a big settee, David in a spacious easy chair. The circumstances of the talk were auspicious. David likes young people,
and the Prince has an easy down-to-earth manner, inherited from
the Duke of Edinburgh, and an unpompous natural dignity like
that of his mother, the Queen. Charles was also a Frost fan of
long standing.

He was told the questions David proposed to ask, but the confrontation became an informal exchange rather than an interview.
Charles talked freely about his earliest memories ("sitting in a
pram") and about some of his youthful escapades ("wandering
about on the roof of Windsor Castle"). The conversation turned
to Cambridge, the alma mater they had in common, royalty and
duty, royalty and money ("There aren't many occasions when we
need it").

When it touched on Charles's stage performances at Cambridge University, David asked, "Were you Macbeth?" The
Prince said he was, and David told him, "I was only Banquo, so
they could kill me off in the third act."

"You have never visited America?" David remarked. The
Prince recalled that he had spent one hour in New York and one
hour in San Francisco. "Both times," he said, "I just saw hundreds
of policemen and hundreds of photographers and was led from
one waiting room to another and on to the inside of one of those
sausages that attach to the airplane. That was all." Of course, he
wanted to see America (he and his sister, Princess Anne, have
since been President Nixon's guests at a young people's party at
the White House), but although he had no particular desire to
see a baseball game, he said he'd like to see a cattle ranch in the
Midwest, the South possibly, and parts of New England where
the Pilgrim fathers first landed.

David brought the interview to an end with a characteristic
remark. "I couldn't have enjoyed it more," he said. When shown
in England, the film produced one comment of the kind to which
David reacts in sorrow rather than in anger. "Prince Charles out-
smarts and outshines David Frost," a reviewer wrote, as if the
interviewer ought to have tried to score off the Prince.

The Frost team in New York, in the meantime, working on the fringe attractions for the show, encountered a few minor difficulties. When Bob Carman asked American showbiz people to come on the *David Frost Show*, the answer frequently was, "The What show? How do you spell it?"

"F-r-o-s-t," Bob spelled, explaining patiently that a new star was rising on the American talk-show scene. It was a passing phase. David, in turn, back in the thick of it in New York, was none too familiar with the names of showbiz people other than international stars.

What surprised Bob Carman and Billy Taylor was David's reaction to these teething troubles. He did not try to cover up his ignorance with bluster or avoid areas with which he was not acquainted. "He was unfamiliar with the musical scene and did not instantly know who was available and who was not, but he was perfectly willing to learn," said Billy Taylor. "He was prepared to listen and to rely on my judgment."

He learned quickly. During these days one of David's London associates told a story of a train trip they had made together. "I expected David to bring some highbrow publications to read on the journey," the man said. "Instead he bought *Melody Maker*, a pop artists' mag." It was said contemptuously, but reading pop magazines in Britain and in the United States provided David with information that was often useful in his work.

Extramural activities demanded rapid changes of scene. Arriving in London by scheduled airliner, David switched to a private plane for Newcastle, whence a car took him to Whitby, another fifty miles away. The reason for this costly dash was to inaugurate a new manse in his sister's home town and to read the lesson from the pulpit of the Methodist church in Sleights.

Within hours he was back in London to work on his stockpile for New York. One show he prepared was a visit to 10 Downing Street, where Mary Wilson conducted him round the Prime Minister's residence in the style of Jackie Kennedy's television tour of the White House a few years earlier. Other interviews David taped were with Rex Harrison and John Lennon.

He worked for America in England and for England in America. To penetrate the mysteries of the forthcoming American moon shot—or find out as much as he needed to host a program on the moon shot on commercial television in England—he traveled to Houston, Texas, and spent a day in the fabulous astro-world of Mission Control for Apollo Eleven. This was one of the experiences that made his work so gratifying.

His free weekends were no less energetic. The beach and the house in Bridgehampton, Long Island, which he shared with Clay Felker reverberated with his vigorous activities. One Sunday he went fishing and caught ninety-four bluefish in three and a half hours. Other weekends were spent in even more strenuous exercise.

Encountering a group of youngsters playing soccer, David quickly insinuated himself into their team. He abandoned his books, papers, and scripts and joined his new friends in a game against local opponents. "Who won?" Clay Felker asked when David returned with a flushed face.

"We did," was the proud answer, "six to three." Did he score any of the goals? "All six!"

The house in Bridgehampton was rarely without guests. Ambassador John Freeman and his family came to spend a vacation, and David's mother flew in from England for her first visit to the United States. (It was not long before her son's American fans started to write her letters addressed to "David Frost's Mum, England," which were duly delivered to her at Beccles.)

Another visitor to Long Island was Jenny Logan, although she and David were no longer seeing as much of one another as they had. "We realized there were more 'good-byes' than 'hellos' in store for us," David said. He spent most of his time in New York deeply involved with the debut of his show, which was almost upon him.

Westinghouse executives were keeping their fingers crossed. "New shows always bring hazards," Chet Collier said later. "Difficulties in the beginning are something you expect, but you still hope they might not happen."

David himself seemed nervous, giving his colleagues the impression that he was wrestling with problems. He obviously realized the magnitude of his undertaking, a much bigger proposition than his London shows, none of which ran longer than fifty minutes. Five ninety-minute shows a week—a total of seven and a half hours on camera—and the need to cope with commercial breaks at ten-minute intervals required considerable readjustment.

Gregarious at most times, David now preferred to keep his own company. He did not seem overeager to go down to the studio, where the first few shows were being put together—in the most elementary sense of the expression. There was no cause to worry about the ingredients, which were first class. The difficulty arose when it came to welding them together into homogeneous shows. Also, the temptation to make a spectacular start by firing off all the big guns at once carried with it the risk of being left empty-handed before long.

After a good deal of heart-searching, four rather disparate items were selected for the opening show. One was the interview with Prince Charles; another was a conversation between David and Ed Sullivan, host of the C.B.S. Sunday-evening variety hour ("Why have you never married?" Ed asked David, who promptly replied: "You present variety, and I enjoy it!"). A third item was a snippet introducing the Rolling Stones.

The pièce de résistance was a discussion about the Women's Liberation movement, with participation by partisans and opponents strategically placed in the audience. When Lionel Tiger, author of *Men in Groups,* took his place opposite David, a number of embattled females upped and walked out in protest. This was lively television, but the discussion between the sexes which followed did not catch fire. David's monologues linking the items sounded disjointed.

Heralded by a shower of publicity, the show was finally unveiled for viewers on July 7, 1969, and David was eagerly awaiting press reactions. The first newspaper he picked up was *The New York Times,* which carried a review by Jack Gould. "If there is one rule applying to television talk shows," Gould started out, "it is never to reach a very firm judgment on the basis of only one outing." He nevertheless suggested that David Frost appeared to be suffering from Americanized inhibitions. "He was a visitor in search of a format," Gould wrote, "seldom very amusing, and deferential enough to be an assistant to a television vice president."

Television vice-president Chet Collier was not dismayed. "It was a mistake to bring material with him, because it had no continuity," he said, "but we were sure we had the right man in David. What we had to do was to put things right around him."

David was also philosophical. "The critical reception was

mixed—that's a euphemism for bad," he said, but added as if speaking to himself: "You have to be certain that it is going to work, that you will make it work!" He kept his nerve. Anyway, Gould had added that he intended to take a second look when the show had settled down.

By that time David was in Los Angeles, and his second show was on the air, a rather sensational interview with Adam Clayton Powell. Living up to his reputation, David pursued his elusive quarry with the doggedness of a British terrier. The show truly erupted when Powell claimed to have evidence that the assassination of Martin Luther King was the work of a conspiracy. "I have facts, I have facts," Powell exclaimed.

"I don't think," Frost retorted firmly, "you can go on to say you have evidence of a conspiracy, that's all. Unless you can give more facts of where the money [for Martin Luther King's assassin] came from——"

Powell: "I know where it came from, and I will not tell you. But when we leave here, I'll tell you."

Frost: "No, no, no. Don't let's have private chats. Let's talk to the people!"

Powell: "No, no."

Frost: "You said they've got a right to know. Tell them!" There was applause, which grew stronger when Frost warned Powell, "You're getting away from the question."

David was not easily put off. "You're talking rubbish," he told Powell at one stage. "If this is important and you know, speak. Either it's unimportant, or you don't know. Which is it?"

Powell: "I'll shut my mouth."

Frost: "If you do know, and you are shutting your mouth, that's the most irresponsible thing you have ever done."

Such exchanges were new to American television. It was a riveting show. The Los Angeles *Times* reflected popular reaction. "Amid the torrents of trivia that flow from television's nightly talk shows," Cecil Smith wrote, "the new David Frost dialogues are like rare beefsteak in a marshmallow sundae world." Mr. Smith praised David for his determination to get answers, for not allowing himself to be diverted by the old ploy of changing the subject, and for being as "persistent as a dentist's drill." If he was indeed cut up about the criticism, this was balm on David's wounds.

He was due to tape an interview with Dean Acheson. His distinguished guest arrived at the studio with a forty-minute opening statement, which he proposed to read. "It wasn't quite the format of the show," David recalled.

Gently he explained to the former secretary of state that conversation, not prepared speeches, was the characteristic of the *David Frost Show*. With some effort Dean Acheson was persuaded to abandon his statement, but there were new complications. David's guest was not conversant with the routine of television, and when told that there would be periodic breaks for commercials, asked, "Do you mean they are coming to stand in front of me and sell things?"

The *David Frost Show* was getting into its stride. Change of pace, change of subject, surprise, and spontaneity were the keynotes, even though the stockpile was not yet exhausted. Before the first week was out, Tommy Steele had joked his way across the screen, Israeli leaders Golda Meir and Moshe Dayan talked earnestly about the Middle East struggles, and John Lennon and Yoko Ono made their bow. On the last show of the week it was Rex Harrison's turn.

Another three weeks, and David Frost received an extraordinary piece of praise. Jack Gould was as good as his word. He offered his second thoughts on the show. "His premiere clearly had been thrown together to meet a deadline and was atypical," *The New York Times* critic commented. David, he said, had since introduced the element of intuitive reportorial curiosity and had provided an agreeable and sophisticated alternative to Johnny Carson, Merv Griffin, and Joey Bishop. Gould particularly liked the manner in which David brought out Mary Wilson's deep interest in poetry and remarked on his skillful handling of another guest, Dr. Benjamin Spock, who told David that the pendulum might have swung too far in the direction of permissiveness. In Jack Gould's opinion the advent of David Frost (and Dick Cavett) upgraded the talk shows in tone and content.

The novelty of David's approach was being welcomed on all sides. Viewers' letters bore the critics out. "Merv Who?" one new fan wrote. "The David Frost Show had wit, élan, and intellectuality that Griffin could not touch!"

As David basked in his American triumph, London called—on two wavelengths. Another series of the *Frost Programme* was due, and in view of the impending German general elections David decided to open it with an interview with Adolf von Thadden, leader of an extreme right-wing party with Nazi overtones, who was campaigning for a large vote to carry him into the Bonn Parliament. A Von Thadden success, observers predicted, would bring another "night of long knives" in German politics. A meeting in a German provincial city between David and the man who has been called a latter-day Adolf was arranged.

Other news from London was disturbing. Trouble was brewing at London Weekend Television, which had ended the first year's operations with a loss of one million pounds. This had been anticipated, but all was not well in overall terms. The board called for the resignation of Michael Peacock as managing director. Six program executives resigned out of personal loyalty to Peacock and in the belief—mistaken, as it turned out—that programs were about to be interfered with. Programs, in fact, remained the province of Cyril Bennett (and later Stella Richman). It was on Peacock's performance as chief executive that the board had made its headline-grabbing judgment. Meanwhile, television people talked about the sudden revolution at London Weekend.

At the last moment David changed his mind. Instead of flying from New York to meet Von Thadden in Germany, he altered course and made for London, where the Battle of Wembley (London Weekend's headquarters) was in full swing. For David it was a matter of "the show must go on." To celebrate his return to the British screens, London Weekend announced a party—"If they can get the bloodstains off the carpet, that is," one observer remarked.

Busy in New York, David had not been involved in the decision to oust Peacock, though he strongly supported it. To succeed Peacock the board appointed Dr. Tom Margerison, the scientist-journalist turned television executive. David was going on with two shows a week in London, the first to go out live and in color, in addition, of course, to his five days for Group W Productions in New York.

In spite of this punishing schedule his work on other projects continued unabated. One to which he devoted much thought was an idea for a show by Ronnie Barker, author and star of many Frost quickies, which appeared most promising, although it seemed too long for television and too short for a film. At his Claridge House offices David discussed the project with Richard Armitage and his Paradine Productions general manager, George Brightwell. As he commuted to the United States the conversations were continued over the transatlantic telephone: "We were talking to David at the rate of five hundred dollars a week," Armitage recalled. Finally David decided to finance the project out of his own funds and take a gamble, investing more than would normally be put into a television show and turning the venture into a film. "We allocated a budget of around fifty thousand pounds," said Armitage.

There were problems. Bob Kellet, who was producing and directing, could not find a studio to fit in with the small budget. After a long search he discovered a house some twenty miles from London and rented it for a fortnight. "It was a tour de force," according to Armitage. The result was *Futtock's End,* a film starring Ronnie Barker, all effects and music without the spoken word, which was shown as a television special in the United States. Offered to movie theaters as a film, it became a big distribution success and earned more than double the investment.

Among those booked for David's London shows were Paul Newman and Tiny Tim, who did not really warrant the suggestion that David's American slip was showing. Tiny Tim, in any case, redressed the American balance by rendering in his unique falsetto a song after David's own heart: "There'll Always Be an England!" In New York the Archbishop of Canterbury came on the show and appeared no better acquainted with television proceedings than Dean Acheson had been. "Why are we taking a break?" he asked David.

He promptly replied, "They're short semireligious rituals we have."

Westinghouse was once more gathering the faithful for a conference in London. One of their parties was held at Madame Tussaud's, where a waxen image of David Frost was unveiled. "Seriously," David quipped, "it's a wonderful addition to the Chamber of Horrors." David Frost—the one in wax—joined the Queen, Edward Heath, Harold Wilson, and the Pope in this peculiarly British Hall of Fame.

CHAPTER 16

"You're Smashing"

IN MAY, 1970, David Frost took his team to the Coast to tape a number of shows in Hollywood. "We had a lineup of guests which included Jack Benny, Carol Burnett, and George Burns," he recalled. He had a brief reunion with Carol Lynley, with whom he was seen in public once or twice, often enough to start the obligatory rumors of marriage plans, which he promptly denied.

It was neither his shows nor his rendezvous with Carol that made this Hollywood visit a memorable occasion for him. An alert gossip columnist spotted him with a girl friend at the Now Grove of the Ambassador Hotel, where Diahann Carroll was appearing. David had never met the talented, beautiful star of nightclubs, film, and television who made her debut in the films *Carmen Jones* and *Porgy and Bess*, became "Julia" in the long-running television series of that name, and has no rival as a diva of floor shows.

Looking even more alluring than on the screen, Diahann, she of the delicate features and the smoldering temperament, gave her usual sophisticated performance, captivating the audience—including David. When told that he was watching the show, she sent a note asking him to have a drink with her in her suite, the usual courtesy from one star to another. David and his friend joined Diahann, who was with her agent, Roy Gerber, and other members of her entourage. "We immediately hit it off in conversation," David said a little dreamily, "and decided to go to dinner—Diahann, her date, my girl friend, and I."

They went to Bumbles, the discotheque, and played pool. There was a mutual attraction between Diahann and David but no word, no specific exchange, between them. The only conversation was one that tacitly acknowledged the situation.

David asked her, "Will you be coming to New York? You must come and do the show!" It was almost like a code, an assignation for the future. The party did not break up until 3 A.M.

After that there was a complete fadeout. David returned to New York and his hectic routine, but his thoughts kept turning back to the Hollywood encounter. Some weeks later, associate producer Bob Carman told him that Creative Management Associates had relayed the information that "the great Diahann Carroll" was coming to New York. Though she never did talk shows, she would be happy to come on the *David Frost Show*. Bob was surprised and delighted. David was delighted but not so surprised. Thursday, June 11, was fixed as the date for the interview.

It coincided with a unique week in David's life. On Monday, June 8, he flew to Boston to appear as commencement-day speaker at Emerson College, which conferred a Doctor of Laws degree upon him. His adroit interviews with entertainers, statesmen, and people from all walks of life had brought a new focus to the world of television, the citation said, and quoted a piece about David Frost by Ben Gross, the dean of American television critics: "With a seemingly gentle hand, but one that is never side-tracked from its target, he relentlessly cuts, digs and removes layer after layer of the protective surface until the inner man is revealed." These probings into the minds and hearts of his television guests had made him the most influential and acclaimed interviewer on the air.

The applause had hardly died down when David was on his way to receive an even greater accolade. That same evening he was at New York City's Carnegie Hall, attending a ceremony that (along with a simultaneous ceremony in Los Angeles) was shown nationwide on television. All eyes were on him as Dinah Shore, with Jimmy Durante assisting, made the announcement that the National Academy of Television Arts and Sciences had awarded him the golden Emmy statuette (television's Oscar) for his show, which was judged the outstanding series in its category for the 1969–1970 season.

David was visibly moved. "The honor leaves me speechless," he muttered at long last, "which is something that is not supposed to happen to talk-show hosts." He thanked his associates and the television industry: "This has to be the friendliest industry there is! You're smashing!" ("It is a substantial achievement at the end of his show's first full year," the *Times* of London commented.)

Three days later at the appointed time, Diahann Carroll presented herself at The Little Theatre in New York and faced David in the studio. They were having their first private conversation—in front of millions. Diahann was vivacious and amusing as she looked back, for David's benefit, on her early life and her first public appearance—in a child's choir in Adam Clayton Powell's Harlem church. She recalled how, a few years later, she was awarded a scholarship to study singing: "It interfered with my greatest aspiration . . . to become a champion roller skater." She laughed. "Will you join me in a whirl on skates?" she asked David.

"That's one way to get violence on stage," David countered. He accepted the challenge, but fortunately for him the skates did not fit, and he was not put to the test.

In a more pensive mood, Diahann reflected on herself as a black artist and the prejudices she encountered. She spoke about her close relationship with her parents and her daughter and about the possibility of a second marriage. The personal character of this conversation on the air was quite obvious to onlookers and critics alike. Commenting on the interview in the Los Angeles *Times*, Joyce Haber suggested that never had such electricity been generated between two people since that great movie *A Man and a Woman*. "The mutual attraction on the air was so evident," according to David, "that people asked whether we were going out together."

After the show he and Diahann went out for supper. The following evening, Friday, June 12, David had to fly to London for a business meeting, which took place on Saturday morning. He was not staying a minute longer than necessary. In the afternoon he was on his way back to New York—and Diahann. They went to Le Pavillon, which was packed that night, and the private dinner became public knowledge.

That day it was announced from Buckingham Palace that the

Queen had awarded David Frost the Order of the British Empire. To round off an amazing sequence David was shortly after invited to Washington to receive yet another award, this one in special communications, from the Religious Heritage of America, an interfaith organization for the preservation of religious freedom. That was a brief period that stood out in a year in which David was flying higher than ever—and not only by jet. The *David Frost Show* was already an institution. Celebrity after celebrity occupied the chair opposite David in the studio. By the end of 1970 the number of prominent personalities who had accepted the compliment—or submitted to the ordeal—of appearing with David Frost was well over fifteen hundred.

In July, 1971, Diahann Carroll returned to the *David Frost Show* as guest hostess. With great professional skill she talked to composer Richard Rodgers, who first launched her on her singing and acting career. They recalled the events that led to her part in *No Strings*: "You were the inspiration that made me write and produce the show," Rodgers confessed. Diahann was quite as successful as David himself in drawing out her guest: "Once I introduced another composer's song into one of my shows," Rodgers said. "It was the best song in the show!" The other composer: Irving Berlin.

To return to 1970—preparing a new book as a record of his American dialogues, David was hard pressed to find room enough even for the highlights. This instructive volume, *The Americans*, could only skim the cream. His first eighteen months as a talk-show host, however, were also punctuated by behind-the-scenes happenings known only to insiders. They throw a light on the origin and background of some of his shows.

There was David in the early days of the show, lunching at Sardi's, as he still frequently does, and spying two friends at a nearby table. "Hello, Gayle! Hello, David!" he greeted namesake David Hemmings, star of *Blow-Up*, and his wife, Gayle Hunnicut, who were having a quick bite before catching an early afternoon plane to London. "How about coming on the show?" Frost suggested.

The couple demurred: "We'd miss our flight." David pressed them ("He is a difficult man to say 'No' to," producer Peter Baker commented), and they were persuaded to postpone their departure. They accompanied David to the studio next door to tape an interview. As a little extra he offered a painting by Hemmings for auction, received a bid of thirty dollars from the audience, and doubled the sum.

The ad-hoc invitation to the two was one of the many occasions on which David recruits prominent guests while on his social outings; some of his friends insist that this is the real reason for his excursions into the night life of New York, Las Vegas, or Los Angeles. His recruiting drive never stops. When he meets Aristotle Onassis in New York or London, they often lunch together. Invariably David asks Ari, "How about coming on the show?"

"Yes, of course," Ari answers, but it has not happened yet. It will.

Since then David has brought off a scoop by getting Maria Callas to talk about her friendship with Onassis, which she had hitherto steadfastly refused to do in public—if not in private— conversation. On David's show she discussed Ari with surprising frankness: "I have never met her," she said, referring to Jackie Onassis. "It's not wanted on the other side," La Callas said, but she added that her friendship with Ari had survived his marriage. As far as her own marriage was concerned, she announced publicly for the first time her intention to seek a divorce once the new rules on divorce in Italy became law.

Early in the *David Frost Show* Hubert Humphrey came in for a second interview. The talk flowed freely, and as is his practice, David kept it going while there were topics of high interest on the agenda. The former Vice-President was critical of President Nixon for not following through on President Johnson's plans for a summit talk with the Soviet premier. "I understand Mr. Johnson wanted the summit meeting," David said, "and checked with President-elect Nixon, who said, 'Please don't.'"

"I am sure that is true," Humphrey replied. Expansive and stimulating, Humphrey stayed on the air longer than expected. Other guests booked for the show were kept waiting.

It so happened that they were not the only ones who were cooling their heels. Hubert Humphrey, who had arranged to appear on the *Merv Griffin Show* that same day, was still deeply involved with David by the time he was supposed to be meeting Griffin. Did David know, was he deliberately prolonging the

talk—and the agony of the Griffin camp? "Certainly not!" he said
with brisk finality.

Another interview with a piquant background was Ned Sherrin's appearance on the show. Television people thought there
was a rift between David and the man acclaimed as his discov-
erer, but though their professional outlooks no longer harmo-
nized, their personal relations remained intact. Sherrin was in
New York for the premiere of his film, *The Virgin Soldiers*, and
there was no better publicity than an interview with David Frost.
"David was most generous in asking me on the show," Ned Sherrin said. The interview recalled their old times together, *TW3*,
and all that. "It was a curious feeling," Sherrin remarked later,
"the two of us facing each other in the studio and going over all
this on the air."

Things were going well at The Little Theatre and David was
the first to acknowledge it. "Soon after the beginning of the
show," Billy Taylor said, "David took me aside and told me I had
delivered what he expected. That made me feel good. It was the
first time in a long career that I got the stamp of approval that
quickly from anyone."

David was still struggling with the intricacies of the musical
scene. He asked Duke Ellington to come on the show and
searched for a novel way of presenting him. "Why not get Willie
'The Lion' Smith on with the Duke?" Taylor suggested.

"Willie 'The Lion' who?" David queried. Billy Taylor explained
that Willie was one of Duke Ellington's friends and early influences. "Let's ask him, then," David said in agreement. Three
pianos were put on the stage, and the three—Duke Ellington,
Willie "The Lion," and Billy Taylor—played and talked.

Not much later Billy persuaded David to invite Roberta Flack,
a girl singer from his hometown, Washington, D. C., who had
just made her first record and, Billy thought, had a great future.
David was willing, and that is how Roberta was "discovered."
"She never looked back," Billy Taylor said.

It was not long before David was involved in a musical inter-
mezzo that revealed the chink in his armor. Danny Kaye was at
his hilarious best in a knockabout interview with David. They
were getting on famously until Danny asked his host to join in a
song and suggested "Hello, Dolly." David would have none of it,

but Danny insisted, the band struck up, and an embarrassed David Frost mouthed the words, for once making sure that the microphone did not pick up the faintest sound of his toneless singing voice. "The American public has done nothing to deserve that," he explained.

He was obviously happier with weightier subjects, such as Jacqueline Susann's literary stature. David's interview with the author of the best-selling *Valley of the Dolls* and, more recently, *The Love Machine* commanded a good deal of attention. Three eminent critics shared the stage with her, and David started the proceedings by asking where she placed herself in a literary sense: high, in the middle, or wherever?

"To answer that would be as bad as if I had to say where do I place you," Jackie answered, turning the tables on David. "I mean, like Johnny Carson, or are you like Merv Griffin? I think you are unique. I am so glad you're here. We need you here. And you're different. You're human."

Frost: "Drat. Can't say anything nasty after that. I wasn't going to."

They talked about love machines: "Lots here in the audience tonight," David said, and introduced the three distinguished critics. One of them, Nora Ephron, praised Miss Susann: "In her book every six pages someone wants someone else ... and it's delicious if you're a woman."

Where did others place Miss Susann on the literary scale, David wanted to know. Critic Rex Reed replied, "I don't think of her as a writer so much as I think of her as a show-business tycoon. I think she has really found a pipeline to public interest."

The audience joined in the discussion, and there developed a free-for-all about sex and literature, a lively, entertaining, and very frank exchange such as American viewers had not heard on television before. There was controversy. Another critic, John Simon, told Miss Susann, "I'm not calling you Dumb Jackie Susann or [*bleep*] Jackie Susann or Swinish Jackie Susann ... I'm calling you Miss Susann, and I'm asking you, do you think you're writing art or do you think you're writing trash?"

"I'm writing stories," Miss Susann replied.

David was not afraid to confront some scientific heavyweights on the show. One of them, Dr. Edward Teller, asked David not to introduce him as "the father of the H-bomb." "I don't mind myself," he said, "but I have a son, and he fears that the hydrogen bomb might be referred to as his kid brother."

A guest from the other side of the fence was Herbert Werner, a World War II U-boat commander in the German Navy. Werner did not respond too readily to questions and was either evasive or silent until David lost his patience—but not his sense of humor. When Werner refused to answer yet another question, David raised the specter of the Gestapo and told his guest with mock menace in his voice, "We have ways of making you talk!"

Ted Sorensen, who can be rather ponderous, unbent sufficiently vis-à-vis David to speculate that in view of Chappaquiddick, perhaps Teddy Kennedy ought not to run for President in 1972. Remarks like this put David's show on the front pages of the American and world press. Another prominent figure he quizzed was H. L. Hunt, the Texas oil man, who talked freely about the seer he often consulted before making important business deals. Fellow talk-show host Johnny Carson, in great form facing David, shocked the studio audience with a four-letter word that was bleeped out before the shock waves could reach the home viewers.

Some time later Senator Edmund Muskie was talking to David with quiet conviction. The conversation was turning on the dramatic events surrounding the 1968 Democratic Convention in Chicago when the floor manager signaled that it was time for a commercial break. David disregarded the signal. The floor manager furiously waved his board, indicating the minutes as they slipped away. Still David ignored him. Not until the senator had completed his account did David turn to the audience with his customary, "We'll take a break now."

Afterward he was emphatic: "It would have been ridiculous to interrupt the senator when he was at the most interesting point," he said. He insists on keeping the time for commercial breaks flexible until they become in fact "natural breaks," as they are euphemistically described.

Frequently in David's interviews the humorist and satirist came to the surface. When his conversation with Senator Robert Packwood turned on the abortion-reform and population-control bills the senator had placed before Congress, an irate woman in the audience shouted: "How do you feel about unwed mothers?"

"Not responsible," David replied.

As Zsa Zsa Gabor and her friend Pamela Mason engaged in a deliciously feline bicker match on the show, David turned to the audience: "Welcome to *Girl Talk*, with David Frost!" Erich Segal, who wrote *Love Story*, engaged David in an animated exchange about the private lives of ancient Roman and Greek writers: "You know, we are gossiping about men long dead," David said.

Segal replied: "If it is old enough, gossip becomes scholarship."

Truman Capote explained to David why he once said that "sex is like sneezing."

Quick as a flash, David exclaimed: "If there is anyone at home with a cold, lucky you!"

People were beginning to collect Frost bons mots: "The mini-skirt is a gift of the gods." "Maxi-length clothes are a barbarous invention of designers." "I'd love to meet Cleopatra, to see whether she looked like Elizabeth Taylor." "It's better to give than to receive. And if you give enough, you'll wind up in the hands of the receiver." Asked about his ambition, David said: "I'd like to do a program via Early Bird satellite with Charles de Gaulle on the third morning, when he rises again."

David continued to talk himself into American hearts. To Chet Collier's delight the ratings registered David's success, but even a hard-bitten television expert like Collier drew as much comfort from the reaction of those close to him. "I saw him," Chet's sister said after seeing the *David Frost Show*. "How did you find him?" she asked. "He is marvelous! I love him!"

Viewers were establishing the kind of intimate rapport with David which was a feature of his relationships with his guests. Noel Harrison told him that he and his wife, Sara, had parted—the first that even the couple's friends knew of it. When André Previn, known to be married, was on the show, Mia Farrow joined in the intimate conversation with the man she hoped to marry, and for the first time they publicly admitted their intention. (They have long since married, of course.)

Asked if he believed in the institution of marriage, Henry Fonda told David, "I must; I have gone into it often enough."

The much-married Artie Shaw coined a phrase: "A good marriage is an endless dialogue between two people."

In the middle of his conversation with David, Tennessee Williams pulled himself up. "I'm talking too intimately to you," he said.

Women used to figure only rarely on David's London programs. On his American show he paraded some of the most attractive in the world and had a rewarding response. He talked to them as readily during the commercial breaks; the outcome of these private conversations quite often was a dinner date. On camera the female guests frequently produced unexpected gems. Raquel Welch (who appeared on the same show with Clare Boothe Luce) came up with, "The mind is an erogenous zone."

"That's a great phrase" was David's spontaneous reaction.

He was uninhibitedly admiring when talking to Lee Radziwill, Jackie Onassis's sister: "I've seen her in many different circumstances, and she always looks superb," he said later. A commentator thought she appealed to David's sense of empire because she was "something of a princess." (When asked to name his favorite woman of history, incidentally, David chose Cleopatra.)

While in his car, racing to the airport at great speed, David frequently dictates letters to Cate Ryan, who has a tricky job consigning the rapid flow of his words to paper. The car was doing eighty miles per hour on one occasion while David calmly dictated a long letter to "Lady Bird" Johnson. "I only just managed to take it down," Cate said, sighing.

Shortly after, David was on his way to London to inaugurate a Congress of the Methodist Association of Youth Clubs and preside over a lunch at which Princess Anne was the guest of honor. Later, at the Royal Albert Hall, with David at her side, the Princess presented awards to successful volley-ball teams.

Slipping away from New York unnoticed on one occasion, David went to Mexico and on his return told David Henderson, by this time head of Group W Productions, "I have been talking to Richard Burton and Elizabeth Taylor, and they have agreed to come on the show next week."

"Good!" Henderson said.

"However," David continued, "I promised to take the show to Los Angeles to tape the interview next week." It was no sooner said than he was gone, leaving Henderson to carry out the major operation of transferring the show to Los Angeles.

"It was a great worry," Henderson recalled. In the first place it was impossible to contact the Burtons, who have no telephone in their Puerto Vallarta home. "You have Richard Burton and Elizabeth Taylor coming into the country," Henderson explained. "They need permission from the immigration authorities to perform!" It was impossible to coordinate the application with them, though.

While laboriously setting the process in motion, Henderson pondered the other problems: "You have to build scenery on the West Coast. Shut down the operation on the East Coast. Turn the production staff loose to do an urgent research job. And only a week to do everything." Arrangements with the Burtons had to wait until they reached Los Angeles. Another problem was a party for the couple, which would also be David's real introduction to Los Angeles. Fortunately, Andrew Franklin, the British consul general in Los Angeles, volunteered to play host to David and the Burtons at his home, although there was little time to send out invitations.

David's on-screen meeting with the Burtons went well. Richard gave an animated account of some of his stage experiences. There was some amusing banter between the couple on the air, and Elizabeth Taylor was persuaded to show David and the viewers her famous diamond ring. "Fantastic!" said David—as a matter of fact, he said it several times—and though the show was received with rapturous praise in the States ("A brilliant, scintillating, unconventional exhibition of vernal virtuosity—the most fascinating show of the evening," wrote Ben Gross), when it was shown by the B.B.C. in London, English critics reproached David for his "fantastic," "super," and other exclamations of boyish enthusiasm. ("Fantastic!" said Chet Collier. "That's a word he stole from us.")

The party after the Burton taping was spectacular even by Hollywood standards. The photographers, in the words of one guest, "went cuckoo" and did not know where to turn their cameras first. Ex-governor of California Pat Brown and Los Angeles mayor Sam Yorty headed a strong political contingent. The stars were there in force: Elizabeth Taylor and Richard Burton were joined by Lucille Ball, Edward G. Robinson, Gig Young, Walter

Pidgeon, Lee Marvin, and countless others. Carol Lynley was
never far from David's side.

"David was adorable," gushed the gossip columnist Suzy
(Aileen Mehle), who conferred the social praises of her column
on the occasion, but there was also some jealousy from predictable quarters. Almost a year later the party still stuck in the gullet
of Mort Sahl, who grumbled with questionable logic (in an interview with Donald Zec, of the London *Daily Mirror*): "Hollywood—it's all David Frost. Sean Connery came here to make a
movie, but the British consul did not throw a party for him!"

Press reactions to the *David Frost Show* were extravagant. "Mr.
Frost would have to commit mayhem on camera to get an unkind
word from me," wrote a critic in the Baltimore *News American*,
and the Boston *Globe* called him "the sophisticate in blue suede
shoes." The Denver *Post* described him as

> a revealing example of the kind of young man one finds
> succeeding in London these days. . . . All that intelli-
> gence sort of swims around loosely like a freewheeling
> jellyfish waiting to immobolize whatever random victim
> happens to present himself. It was Frost's bloody-
> mindedness, even savagery that endeared him to British
> audiences. On the current American show, he is gentle,
> friendly, restrained, more like a calculating diplomat
> than a knight errant.

Like an avalanche, the massive publicity campaign with which
Westinghouse supported the *David Frost Show* covered the country with information about the new host and his eminent guests.
However voluminous the output from the office of the creative
department under the highly skilled Owen Simon, he and his
staff had their work cut out for them, gathering in and process-
ing the escalating returns—news items, gossip paragraphs, articles,
cover stories, and photographs in magazines and newspapers from
one end of the United States to the other. Each show in addition
generated its own public reaction, linking David's name with
those of the country's most prominent figures.

When the media took up his association with Diahann Carroll, the confluence of their publicity swelled into a raging stream that all but burst the banks of tolerance. Even minute references in minor publications carried interest beyond the seas. One evening in August, 1970, David was the The Little Theatre, already made up and about to go down to the studio, when a reporter and photographer of the London *Evening Standard* turned up to record "his engagement to Diahann."

They had been alerted by a paragraph in *Jet*, a slim, pocket-sized magazine, which had suggested that "Julia" might not be single in real life much longer. "Actress Diahann Carroll and television personality David Frost," it speculated, "were seen looking very much in love in Hawaii. Their being together lends support to rumors that they will be married soon."

David and Diahann were seen together not only in Hawaii but also in New York, Hollywood, and Las Vegas—and seen to be very much in love. The rumors persisted or rather came up, subsided, and surfaced again on both sides of the Atlantic. During one of his brief sojourns in England, David took Diahann—like all his previous "young ladies"—to Beccles to meet his mother.

Dutifully David denied that he had any marriage plans, but his stereotype rejoinders that he had no intention of getting married for a few years yet no longer sounded as firm as they had of yore. With Diahann tied to Hollywood and him commuting between New York and London, they could not snatch more than brief weekends together without impairing their all-consuming careers. When it was reported that David had bought a country house in England and was looking for a house in the Bahamas, though, it was taken as a hint that he might be planning to take things a little easier—a wrong guess, obviously.

Though America demanded an increasing share of his time, big occasions always saw him on the English screen. He was the obvious choice to host commercial television's mammoth general-election coverage in June, 1970, in opposition to the B.B.C. It was a typical Frost exercise.

On Monday, June 15, he flew into London from New York, arriving at 9:40 A.M., and thirty-five minutes later he was being fitted with a new television ear-piece. At 10:30 he joined two directors of Paradine Productions for a half-hour meeting, which was followed by an hour's discussion with the executive producer of the election program. At 12:30 he was back at the London airport and off to Geneva, Switzerland, for two business meetings. Catching a return flight at 9:30 P.M., he reached the London airport again at 11:00.

Things built up during the next two days, reaching a climax on the day of the election, June 18, 1970. Scheduled to spend most of the next twenty-four hours tied to the studio, David nonetheless started the day with a 10 A.M. meeting at home to discuss a film script. Seventy-five minutes were devoted to a conference about the details of the election show, but he squeezed in a meeting (12:15 to 12:45) with Paradine Productions executives before settling down—if that's the word—to a working lunch.

By 2:30 P.M. he was at Television House, the headquarters of Thames Television in Kingsway, for a final full discussion with the production team. He had a haircut at 4:00 and a quarter of an hour later was at the Euston Road studio of Thames, a mile or so down the road, for a lineup and camera rehearsal. That was immediately followed by work on the complicated coordination with the Independent Television News team, which was providing the election results and news.

David went on the air at 10 P.M. for his first stint before the cameras. When he came off an hour later as results started to come in, he went to a conference to decide on last-minute bookings for the later part of the program. As the program was being shaped and reshaped according to the fluctuating state of the election results, it involved urgent but difficult decisions on the personalities to be invited for a running commentary. At 2:30 A.M. it was David's turn on the air once more.

Between 4 and 7 A.M. he worked without sleep before coming on again at 7:10 to preside over a round-table discussion, during which his thirty-odd guests nibbled at breakfast while he engaged them in informal talk. What viewers saw and heard was an easy-flowing exchange, closely aligned to the latest news and unobtrusively guided by the watchful host, who saw to it that everyone got a word in. It looked simple but was a considerable accomplishment. The Tory success over Labour, which came as a total surprise, did not make David's task any easier.

His schedule for that day, Friday, June 19, provides an inkling of his capacity, even after a virtually sleepless night, to switch his mind abruptly from one subject to another. As dictated and annotated by him, it read as follows:

7:10 A.M.	On air till 10.
10:30 A.M.	Downing Street to interview Mr. Wilson.
12 noon	Paradine Board Meeting.
1:00 P.M.	Working lunch with Richard Armitage.
2:15 P.M.	Meeting Willi Frischauer.
3:00 P.M.	Meeting—Paradine to discuss future series with artists.
5:00 P.M.	B.B.C. T.V. centre—meeting and viewing of T. Williams tape.
7:00 P.M.	Return to office to make phone calls to New York to plan next week's programmes.
8–9:15 P.M.	Letters.
9:30 P.M.	Private dinner.

Checking the typescript of the schedule, David could not resist adding a few marginalia. Next to "Willi Frischauer" he scribbled, "the well-known soothsayer." The "T. Williams tape" bit referred to his New York show, which had to be cut down to sixty minutes for screening on the B.B.C.

His Downing Street interview with Harold Wilson, which took place immediately after the Labour leader conceded the election to the Tories, was a classic. It was one of the rare occasions when the outgoing Prime Minister, under David's gentle prompting, showed signs of deep emotion in public. The spontaneous comment from Alastair Burnet, editor of the *Economist*, who followed David on the screen, was "That's one for the history books." A weekend crowded with talks at his London home was ahead of David. By midday on Monday, June 22, he was in an airplane on his way back to New York.

The Burton-Taylor and Tennessee Williams interviews were among a batch of *David Frost Shows* the B.B.C. bought in spite of David's involvement with rival London Weekend. The interviews included his Sammy Davis, Jr., show, which David—and American television critics—regarded as one of the most successful in his career. In the B.B.C. version of his Jack Benny and

George Burns interviews the host took a modest back seat and confined himself to a few encouraging ohs and ahs while his guests talked and acted out some of their most popular routines.

What delighted American audiences did not go down half as well with English critics, who judged these shows by the standards of David's satiric exploits and his "trials by television" and could not reconcile themselves to David Frost, the genial and appreciative foil to some of America's greatest performers. "Where was the acid David Frost?" one of them asked.

"Why should I be acid with Jack Benny?" David replied.

"Over the years," said a radio interviewer, "haven't you got older and softer?"

There was a slight pause. "Yes," said David, "I must admit you've got me there. Over the past eight years I have certainly got older. Almost eight years older, in fact!" Although he insisted that his approach and manner were the same in England and in America, there was a tendency to put these shows in the same category as other American television imports, which were a favorite target of sophisticated English critics. Latent anti-American sentiments, envy, and English suspicion of too much success combined to plague David.

He was beginning to pay for his American success with the hard currency of his English reputation. Milton Shulman, of the London *Evening Standard*, whose views carry weight in English television, wrote about the Frost imports. "This sort of stuff may be doing him the world of good in America but it is bound to diminish him powerfully here."

"I am so glad the shows were seen in England," said David, meeting the criticism, as usual, head on. "The audience response was terrific, though I do wish one or two of the press had remembered that because the B.B.C. had picked the showbiz shows—they were timeless—it did not mean that all my American shows were solely showbiz. Of course when the Vice President Agnew–student confrontation was seen in London later, that became doubly apparent." David disputed the suggestion that American audiences prefer less-demanding fare than the English: "They are every bit as demanding," he said. The comment of *Sunday Times* writer Elkan Allan, who had held the ladder for David's first steps to the top, was that David would have to be tough to restore his tarnished image when he returned in September with another live show for London Weekend.

After talking to Mort Sahl, Donald Zec put his finger on another phenomenon. "It is curious," he wrote, "how baiting David Frost has become a new game among his immediate and maybe less successful competitors."

Yet David was in great form when he did return to the English screen with a new series while guest hosts (Otto Preminger and Orson Welles among them) took over the *David Frost Show* in New York. An early guest was Zambia's President Kenneth Kaunda, who exploded a few diplomatic bombshells on the show. Talking soon after his meeting with Tory Prime Minister Edward Heath, Kaunda admitted that he had walked out of a Downing Street reception. The repercussions of his confidences on David's program occupied the press for days.

The liveliest show to be seen on television in a long time was David's interview with Yippie leader Jerry Rubin, the self-styled "orphan of Amerika," his lieutenant Stewart Albert, and other associates. Abetted by supporters who had infiltrated the studio audience, Rubin, under sentence for his part in the "Chicago Conspiracy," deliberately disrupted the show, called David a "plastic man," and squirted water in his face. When the tumultuous fellow asked those of like minds to join him on the stage, David demonstratively stepped down and took his place with the audience. "Your behavior is a commercial for law and order," he told Rubin. For the second part of the show, an interview with American author Robert Ardrey, David escaped from the upheaval to another studio, which had been prepared for just such a contingency, while Rubin and his rowdy friends were dealt with.

By way of contrast, that same weekend David visited Buckingham Palace to collect his O.B.E. and took part in a most spectacular British charity show in aid of Lord Mountbatten's United World Colleges, a cause close to the Duke of Edinburgh's heart. Bob Hope, Frank Sinatra, and Raquel Welch were among the performers introduced by Grace Kelly—Princess Grace of Monaco. At one point in his act Bob Hope cut in as David danced with

Raquel and continued the dance—with David. It was the first time Hope had done the routine in fifteen years. His original partners then had been Laurence Olivier and Vivien Leigh.

There was another uproar at the London Weekend studios later in David's series when at the height of a slowdown by power workers which disrupted electricity supply throughout the country he asked a group of rank-and-file power workers to state their case and defend it on the program. As usual he identified himself with the vast majority of his viewers, who were sick and tired of the strike and the inconvenience it caused. The program attempted to show what rank-and-file shop stewards and rank-and-file public were feeling. The result was that some felt the program did not adequately represent the union case. The program produced at least two classic statements from the union men, however: "We are not responsible—we are helpless prawns [sic]" and "When they offered us ten percent increase, we deducted——"

"What?"

"We deducted that something was afoot."

The audience included some irate opponents of the workers, and at one stage a farmer who had already gained notoriety by dousing an electric-power plant with manure in protest jumped onto the stage and began to exchange blows with one of the workers. Pandemonium threatened, but David kept his cool and restored order.

Some militant workers later blamed David for the inadequacy of their own men, and his name was bandied about at meetings. Britain was seething with labor unrest, and one shop steward, while addressing a meeting that was being televised for another program, reassured the workers, saying, "Don't worry! David Frost is not hiding behind the cameras."

David was again back in New York when London Weekend Television went through another crisis—poor programs, shortage of funds—but however distant from the organization he created, David Frost was associated with it in every public reference to the difficulties. Another big reshuffle was under way. It came when Rupert Murdoch, a youthful and energetic Australian newspaper proprietor who had only recently acquired a stake in Fleet Street and revitalized the fading *Sun* newspaper, put half a million pounds sterling (1.2 million dollars) into the London Weekend kitty. Remembering an earlier David Frost interview with Murdoch which became rather acid, the pundits predicted that Murdoch's advent would swiftly be followed by David's departure from London Weekend. The prophets did not know their David Frost—or their Rupert Murdoch, for that matter.

The rules governing British commercial television did not permit Murdoch—or any newspaper proprietor—to hold a dominating position in a television company. When the chief executive, Dr. Tom Margerison, and some of his colleagues departed, the press speculated on David's television future in his native country. They need not have worried. He was already busy behind the scenes—on the telephone from New York to Australia (where Murdoch was on a visit to his antipodal interests) and London —and came up with a brilliant solution of London Weekend's managerial problems. Since Murdoch himself could not be chief executive, David suggested, why not approach John Freeman, the retiring British ambassador in Washington, a close friend who had been David's original choice for a major post in the company?

Freeman not only had the necessary television expertise, but he also commanded great respect. He was just the man London Weekend needed to revive its flagging spirits and restore it to prestige and popularity. The suggestion was taken up with alacrity. Within a few weeks John Freeman emerged as the effective head of the organization.

It did not stop there. London Weekend also required a new program controller, and it was no coincidence that the man chosen for the job was David's longtime collaborator Cyril Bennett. The old gang was together again. The British public knew nothing of David's part in this major reconstruction of the television organization that owed him its existence. Some inveterate British critics were still sniping at him, but if David Frost was having a rough time in his own country, America soon offered him ample compensations.

CHAPTER 17

Frost at the White House

———

IN THE UNITED STATES David was still riding high. The show's ratings were rising, and a significant comment on his success was the recurring question "Where can he go from here?" Before the end of 1970 he might well have answered, "To the White House!"

Early in December David Frost was formally invited to perform for President Nixon and his guests at the White House Christmas party. The U.S. Army Chorus was taking part, but David would be the sole entertainer. The theme of the evening was almost automatically suggested by a record that had just been released under his auspices. Entitled *David Frost and Billy Taylor—Merry Christmas*, it included readings by David and carols played by the musical director of the *David Frost Show*.

For the benefit of the President, his family and his guests, David proposed to present a historical review of Christmas through the ages with musical accompaniment by Billy Taylor, an idea warmly approved by the President. In the few remaining weeks preparations and planning took up every free moment of David's time. After intensive research and scrutiny of hundreds of historical references, he decided to alternate—in the typical Frost style—between solemn readings and a lighthearted monologue in the manner of his satirical repertoire. Gradually he reduced a mass of material to a varied but homogeneous program that essentially represented his own taste and religious outlook.

David was elated. For an Englishman to be honored in this way by the President of the United States was a rare distinction.

Keeping a promise, made half in jest after receiving the Order of the British Empire at Buckingham Palace, David brought his mother to the United States to join him at the White House party. With Billy Taylor, production manager Bill Weyse, Peter Baker, and Neil Shand, the *David Frost Show* stalwarts, they flew from New York to Washington on December 18. David and Mona Frost went to the British Embassy, where they stayed as the guests of Ambassador John Freeman.

The following morning, the day of the White House show, David and his crew drove to Fort Myer, the army camp near Washington, to rehearse with the Army Chorus, time the readings, and coordinate the musical numbers. He was back in Washington in time for a small lunch at the Embassy. Among the guests was Martha Mitchell, the attorney general's wife, whom David hoped to interview on his show one day.

That afternoon he went to the White House and was conducted to the East Room, on the first floor. High-ceilinged, magnificently furnished in the style of a patrician residence of the eighteenth century, the room was decorated for Christmas with red candles and a Nativity crèche. In the setting for the evening's performance he spent three hours rehearsing with Billy Taylor and the Army Chorus. One surprise act was in the cards. The President told Frost in confidence that he would play "Silent Night" on the piano and ask the audience to join in.

A group from the Far East, a children's choir known as The Little Angels of Korea, was touring the White House, where President Nixon was conferring with British Prime Minister Edward Heath. The little Koreans sang for the President and the Prime Minister, and President Nixon asked what they were doing in the evening. When the reply was "Nothing in particular," the President asked them to come back and sing at his party.

Mrs. Bailey, the President's housekeeper, gave David her office to use as a dressing room. He was only there for a few minutes when the telephone rang. Answering it, David asked whether there was anything he could do, only to receive a request for some domestic items. "David Frost, White House housekeeper—one ambition fulfilled," he thought to himself.

By 8 P.M. he, Billy Taylor, Peter Baker, and Neil Shand went to the East Room, where the guests, some two hundred of the President's friends, officials, and political associates, were gathering; among them were Mamie Eisenhower, the Reverend Billy Graham and his wife, Ambassador and Mrs. Freeman, onetime Presidential candidate Thomas E. Dewey, Chief Justice Warren E. Burger, and Presidential adviser Arthur Burns. It was a well-heeled, elegant company. As they settled in their seats, Mrs. Frost took her place in the first row, by the side of the President and his family.

First to take the stage were the Korean children, who sang carols and "America the Beautiful," rendered bravely in phonetic English. The President personally introduced David, whose readings included early reports of a Puritan Christmas and passages from Charles Dickens, Robert Benchley, and Dylan Thomas. A favorite item—pure Americana—was an editorial from the Christmas, 1907, issue of the *New York Sun* (in reply to a letter to the editor from a little girl, Virginia O'Hanlon, who said, "My friends said there is no Santa Claus").

As planned, part of David's act was a satirical monologue, with his version of the Creation (dating back to *TW3*) and a few crisp topical jokes. "This Christmas at the White House, Santa Claus came down the chimney and met Wally Hickel going up"—Walter Hickel, the ex-secretary of the interior, had recently left the Nixon administration. It caused much hilarity. The Army Chorus sang Billy Taylor's new song, "Stable down the Road." The composer was at the piano.

The applause testified to the impact of the performance. Thanking David, the President said that there had been some great nights in the White House but that this was an evening that would be very hard to match. He had planned to play the piano, but David's was an impossible act to follow, and his own "performance" would have to wait for the next year. David's mother was congratulated from all sides. "You must be very proud of your son," people said to her.

The President looked pleased. He invited David to join him, Mrs. Nixon, and Mamie Eisenhower in the receiving line that guests were passing on their way to the West Room. "I know," Mr. Nixon said, "that people like to meet a celebrity." Standing in the lineup between the President and Mrs. Nixon, David shook hands with all the guests, most of them celebrities in their own right. The President's gesture was a spectacular honor, in the light of which a subsequent scurrilous report by a gossip-writer about his alleged displeasure with David's monologue becomes incomprehensible.

The party continued in the West Room with a huge buffet. Champagne was served, and the Army Band played. There was dancing, and David, not usually the most energetic of dancers, was among those who took the floor. His mother left with the Freemans around midnight, but he stayed on until 2 A.M.

When he woke up the following morning, he found a telegram from Billy Graham, which read, "I thought you gave a magnificent performance reciting the history of Christmas. My wife and I enjoyed it and I heard extremely favorable comments from other guests. God bless you, Merry Christmas." At the same time Dr. Graham asked for a copy of the readings for his own use.

The wire services duly reported the occasion, and lest some feathers were ruffled by the President's choice of a non-American to entertain his party, Connie Stuart, Patricia Nixon's press secretary, said that David Frost had been invited to do the show partly because this year was the hundredth anniversary of the death of Charles Dickens. "We wanted someone who could give readings from Dickens with a English flavor and who at the same time knows Americans and American sense of humor."

"Someone . . . with an English flavor . . . who at the same time knows Americans and American sense of humor" is a description that fits David Frost well. It goes some way toward explaining the phenomenon of his rapid rise to great heights of esteem and popular appeal. You can't have popularity without respect, he once said. And when critics pay a public personality—politician, creative artist, or performer—the respect of measuring him by the highest standards, the occasional lapse from his level instantly evokes adverse comment that often comes most vociferously from his strongest supporters.

David lays his reputation on the line every day of the week (and occasionally ten times a week) by matching his wits against those of the most eminent people in the land—in the world. One criticism frequently voiced is that he approaches some of his guests with too much regard, that his natural curiosity, one of his greatest assets, is sometimes tempered by too great humility or obsequiousness, that he is too easily impressed—in other words, that he is not always rude enough. He rarely replies to such criticism but always maintains that he asks the questions his viewers want to hear answered, which implies that he is liable to adopt the attitude of his viewers toward a particular subject. He does indeed try not to express his own views, whether preferences or distastes, so strongly that they might swamp the personalities of the people he interviews.

Though he does not easily lose his temper, if he feels strongly enough about a topic under discussion, his views come through. Religious, kind, and largely free of prejudice as his disposition is, he will come down hard on evil as he sees it—destructive revolutionary tactics or violence (like Jerry Rubin's), insidious suggestions unsupported by evidence (like Adam Clayton Powell's), irresponsible attitudes to drugs (like Dr. Petro's), and rampant color prejudice (like Governor Wallace's) rouse his ire. But in all but the most flagrant cases, he is prepared to give people the benefit of the doubt.

His friend and erstwhile colleague Bernard Levin, who nominated him "Britain's Man of the Sixties," also has remarked that "David Frost had said no memorable thing. . . . Rather had the memorable things been said to him." That, David would answer, is in the very nature of the job he is doing. He is doing it with skill, vitality, perseverance, and perception. A mirror of the age rather than a sage, a disseminator of views rather than a propagandist, a digger for truth rather than a builder of theory, he gives millions the opportunity to see and to hear with their own eyes and ears what they have no other means of finding out.

There is no reason that David Frost should not go on for a long time to fulfill the function of his choosing. As active off the screen as on camera, his entrepreneurial activities are constantly expanding and may from time to time curtail his public appearances on one side of the Atlantic or the other. There is no saying how far he will go as a major figure of the television age, what new opportunities he will explore, what new techniques he will devise, and in what guise he will present himself in the years to come.

He is, after all, only thirty-two years of age. If for no other reason, this last page of *David Frost* is not the end. It is only a beginning.

Bibliography

BBC Book of That Was the Week That Was, The. London: British Broadcasting Corporation, 1963.

Booker, Christopher. *The Neophiliacs: A Study of the Revolution in English Life in the Fifties and Sixties.* London: Collins, 1969.

Davies, Rupert E. *Methodism.* London: Penguin Books, 1963.

Frost, David. *The Americans.* New York: Stein and Day, 1970.

——. *The Presidential Debate, 1968.* New York: Stein and Day, 1968.

——, and Jay, Antony. *To England with Love.* London: Hodder and Stoughton-Heinemann, 1967.

——, and Sherrin, Ned, eds. *That Was the Week That Was.* London: W. H. Allen, 1963.

Levin, Bernard. *The Pendulum Years.* London: Jonathan Cape, 1970.

Reyburn, Wallace. *Anatomy of a Success.* London: Macdonald, 1968.

Worsley, T. C. *Television: The Ephemeral Art.* London: Alan Ross, 1970.

Index